Teach the Children to Pray

Rebecca Harwick

Kastanien Press
Berlin

Copyright © 2024 by Rebecca Harwick

All rights reserved.

No part of this publication may be reproduced, distributed, or transmitted in any form or by any means, including photocopying, recording, or other electronic or mechanical methods, without the prior written permission of the publisher. For permission requests, contact Kastanien Press, Saarbrücker Str. 33 10405 Berlin, Germany.

This is a work of fiction; therefore, the novel's story and characters are fictitious. Any public agencies, institutions, or historical figures mentioned in the story serve as a backdrop to the characters and their actions, which are wholly imaginary.

Book Cover by Heather VenHuizen

Map by Elbie Bentley

First edition 2024

For all war's children

Contents

Prologue	1
Part 1	5
1. The Devil in Ellwangen	7
2. Baker's Boy	20
3. The Girl Who Fell to Earth	32
4. Ploughshares into Swords	43
5. Little Warrior	52
6. The Many Uses of Flowering Plants	65
7. Blood and Plunder	82
Part 2	93
8. The Boy Who Believed in Goodness	95
9. Bathing Day	108
10. The Wildflowers of May	117
11. A Place of Open Arms	132
12. The Sweet Taste of Honey	145
13. Waiting	156
14. What a Woman May Choose	165
15. The Man War Could Not Touch	184

16.	Fool	199
17.	The God Who Gives and Takes	209
18.	Ordinary Time	221
19.	Magdeburg Mercy	232
20.	Gottschalk	244
21.	Eleonore's War	259
22.	Death and Birth	272
Part 3		285
23.	Wonderful, Difficult Things	287
24.	For Everything a Season	299
25.	Siege	315
26.	The Quick and the Dead	328
27.	The Deacon	340
28.	A Loss of Vital Parts	353
29.	The Black Nail	368
30.	Out of the Wilderness	376
31.	God Help Us Night and Day	385
32.	Now All the Woods Are at Peace	403

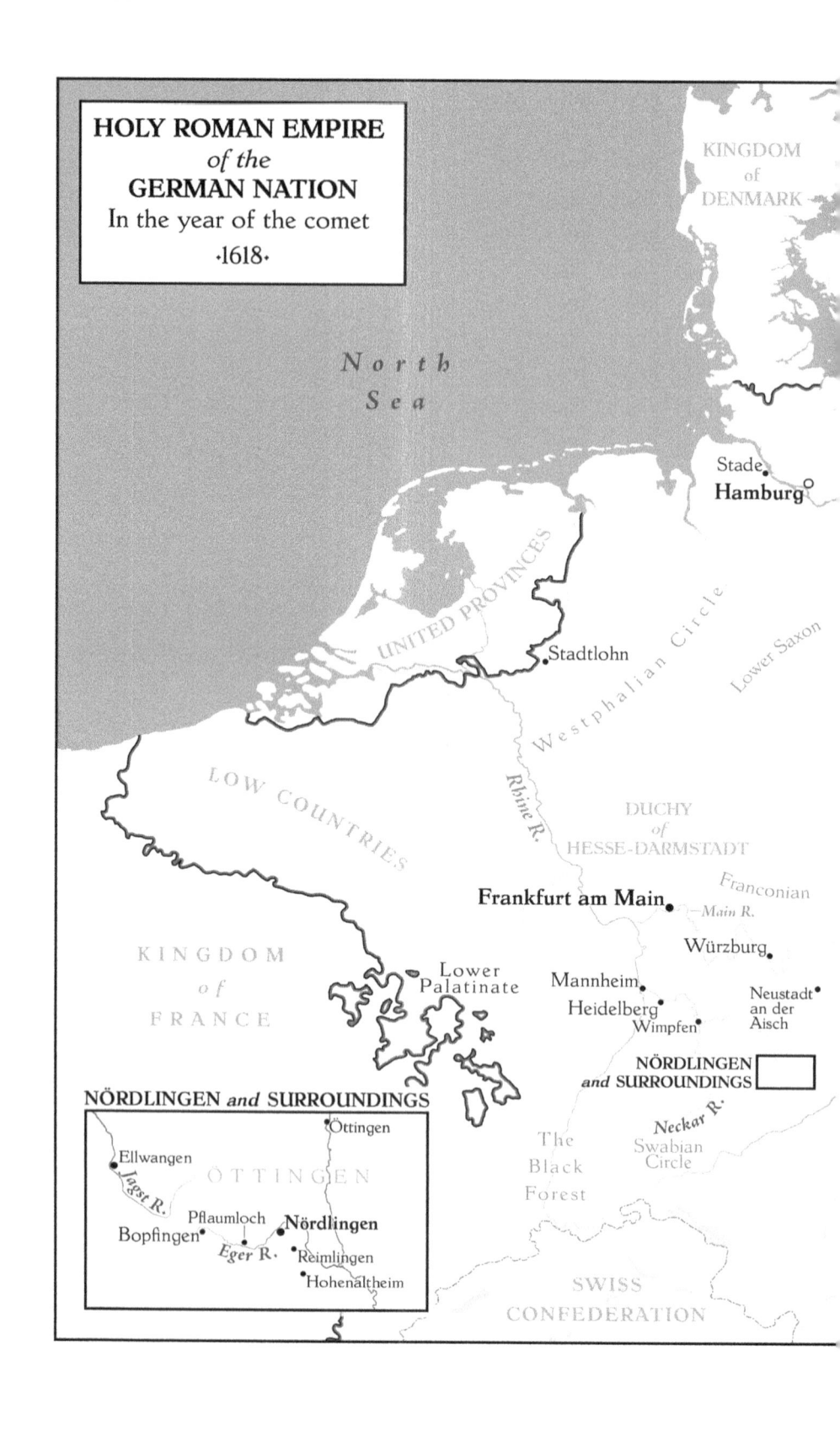

HOLY ROMAN EMPIRE of the GERMAN NATION
In the year of the comet
·1618·

North Sea

KINGDOM of DENMARK

Stade
Hamburg

UNITED PROVINCES

Stadtlohn

Westphalian Circle

Lower Saxon

LOW COUNTRIES

Rhine R.

DUCHY of HESSE-DARMSTADT

Franconian
Frankfurt am Main
Main R.

Würzburg

KINGDOM of FRANCE

Lower Palatinate

Mannheim
Heidelberg
Wimpfen

Neustadt an der Aisch

NÖRDLINGEN and SURROUNDINGS

Neckar R.

The Black Forest

Swabian Circle

NÖRDLINGEN and SURROUNDINGS

Öttingen
Ellwangen
ÖTTINGEN
Jagst R.
Pflaumloch   Nördlingen
Bopfingen
Eger R.   Reimlingen
Hohenaltheim

SWISS CONFEDERATION

KINGDOM
of
SWEDEN
Baltic
Sea
Copenhagen
Stralsund
DUCHY
of
MECKLENBURG
Elbe R.
Electorate
of
Brandenburg
Circle
Berlin
Frankfurt
an der
Oder
Magdeburg
KINGDOM
of
POLAND
Breitenfeld
Leipzig
Electorate of Saxony
Oder R.
Circle
KINGDOM
of
BOHEMIA
Bayreuth
Prague
Bamberg
Upper
Nuremberg
Palatinate
Regensburg
Harburg
Donauwörth
Ingolstadt
DUCHY
of
BAVARIA
DUCHY
of
AUSTRIA
Augsburg
Linz
Vienna
Danube R.
KINGDOM
of
HUNGARY

Prologue

1647

A priest first suggested I write out the story of my life—how it was I came to follow the armies and learn my trade and all the things, good and bad, I'd experienced since this endless war's beginning. He thought it might do my soul good to recall the ways God had worked in my life; he thought it might bring me some measure of peace.

Peace! Peace was the first casualty of this war. God was the second.

The year it started, an ill omen, a comet, blazed across the sky, blotting out the stars. Blame the comet. Blame the stars. Like a bad harvest or a plague or a bolt of lightning, it's easy to slip into believing this war was God's idea.

But God's got nothing to do with it. Princes make war. Emperors. They offer money to starving men, eight gulden a month, and put pikes in their hands, and they drill them to march in squares and bury their spears in men's guts and give thanks to God it doesn't happen to them. And when the princes don't want to pay, they set the soldiers on the rest of us. They bleed our contribution out of us with the sharp of their blades—a field of rye, storehouse of beer, a flock of sheep, a daughter's dowry. And if you don't pay, if you've already been bled dry, they'll burn your house down for spite.

My own war started the day my mother died, long before I saw my first army. That day, I found myself homeless, townless, condemned to wander the roads of this Godless country alongside my father. The bitterness of those days cut deep into my heart, a seeping wound that would not heal. By the time I started following the armies, I had already grown fair wild. War doesn't come from the heavens. We all carry a little war in us.

We all carry a little peace, too, my priest would say. My beautiful, foolish priest.

There are times peace seems to me like a house I once lived in, a lifetime ago. All that's left are the timeworn stones of memory: the floral scent of a candlemaker's shop, leafy herbs shimmering with dewdrops in the pre-dawn light, the prickling of my skin as I submerse myself in cold river water, the salty taste of a lover's lips in the ruined shell of an old church. The sound of my priest's voice as he prays.

I have a daughter. She's nearly a woman herself now. Clever, pragmatic, resourceful, she measures the worth of each thing according to how well it keeps the soldiers from our doorstep—silver for officers, leather for the regular enlisted men. A good belt buckle might buy a week of safety, a set of spoons more. Like all the children of her generation, this endless war has raised her.

I've taught her all I know of survival; what about the rest?

Once, when I was still following the armies, I met a woman who had a single strand of pearls for her most cherished possession. It was given to her by her mother. When the armies came, she took the strand apart and sewed each pearl into a different fold in her dress, into her bodice and her cap, so that even if the soldiers found one, they wouldn't find them all.

I can't help but think on that woman as I write now, preparing to turn over the folds of this patchwork life of mine. Let me find the pearls! Let me find them, so that I might have something left to give my daughter, so that even if this war never ends, she might still have some treasure it cannot touch.

Part 1

Girl

I

The Devil in Ellwangen

1608-1618

I suppose I should begin with my birth, ordinary though it was. My mother was busy toiling in my father's tannery when the first of her labor pangs came over her. A stubborn, practical sort of woman, she kept right on working until she could no longer stand for the pain.

My father went to fetch the midwife, but she was two towns over at the time, tending to farmer Ehrlich's mare. So, the horse had the midwife, and I had only my mother's cries and the fulsome scent of tannins to guide me into the world.

Those first years were relatively peaceful, or so I gather. I have little memory of them. The town we lived in, Ellwangen an der Jagst, was an unassuming small place, much like any little town you might find on the border of Swabia and Franconia, with its tradespeople and taverns, its chapter house and church, its storehouses and market square, surrounded by rolling grain fields and forests of feathered spruce trees. The river Jagst, which had its source nearby, was a reasonable stream, good for fishing and for turning the waterwheels, but nothing so boastful as the Rhine or the Danube or the Elbe.

Like the lands around it, Ellwangen is part of that wide territory we call the Holy Roman Empire of the German Nation. But in those days, we gave little thought to the Emperor in faraway Prague or Vienna. The German Nation is not one country but thousands, each with its own prince, duke, or bishop to rule over it. In Ellwangen, which had been a monastery town in days past, it was the Prince-Provost of the chapter house who enforced the laws and took the tax.

My parents were Godly folk and well-respected in the town. My father prayed every morning and night and taught me to do the same. I'd sit on his lap while he guided my small fingers over his amber rosary beads.

He always dealt honestly with his customers. A tanner by trade, he dabbled in leatherwork, and he was happiest with a mallet and stamp in his hand. If he had a fault, it was that he never stopped believing that the world was just and would one day repay him for his suffering according to his virtue.

My mother was the more forceful of the two by nature. What could not be said directly ought not be said at all, in her view, and she rarely hesitated to speak what was on her mind.

Like many folk, my mother was a fervent believer in the prophetic power of dreams. From a young age, she'd make a record of what she dreamt each night and study the imagery for portents. Over time, she became known for her skill and wisdom in the interpretation of these dreams, so that the people of Ellwangen came to her often, bringing the best of larder and loom in hopes of receiving a good sign.

I've long debated with myself whether her dreams contained any real power, or whether it was only my mother's cleverness, her talent for reading people's feelings and desires, and her prodigious imagination at work.

I can recall one dream in particular. In it, she saw crows circling a house. Five times, they circled, but they left when white smoke started to rise from the chimney in puffs. She was sure it was a portent.

That same month, all five of Mrs. Krause's children fell ill with smallpox. My mother, remembering the white smoke from her dream, told the woman to burn the green branches of saplings in her hearth, and soon all five children recovered. For a year after that, Mrs. Krause came by each week, bringing my mother a loaf of bread and a bottle of goat's milk in gratitude.

I remember my mother now in glimpses only, framed in the doorway of our house while hunched over her sewing. She looks up, smiling and calling me by name, but the note in her voice is false: there's a tremor that betrays her attempt at joy. I was too young then to understand such sadness, but I felt it.

Now, this memory appears to me as the portrait of a woman ensnared. The threads that fix her in place are so diaphanous, you'd be forgiven for missing them. I can see them, though; they reach out to wind themselves around me, too, cocooning me for weeks at a time in deep and unrelenting melancholy.

After my mother's death, my father was always quick to insist that she'd loved me. Night after night, he'd repeat it, as if repetition could make the words true. I want to believe it. When I first held my own daughter in my arms, I felt as if my very soul had been transposed into that fragile being. But I've also seen children enough left in ditches, in shallow graves, or in the hollows of trees, sometimes by choice but more often by necessity, to know that the relationship between mother and child rarely follows a straight path.

My mother did not abandon me, at least—not exactly.

Here is what happened: when I was not yet four years on this earth, old Barbara Rüfin—past seventy and her teeth long rotted out—attended Easter Mass, and when the time came to put Christ's body in her mouth, she found he'd gone stale. The Lord Jesus Christ, our Redeemer, proved to be too tough for her tender gums to chew. So, she spat him into her cupped and wrinkled palm, thus profaning the host and making plain to all that she was a witch.

At the time, there wasn't a soul who would dispute the charge. Even my mother believed it. She'd had a dream years before, you see, in which she saw the old woman, or someone very like her, lay a plague on farmer Holhansen's herd. In the end, Mrs. Rüfin's son and daughter-in-law both testified against her, and she was found to bear the devil's mark.

That might have been the end of it, but this wasn't the first time a witch had been found in Ellwangen, and in the years between, the courts had taken the lessons of the past to heart. For the sake of the town, for the sake of the mortal souls of everyone involved, they applied the full and dreadful power of the law to ensure that when all was settled, not a witch would be left alive to poison us with their diabolical corruption.

They brought in an expert, a man by the name of Gruber, who'd successfully drawn confessions out of countless witches in Obermarchtal just a few years earlier. His method was to suspend the accused by the arms and tie weights around their ankles until their shoulders pulled away from their sockets.

Under Gruber's careful hand, the old woman, once so sure of her own innocence, soon saw the error of her ways. Her memory, once empty, now recalled her sins in vivid detail, precisely as her interrogators described them to her.

In addition to hexing Holhansen's cows, Mrs. Rüfin confessed to breaking into St. Wolfgang's cemetery in the dead of night with her coven of witches. There, she said, they unearthed the body of a recently deceased child for use in their sacrament and rendered the fat from his bones for their salves. One by one she gave over the names of her accomplices, women who'd joined her in the unholy rite.

That first year some hundred people were arrested and sentenced to the pyre for witchcraft, including Mrs. Rüfin, although the Prince-Provost took mercy on her and ordered her head separated from her shoulders before the burning.

You might think that would have been enough: a hundred charred bodies, tossed in a pit, their property confiscated by the town (there's always been good profit in witch-hunting), but the devil's hold on Ellwangen was strong, his influence present in every sideways glance or whispered word. You could hardly kick a stone in those days without hitting a witch.

I was six or seven the first time I remember my father pleading with my mother to let him pack up and take her—*us*—away. But my mother was a wall. In the first place, she insisted, her dreams were harmless. Countless holy men and women in the Bible had both dreamed and interpreted dreams, and who would dare accuse the likes of Abraham or Daniel or Joseph, husband to Mary, of witchcraft? In the second place, it was no easy thing to pack up and find work elsewhere: would my father have us become vagrant wanderers, homeless, townless? And finally, she said, it wasn't yet her time.

Year after year, they reenacted the old argument, but the conclusion was always the same: my mother embracing my father and telling him, "It's not time." I don't know if he ever asked her, *time for what?*

Year after year, the population of the town grew smaller, and both my mother's and father's faces grew haggard and wan from swallowing so much grief. The reek of charred flesh hung perpetually in the air, and even in the quiet months, when there was hardly a burning or an accusation, you still smelled it, out of habit. Women became fewer on the streets, and the young men were forced to go elsewhere to find wives. A thriving town of more than twelve hundred shrank to two-thirds that number. On lane after lane, houses sat empty; there was no one left to live in them.

The living tried their best to forget the dead, but the dead always had the last word. The Prince-Provost insisted that it was all necessary to save the town from damnation. But no matter how many witches the town destroyed, still there was no end to disease and misfortune, to the curse the devil had laid on Ellwangen.

It was the summer of 1618, my tenth year, when the devil finally came to our door. It had been a hot, dry spring, and lightning storms had already set several fields ablaze between Ellwangen and Rindelbach.

My best friends at that time were the twins, children of one of the secretaries who worked for the court, taking down confessions. The older by two minutes, Albrecht, was a quiet, thoughtful boy who had not spoken a word in the first three years of his life. Everyone had been convinced he was an idiot, until the day his tongue finally loosened and all at once he started speaking complete, faultless sentences. His sister Anne spent their early years chattering enough for the two of them, and even after he'd begun talking, she was the loudest of the three of us and, therefore, in charge.

My mother wanted me home that day, helping with the washing, but Anne had taken the idea in her head to explore an abandoned barn outside the city, so I asked my father to let me go, and he did. *You're only a child for a season,* he told my mother.

So the twins and I set out early that June morning, cutting through the tall grass that sprang up and threatened to consume the road into town. Fewer and fewer wagons traversed it in those days.

The heat of the day sticks in my mind. We were not halfway across the field that separated the town from the river when our clothes began to cling to our skin. When we finally reached the water, Albrecht and I had forgotten our mission. We stripped and ran into the shallows, splashing and laughing, while Anne looked on, disapproving.

"You two are such children," she chided, clicking her tongue.

"And what are you?" I shouted back, laughing and swallowing a mouthful of river water as Albrecht slapped the surface and sent it spraying into my face. I lunged at him, pulling him beneath the gentle current, but he shook free.

Anne stared at us from the bank. "Are you finished?"

"My sister was never a child," her brother explained, wiping the liquid from his eyes. "The elves took her at our birth and brought her back grown."

"Liar," Anne snapped back.

"Doppelgänger," Albrecht teased, splashing water at her ankles.

Anne raced down the muddy bank toward her brother and plunged into the water without bothering to undress.

I don't know how long we played. Minutes, hours—time is cheap when you're young. I only know that my sides ached from laughing, and we might have forgotten the barn entirely, but for the clouds.

Never in my life have I seen a bright day turn black so fast or felt such a chill as when the wind swept across the river and touched my bare, wet skin: fingertips on my spine. We scrambled up the muddy bank, seeking hand- and footholds among the rocks and roots, and hurried to dress ahead of the coming rain. Anne ran ahead, and I followed close behind, with Albrecht in the rear, struggling to pull on his boots. Eventually, he gave up and chased after us, barefoot.

We'd just reached the edge of the field where the old barn stood when the sky burst open in front of us: a white-hot flash, blinding, accompanied by a sound so terrible I didn't so much hear it as I felt it rip through my body. And after: darkness, silence, and the peculiar sulfuric scent of approaching storm.

When I could see again, all three of us had lost our footing and were lying on the ground. Albrecht was rolled on his side, curled up like a bug, hands over his ears. But Anne was looking straight ahead, mouth agape, at the field in front of her.

Once, it had grown wheat and rye, but the last two seasons it had lain fallow with no one to plant it. In the official records, it belonged to the town now, having been confiscated when the farmer that worked it was arrested for his sins against God and humanity, but farms are worthless without hands to plough and plant and harvest. So it was overrun with tufts of wild grass and dandelions. They'd ignited the instant the lightning struck, and Anne and I stared, half-dumb, as the field spit up sparks and white smoke.

The rain brought us to our senses. It followed close behind the lightning, coming down first in heavy drops that struck us like hammers, and then more rapidly, thousands of needles pricking our skin. I took Albrecht by the arm and helped him to his feet, and we raced for the barn.

By the time we reached it, the fire had been doused, but we were soaked through. There was a chain fastening the door, but the wood at the latch was so rotted, one quick tug splintered it without resistance. Inside, the barn stank of wet straw and old manure, and the rain that pounded the roof slipped through the cracks and puddled on the muddy ground. Albrecht collapsed into the dirt, sputtering and stammering, and Anne knelt next to him, choking back sobs.

I was the first to notice the intent gaze of a pair of wary eyes, watching us from the shadows of one of the stalls, glinting with each flash of lightning. Beneath the din of raindrops rattling against the roof came a low, weak growl, resolving in a high-pitched whine. I moved cautiously toward the sound, heart in my throat, not sure if I expected something living or dead.

The bitch lay in a pile of moldy straw, her brown coat patchy with mange, her hide revealing the shape of her ribcage with each fresh intake of breath. She'd whelped recently, and four of the pups still suckled greedily at her swollen teats. She renewed her growling as I approached, baring sharp yellow teeth set in black gums, but she made no move to stand, and from the looks of her legs, bone-thin and trembling, I do not know if she could. Here and there, her neck and shoulders were pocked with white pustules—ticks that had planted themselves in her skin and gorged themselves on her blood. A frayed length of rope hung loose around her neck, the only sign that she had once belonged to someone.

Since then, I've seen many such creatures—dogs half-starved and half-feral wandering the roads, horses rendered lame and abandoned to their suffering or killed, and humans treated no better—but for all that had happened in Ellwangen in the years since my birth, I was still young, still unready to comprehend the depth of the world's miseries. All at once, the shock of that afternoon struck me—not just the ugly sight in front of me, but the lightning, how close we'd all come to death. I doubled over and emptied my stomach into the neighboring stall.

Then there was nothing to do but wait for the storm to pass.

"We should tell someone about her," Albrecht said. He'd regained his speech and was seated on the ground, leaning his head against his sister's shoulder.

"Of course we will," I said.

"Don't be ridiculous." It was Anne. "Do you think if there was anyone to take care of her, she'd be here? She's an unwanted creature." She snapped a stalk of straw between her fingers.

"Maybe they don't know she's here," I said, looking toward the animal, its eyes crusted but still shining.

Anne shook her head. "That sick thing? No one wants that."

"Hardly seems fair," said Albrecht, with a philosophical cock of his head. "A healthy dog doesn't need anybody, and a sick dog, nobody wants."

"It's just how it is," said Anne, and that was the final word.

The rain slowed and the dripping of water from the eaves grew sluggish. I crossed the barn once more to check on the bitch, but she'd fallen asleep, her pups curled against her. I thought to pick them up, but fear stopped me. Fear, and Anne's words, echoing in my mind: nobody wants them.

When we left the barn at last, the clouds had cleared, and the sky was painted with the pale hues of the evening sun, bearing no evidence of the storm that preceded it. We hurried back the way we came, through the grassy meadow, cool in the aftermath of the storm. As we waded across the river, we did not speak. The mood was leaden with the signs we had witnessed that afternoon.

The next day, court officials arrived at Anne and Albrecht's house and arrested the whole family.

The arrests happened on a Thursday. By Saturday morning, they had confessions, extracted in the usual way. The entire family had admitted to making a pact with the devil. Among the eyewitness testimony submitted to the court: the children had been seen at the abandoned barn alongside a third unidentified child, summoning lightning in the field, with the intent of setting the whole town ablaze.

My parents' old argument started again. *We should go*, my father insisted. This time, my mother did not contradict him. *Yes*, she said.

Yes, tell Josefine and pack up what you can. Leave this place and don't look back. Don't ever look back. I wonder now if she knew what was coming. I wonder now if she had seen it in her dreams.

Saturday afternoon, they hanged the twins from the gallows and tied their parents to the pyre.

While the smoke rose from beyond the fortress walls, the town priest knocked on our door. He'd been a vocal skeptic of the witch executions, and for his troubles, his sister had been accused and put to death. Now he came to our house with a warning: under torture, my mother had been named. If that were not enough, the twins had testified that I was the one in the field with them when the lightning struck. The court was preparing the warrants.

In the official record, the twins' parents said that my mother had introduced them to the devil. They said she knew how to summon demons to her like swarms of bats, lifting her into the air and carrying her across miles and miles of land. By this means, she could travel halfway around the world in a single night to meet with other witches in their dread sabbaths, profaning the host and fucking the devil's soldiers.

How I've wished the stories were true. Not a single night has gone by since that time that I haven't wished they were true. Perhaps then instead of what happened, she could have taken to the sky and called down her diabolical army on the whole town, leaving it a smoldering ruin. Let all the judges in the courthouse, all the witch-hunters and interrogators with their implements of torture feel the flames rising around them, let them choke on the scent of sulfur and melting flesh.

Instead, she told my father she was going to buy bread for the journey. Then she left him and went down to his workshop, to the very place where she'd birthed me almost a decade earlier. There, she took rope, tied the knot sure, looped the cord over the eaves, and kicked the chair out from beneath her. There she fell, suspended between Heaven and earth, until the last breath went out of her.

I can't know what went through her mind that afternoon. Did she think she could save us by sacrificing herself? Or had she perhaps dreamed of her own death long before? Was she trying to escape her fate, or was she flinging herself into its arms? How many times had she told my father, *it's not time*? And why had this day been different? Oh, the countless hours I've wasted, wishing I could summon her here and make her answer for herself.

After waiting into the night for my mother to return, my father went down to the workshop to pack up his tools and let out a wail so loud I heard it in the rooms above; so loud it pierced my heart like the sharp end of a pike.

I went to my bedroom window, and I saw her, drifting down the lane that led to the town gate. Her white-blonde hair fell around her shoulders, and her dress shone just as if it were made of moonlight. I watched her until the darkness swallowed her up. She didn't look back. I didn't need to go down to the workshop to see it; I knew then she was gone.

When he'd finished his wailing, my father cut my mother's body down from the rafters and dug a shallow grave behind the workshop. Then he packed his few belongings into a leather rucksack and arranged a ride for himself and his only daughter on the back of a wool merchant's wagon.

As the wheels turned over the uneven track out of town, I thought I saw her again, her back still turned to me, her feet only grazing the earth, silver light streaming in her hair.

I leapt from the wagon and ran after her. My father's shouts following me, I chased her toward the field where the lightning strike had seared the ground, all the way to the old barn, the door still swinging open, just as we'd left it.

There was nothing but empty darkness inside. My mother, if she'd even been there at all, was not to be seen. Only a low, persistent buzzing broke the silence, and the air carried the heavy scent of death.

As I drew close to where I'd first found the bitch and her pups, I saw clear enough why. The poor creature lay lifeless in the moldy straw, a miserable pile of hide and bone. Her whelps had wandered off or been snapped up by some other hungry creature—all but one, a boney runty beast, with one brown eye and one blue. He let out a little whine as I scooped him up and wrapped him in my skirt.

2

Baker's Boy

1618

The war had already begun by the time my father and I set out on the road from Ellwangen, though at the time we were only dimly aware of it.

Sure, we'd heard the story of those unruly Bohemian Protestants in faraway Prague—how they'd tossed three men out of the third-floor window of the castle chancery in defiance of both King and Emperor; how the victims had clawed for their lives at the window casing, crying out to the Virgin to protect them; how the Protestants had looked on in astonishment as all three landed safely on a pile of refuse below and fled.

The story grew more elaborate with each telling, but it was just a story. After all, what had Bohemia to do with Germany? My father and I had enough troubles directly in front of us without imagining new ones, especially so far away.

For even without war, the road was an inhospitable place. It wasn't uncommon in those days to chance upon the still-moaning body of a thief broken and threaded through the Wheel in punishment for his crimes. Or you might hear the buzz of flies as you rounded a bend to find a discarded body beside an overturned wagon. We made the sign of the cross as we passed, and prayed that whatever calamity befell them would pass us by.

That summer we slept in the bottoms of carts, the splinters digging into our backs, or in the woods under the naked sky, waking to the sensation of spiders' legs crawling up our arms. If we were lucky, someone would invite us to unroll our blankets on the floor of their barn, or the local church would open its doors to us in charity. I became used to the coarse pricking of burlap on my cheek, drifting off at night to the heavy scent of shit and mildew, and filling my belly in the morning with horse feed.

The runt I'd rescued from the abandoned barn slept beside me, curled up against my belly or in the bend of my knees. I fed him meat or milk when we had it and crusts of bread when we didn't, and he grew large and gangly. His tail set to wagging at the sound of my voice, and he kept me company in the long days while my father looked for work.

My father took work wherever he could find it—in a tanner's workshop for a day or more often in a farmer's field with the sun beating on his back. But word of the accusations against my mother followed us from village to village and farm to farm like a hound baying at our heels, and my father was just as often turned away, spat on, and forced to begging.

On the outskirts of Ederheim or Neresheim, or I-for-get-which-heim, I saw him knocked to the ground, the hot dust rising around him in a fine cloud to choke him. As he coughed and sputtered in the dirt, flecking the earth with his spittle, they explained that the town had no need of vagrants or devil-worshippers. We'd slipped through the sieve of the world's good intentions.

At summer's end, my father set me on a fallen tree trunk and unrolled the soft leather from around his tanner's instruments. The runt turned in circles beneath me, pawing at the bark and letting out a nervous whine.

My father crouched in front of me and put a hand on my face, and I felt the blisters on his palms, saw how the skin had cracked open, dirt mingling with streaks of dried blood. He smiled at me—a thin, wavering smile. "My God," he said. "You could have been spit from her mouth." Meaning my mother.

He meant it lovingly, I'm sure, but I felt shamed by it. How could I not? Her death was the cause of all our misfortunes. I didn't know how to mourn her, so I blamed her instead.

I squinted into the blacks of his gray-blue eyes, searching for my reflection. It was true what he said. My hair was the same white-blonde shade as hers, and my cheeks, rapidly shedding the soft roundness of childhood, reproduced the shape of her face from her high cheekbones right down to the chin, slightly square.

"You're wrong," I said. "My eyes are blue. Hers were brown."

His smile widened then, revealing a glimpse of yellowed teeth beneath the wiry gray hairs of his mustache. "So they were. So they were."

Then he took out a small knife with a narrow blade, sharp as a razor, and wiped it with a cloth rag. I'd seen him make the motion a hundred times or more in his workshop.

He ran his fingers through my hair, pulling it away from my head in greasy knots. "There's a cousin of mine lives in Nördlingen, where we're headed," he said. "He's a baker. It's good, consistent work. There's always a need for bread."

My stomach grumbled at the word.

"Bakers are always in want of hands," he went on. "Clever, honest boys who don't oversleep and who know their weights and measures." He looked down at the knife in his hand, flexing his fingers around the wooden handle to adjust his grip. "Do you understand what I'm saying, *Häschen*?"

I nodded.

"Can you do that? Can you be clever and honest?"

"Yes," I said, biting down on my lip to stop it trembling. My father had enough troubles without his only daughter mewling like a suckling.

"Good," he said with a nod. Then he put the knife to my head and cut my hair away with quick, jerking strokes. When he was done, the strands covered the ground in clumps, like straw scattered on the floor of a barn. The runt sniffed at it and whimpered. What remained on my head stuck up in uneven tufts, but I spat on my hand and smoothed it down.

Then my father packed up his tools once more, and we set out down the road to Nördlingen.

The Imperial Free City of Nördlingen was the largest town I'd yet seen, twice and twice again the size of Ellwangen, with a wall some thirty feet high ringing the city, and a church tower visible from the hills miles away. The Imperial eagle was blazoned above the city gates.

Nördlingen was a Lutheran city. In those days, before the Bohemian War had reached Germany, Lutherans and Catholics were alike to two old dogs. In their younger years, they'd been at each other's throats, but over time, they'd mellowed, and now they grudgingly tolerated each other's presence. As long as the one did not encroach too closely on the other's space, there was peace; if not, there was a great bellowing and snapping of jaws.

From time to time, you'd hear word of a priest attacked on the road in Bavaria to the south or of Calvinist preachers being driven from a Catholic town, but these incidents rarely made so much as a ripple in the peace. The wound of religion had largely healed, or so we all believed. In Nördlingen, they followed the Lutheran faith and pledged their loyalty to the Catholic Emperor, and few saw any trouble in it.

My father's cousin, Baker Ruppel, was a cheerful giant of a man with a laugh you could hear echoing down the lane. My father introduced me as his son, and if the baker suspected the lie, he was too good-humored to admit it. He put me right to work for two kreuzer a week—a meager sum, but it came with a place for my father and me to sleep in the bakery storeroom.

In Nördlingen, I tried hard to be the person my father needed me to be, but I was ill-suited to the task. Oh, I was clever enough. I could figure without the use of my fingers, and my mother had taught me to read passing well, but as it happened, neither skill was of much use in Baker Ruppel's shop.

Nor was honesty, for that matter. My first day, I saw one of the other boys slice away a lump of dough after it had been weighed. I told the baker's apprentice about the cheat, and he boxed my ears until they rang. Such was the reward for honesty.

As the new boy, I was about as welcome as a tick on a cow's teat, and the others made certain I knew it. I spent my first week carrying wood and working the bellows until my hands split apart with blisters. But I'd have sooner chewed off my own tongue than let them hear me complain.

At night, when the loaves of rye were left to bake in the cooling ovens, and all the others had gone home, I rolled out my blanket on the storeroom floor and waited for my father's return. It was often past dark when he wandered in, his footsteps a slow, ponderous shuffle, and set himself down on the boards with a heavy groan. He couldn't look at me but he sighed and shook his head bitterly.

Being a child, I took myself to be the cause of his misery. If only I didn't eat so much, if only I'd not been born a useless girl, if only I didn't look so very like my accursed mother. Of course, I couldn't have changed any of these things, but I carried them with me anyway. Were it not for the runt, who bounded alongside me wherever I went, the burden of them might have proved too much for me to bear.

It was that year I first met Eleonore.

It was Advent, and Baker Ruppel had started trusting me with deliveries. My last of that day was to St. George's church—bread for the host. The church had three deacons, and Eleonore's father, Peter Kästner, was one of them. I found him in the nave, folding altar cloths. He took one look at the oversized rags I wore and took a loaf out of the sack, broke it in two, and offered me the smaller half.

I shook my head. "I don't need charity, sir."

He had a thin face and a kind smile. "Think of it as payment for a job well done," he said. "Not a piece missing. I know the other boys all take their share."

My stomach growled then, audibly, and my face grew hot. I took the bread he'd offered and turned to leave as hastily as I could.

Out in the street, I whistled to the runt, who hurried to my side, his nails clicking and scraping against the stones. I broke off a chunk of bread and tossed it to him. He caught it in his mouth and gnawed on it eagerly.

When I looked up, she was beside me—a brown-haired girl just a year or so older than I was. Her face was not six inches from my own, bright mischief gleaming in her eyes. I'd seen her at the church before, but I'd never spoken to her and wouldn't have dared.

"You're a very strange boy, you know that?" she said, matching her pace to mine.

"I'm not a boy," I answered in haste. Realizing my mistake, I forced the bread I was chewing down my throat. "But you mustn't tell anyone," I added.

"Who would I tell?"

Her smile was wide and easy. Until you've been stuck on the sharp end of the world's indifference, you might not understand what such a smile can do to you.

"So, what's your name, Not-a-boy?" she asked.

"Josefine."

"I'm Eleonore. Nice to meet you." She eyed the bread in my hand.

I clutched it close. "I didn't steal it, you know."

"I know that. I saw Father give it to you. And what's your dog's name?"

I looked down at the runt, trotting beside me, wide, eager eyes fixed on the bread. I tore off another piece and threw it to him. "I just call him the runt."

Eleonore frowned. "It's not much of a name."

"He's a dog. What does he need with a name?"

"Well, he doesn't look like a runt, either."

It was true. His head came nearly up to my waist by then, and he had the paws of a giant, all out of proportion with the rest of him. I shrugged. "He's grown a little."

She giggled. Then she asked, "So where are your parents?"

"My father's working. He's a tanner."

"And your mother?"

"In Hell."

Eleonore stopped in her tracks, and I knew I'd made another mistake. "You don't mean that."

"She killed herself. Heaven doesn't take those that end their own lives."

I thought she would turn and go, then, and the thought seized me with fear. I hadn't had a friend since leaving Ellwangen, since the twins had gone to the gallows. So, I did the only thing I could think of. I tore off a piece of bread and held it out to her.

Eleonore stared at my offering, then she laughed.

I laughed, too, more out of relief than anything.

She grabbed my arm. "Come with me," she said, tugging me down a side street off the road that led back to Baker Ruppel's shop.

"Where are we going?"

"What good is bread without honey?" came her reply.

We came to a stop outside a small candle shop. She ran right up to the window and pressed her hands against it, looking in. The shop was dark.

"They're closed," I said, feeling the excitement drain from me and the sour taste of disappointment set in.

"No matter," Eleonore said, and she plucked a pin from her hair and knelt in front of the lock.

"What are you doing?"

She didn't look up from her work. "Stand watch, will you?"

I swallowed my protest and turned back toward the road. It was empty and growing darker by the minute as the sun set behind the houses. "Are you out of your damned mind?"

"Who taught you to talk like that?"

"Who taught you to break into shops?"

"You're not telling me you've never stolen anything!"

Was it stealing if it fell off the back of a cart? Or if my dog, big dumb animal that he was, happened to knock it off the market stall with his tail? Was it stealing if your father had gone three days without work, which meant he'd gone three days without bread? "That's different," I said.

"How?"

"I didn't have a choice."

"You always have a choice."

"Starving's no choice."

The door swung open, and Eleonore grinned. Stepping inside, we were engulfed in the intense, heady scent of beeswax, at once saccharine and floral.

"There's honey here?" I asked.

Eleonore was already opening and closing cabinets, searching through their contents. "Mr. Baumgarten always has a few jars set aside somewhere. He likes to offer it to the small children who come into the shop."

"Won't he see they're missing?"

"We'll just take a little off the top. No one will notice. Besides, it's not as if anyone will know it was us."

I looked toward the open door, toward the golden light on the sunset-bathed street outside. "And if someone walks by while we're in here?"

"The runt will bark, won't he?"

"He seldom barks."

"A boy who's not a boy and a dog that doesn't bark. You are quite the pair, you know that?"

"And you're a deacon's daughter who pries open locks with her hairpin and steals honey."

"How else did you think we'd get it? Do you have any money?"

"No."

"Well, there you go. Neither do I." She reached into a low cabinet in the back corner. "Aha! Here we are." She held a honey jar aloft in triumph. I glanced toward the door once more as Eleonore pried the jar open, but all was quiet. The runt lay in the street, licking his paws and stopping only to nip at a flea on his backside.

"Ah, pity," Eleonore said, her nail scraping the top of the honey. "It's practically solid."

"It's too cold."

"Here," she said, sealing the jar again and thrusting it into my hands. "Wrap it up in that silly coat of yours and hold it against your body."

"No." I pushed the jar back to her. "You do it."

"Me?" She looked down at her dress. "And where should I put it?"

"I don't know. Between your knees. But I'm not holding it."

"Why not?"

"Have you ever seen them break a thief on the Wheel? Sometimes they live for days after, hanging there, while the buzzards pick at them."

"They don't use the Wheel on children."

"No, but they'll take my hand."

"And what about me?" she asked.

"Your father's the deacon. They won't hold you to account. This was your mad scheme anyhow. It'd be just as well with me if we left right now."

"Fine," she huffed as she pulled up her skirts. "But don't look. For all I know, you're lying about not being a boy."

The whole exchange left me feeling dizzy and unbalanced. The thick aroma of the candlemaker's shop was no help. I stepped out onto the street and sat down in the gutter, next to the runt. He rested his chin on my knee with a whimper and a lick of his lips. I broke off another piece of bread, and he gobbled it out of my hand, licking my palm with his rough tongue well after the last crumb was gone.

A few people walked past while I waited, their coats pulled tight against the growing cold, their breath puffing in front of them. If they noticed me at all, they said nothing about it. I suppose a rag-shod child in the gutter was no extraordinary sight, even then.

After a time, I felt the light pressure of a toe in my back. It was Eleonore, beckoning me in. I told the runt to stay while I went inside.

As long as I live, I'll remember that honey. It seeped into the bread and stuck to our fingers until we licked them clean. Even after we'd said our goodbyes and gone our separate ways, I could still taste it on my lips, a mixture of wildflowers and sunshine and something I could not then name: contentment. Even years later and miles away, I would taste it whenever I thought of Eleonore.

When we'd had our fill, we stumbled out into the street as if drunk, giggling at our mischief. The sun had already set, so we hurried on our way, before we lost the light.

"Your father must be worried," I said.

"I doubt it. All he cares about is church business since Mother died. He hardly notices if I come or go."

I thought on my own father, sitting wordlessly each night in grief and exhaustion. "I'm sorry," I said. "How did your mother die?"

"Oh, it was stupid, really. Giving birth to my baby brother."

"That's not stupid."

"Well, he died, too. So it was all for nothing, wasn't it?"

I was quiet then, unsure what to say.

Eleonore changed subjects: "How is it I don't ever see you in church?"

I shrugged. "We're Catholic."

"Ah, that's a shame," she sighed. "If you had been a Christian, we could have been friends."

Her words twisted my insides into knots. I stammered a protest. But then I saw Eleonore, hand over her mouth, suppressing a laugh. I stuck my tongue out at her in reply.

"Look!" she exclaimed, pointing skyward. "The comet!"

The Great Comet, they called it. It had been spotted over the city a few days before, but this was my first time laying eyes on it myself. It looked far smaller than I'd expected, for all the fuss that had been made over it. But the longer I watched it, the more it mesmerized me, that solitary star tracking across the sky, dragging a trail of stardust behind it.

They say now that it was an omen, a sign of God's judgment for our sins, portending all the horrors that followed.

"I wonder where it's going," I said.

"Far from here," Eleonore answered, her voice breathy with longing.

We parted ways soon after, and I made my way back to Baker Ruppel's in near darkness.

My father was waiting for me when I returned, and no sooner had my shadow darkened the door than he flung it open and embraced me. He held me so tight, I thought I might be crushed.

I laughed uncomfortably. I couldn't recall that he'd ever hugged me like that before, not even on the night we'd poured the dirt over my mother's grave.

"There's nothing funny about this," he said, and then I saw the streaks on his face where the tears had marked their crooked paths, and I felt a guilty weight form in my stomach. He went on: "I didn't know where you were. The streets were dark, and I didn't know where you were."

"I'm sorry." I buried my face in his, feeling his wet whiskers scrape my cheek.

"You can't disappear like that," he said. "You're all I have left."

It's too much, I wanted to say. *I can't be it all. It's too much.* But it was all I could manage to repeat, "I'm sorry," again and again as he held me.

3

The Girl Who Fell to Earth

1619

In those days I half supposed Eleonore to be a magical being, a fairy from the stories. She had a mind for mischief and a smile so wide you could tumble into it. When she turned it on me, it warmed me from the belly out, thinking that I could be the cause of such brightness. Besides petty theft, her favorite pastimes were sneaking outside the city walls of a Sunday morning and hiding in the watchtowers to dodge her chores.

Her father the deacon viewed me with suspicion if he noticed me at all. The former kindness vanished from his smile when he saw the two of us together, the ragged little baker's boy with the unkempt hair and his good, God-fearing daughter.

Theirs was not an easy relationship, even measured against my own complicated experience of fathers. Eleonore's mother and brother had died when she was just five years old, and since then, her father had given himself over to his service to God, neglecting entirely the fact that he still had a daughter, very much alive. Eleonore had fairly raised herself.

The people of the town doted on her, their beloved deacon's only daughter. They talked of her in the market and the baker's shop with pride and protectiveness in equal measure. Yet she had few friends and, I flattered myself to think, not a soul who knew her as I did.

That winter, we were as cords braided together. It was beyond my fathoming why she'd chosen to pay me any attention at all—a poor, underfed Catholic in ill-fitting clothes—but now I see how my strangeness must have weighed in my favor. In my presence, she needn't be her father's daughter, only herself. I suppose it didn't hurt that her father so clearly disapproved. I think she might have courted the devil himself for his attention.

Whatever her motives, her friendship was nourishment to me. Most afternoons after my day in the bakery was finished, I wandered by the church to find her. She turned up likewise at the bakeshop on Sundays, flinging gravel and birdseed at Baker Ruppel's window.

"Not-a-boy!" she'd call to me, in a teasing singsong.

One such Sunday our path took us along the bank of the Eger river beyond the town walls. The Eger was a retiring stream slipping between the reeds, even less of a river than the Jagst. That day it was frozen over, its banks slick with clumps of snow.

Eleonore picked a spot on a slope high above the stream and tipped out the contents of a burlap sack: brown bread, a wedge of cheese wrapped in cloth, a small pouch filled with walnuts, and two fresh, soft pears, their flesh so sweet and mild it dissolved in the mouth. She'd brought a piece of swine's rib for the runt as well, shreds of meat still clinging to the bone. "Don't worry," she said, "I didn't steal any of it."

We ate and gossiped and laughed until our bellies ached, and afterward, we collapsed on our backs to stare up at the sky. Eleonore tossed the core of her pear into the brush and stretched. My hair had grown out some since my father cut it, and as she lowered her arms, she took a lock of it in her fingers and swept it behind my ear. It was a careless movement, an afterthought.

"You know, your hair wouldn't look half so bad if you combed it sometimes," she remarked.

"I don't have a comb."

"I'll lend you mine," she said, eyes smiling.

It was a small kindness, but it hit my gut with unexpected fire, numbing my senses like a slug of brandy. I can't list half the stupid things I've done in my life on account of a smile and for that smile in particular.

We talked, and as we talked, I told her about Ellwangen. I told her about my mother, furiously recording her dreams each morning. I told her about Mrs. Krause's children, surviving smallpox. I told her about Mrs. Rüfin hexing farmer Holhansen's cows and spitting out the host. I told her about my mother's death and about seeing my mother's ghost the night we left, leading me toward the runt.

I told her about the loneliness that followed.

Eleonore's expression was impassive at first, and I feared she'd laugh and call me strange. Instead, she reached out and took my hand.

My face flushed, but I held on tight.

"You want to know a secret?" she said then.

I laughed. "What secrets do you have?"

"You don't think I have secrets?"

"Well, go on then."

"I tried to run away," she said. "More than once, after my mother died. I never got far. You see that tree by the river?"

It was an old oak, twisted and bent over the water.

"I'd go down to that tree, and then I'd get scared and run back home."

"Why would you want to run away?"

"From Nördlingen? Why wouldn't I?"

"The city's nice. The city's safe."

"It's a cage. Everyone knows me, everyone's watching me. The deacon's daughter. The think they know just who I am. You should hear them, whispering. 'What a fine young woman she is. What a fine godly wife she'll be. A credit to her father.'"

"But where would you go?"

"I don't know. Anywhere. Amsterdam, Prague. You think I'm foolish. I know you do."

"No, I don't."

"Then what is it? Tell me what you're thinking. You're always so quiet, and I think you must be judging me."

"I think if you ran away, I'd miss you."

"If I ran away, I'd insist on taking you with me."

I felt a flutter deep in my gut. Then I thought of my father, alone.

Eleonore jumped to her feet. "Follow me," she said without explanation. Then she charged down the side of the hill toward the river.

I gave chase, but my poor shoes, handed down to me from Baker Ruppel's apprentice, were cracked and worn, and I struggled to find purchase on the slope, patchy with half-melted snow. I tumbled and slid toward the water, caking my breeches and the whole left side of my coat with dirt.

Eleonore stopped in front of that ancient, knotted old oak, its trunk hovering above the river's frozen surface, its branches reaching to the far side. She hesitated for only a moment at the roots, and then started to climb it unsteadily, perching at the start of a large branch that stretched out over the icy stream.

"What the devil are you doing?" I called to her.

"Running away, of course."

She edged her way out cautiously. The branch swayed and bent under her weight, but it didn't break. Then she sat upright, gaining confidence, and straddled it, her legs dangling over the river. "Look." She gave a bounce. "It's sturdy as the church tower."

"Are you mad? You'll fall." I was muddy, sore, and out of breath.

"Stop worrying and get up here."

There was no arguing with her. I stripped off my coat and left it on the shore as I climbed the tree to join her. When I reached the branch, I hesitated, but she reached out and pulled me toward her.

Relief washed over me as I watched the river below. All was still beneath the ice, placid and untroubled. I felt impossibly light, so far off the ground, little more than air beneath us.

"Would you believe this is as far as I've ever gotten?" Eleonore said. "I've seen this tree countless times, but I've never dared climb it. Just a few feet more, and we could be across the river. We could be on our way to Augsburg, to Munich, to Milan."

"We'd freeze before we reached Munich."

She groaned. "Can't I at least imagine? Where would you go if you could go anywhere in the world, do anything?"

"I don't know. I never thought about it."

"Fi."

"My father used to go to Frankfurt for the leather market. I always wanted to go with him."

"Very well, we'll go to Frankfurt. And then... Paris. Look—" She put her hand to her forehead, shading her eyes. "Can you see it, coming into view over the treetops? There's the cathedral, and there's the king's castle. Where next?"

I squinted and the clouds above the trees transformed themselves into rooftops and spires. In one of them the billowing sails of a great ship took form and I saw a harbor. "Rotterdam!" I cried.

"Yes, Rotterdam. We'll board a ship, and sail to England!"

So, we played, conjuring metropolises out of clouds—great teeming cities in England and France and Italy and places further still—Egypt, India, China—describing what we saw there in fantastical detail. Suspended on that branch where nothing could touch us, I believed it all.

And then, mid-sentence, Eleonore's smile faltered, her words dissolving into a moan. The light went out of her eyes as her body listed leftward. I grabbed her by the sleeve, but it tore free under the force of her weight as she fell.

She struck the water insensible, breaking the ice, without struggling or crying out. Unthinking, I jumped down after her. My own muscles went rigid as the cold water encased them.

The river was no more than belly-deep, but it took all my focus to make out Eleonore's dark shape amid the clouds of sediment beneath the frozen surface, and if she had not regained her senses, she surely would have drowned. But she started thrashing just as I grabbed her and came up coughing and gasping. I draped her arm over my shoulders and guided her to shore, where the runt waited, barking.

The steep slope of the muddy bank fought us, pushing us back down to the water's edge, but I seized hold of a tangle of sturdy roots, and used them like a rope to lift us out. On dry ground, violent shivers racked her body, and she choked up water. I could feel little else apart from the hammering of my own heart. I stripped her dress away from her bright pink skin and wrapped her in my threadbare coat.

My memory of what followed is hazy. Somehow, we made it to the edge of town. In the following days, my throat was sore and ragged, so I suppose I must have shouted until someone heard and found us.

That evening, my father, who'd never once raised his voice to me, upbraided me until he was too hoarse to speak: *We are guests in this town, do you understand that? We have nothing. We are Catholics in a Lutheran city. She's the deacon's daughter. He could have us back on the road in a breath. In the middle of winter, no less. I had no idea I'd raised such a foolish child.* Your mother *did not raise you to be such a foolish child!*

My body burned with the heat of shame. I was sure then that I'd done it; I'd exhausted his patience.

That night, I was stricken with fever. The illness lasted weeks, during which time the waking world and the dreaming melted into each other. There were times when I woke in a pool of my own sweat, unaware of where I was, or how I'd arrived there. And there were times when I huddled beneath my blankets and shivered as if I'd never know warmth again.

At some point, they moved me out of Baker Ruppel's storeroom and onto a bedroll in the charity Spital on the tanners' street. There, a wrinkled woman with whiskers on her chin spooned broth into my mouth and wiped my forehead with a damp rag. "*Liebchen,*" I can still hear her voice, fragile as winter frost, calling me. "It's not your time yet."

I only understood later how close to death I'd come. At my father's insistence, they'd summoned a Catholic priest from one of the nearby villages, and he read the last rites over me and touched the host to my colorless lips. The following night, my father sat at my side, waiting for me to pass. The old nurse had to coax him to eat.

I don't know what thread held me there, but shortly after the priest's visit, my fever broke and I returned, blinking, to the sight of harsh daylight spilling through the Spital windows. My father napped at my side, and the runt had his head wedged beneath my hand.

The world shifted and rocked around me, and when I tried to sit up, I felt as if I'd been pinned to my bedroll by an invisible force.

A quiet moan left my lips, and my father stirred at the sound of it, then let out a shout: "She's awake! She's awake!"

Several days went by before I'd recovered enough strength to stand and walk. My father was there each night, lying on the bedroll beside me, and in the day the old nurse tended to me. Eleonore never came, and it took some time before I found the boldness to ask what had happened to her.

My father sighed. "Best to put that girl out of your mind. If I still had my shop, you understand... but it's different now. We're no sort of people for a deacon's daughter, you understand?"

"But she's well?"

His face relaxed then, and he smiled. "Yes, she's well. Right well. And she says it's your doing. She says it was you who pulled her out of the water."

There was such pride in his voice then as I'd never heard before or since.

There's an old story that one day God called a council with all his angels, and Satan was among them. *Where did you come from?* God asked. And Satan said: *From walking back and forth across the earth.* And God said, *Have you met Job? He's a good man, righteous and God-fearing.* To which the devil replied, *It's easy enough to be righteous when you have all the blessings of God heaped on you. Take away everything Job has, and then see whether he still loves you.* So, God made a bet with the devil, and the wager was Job's peace.

I don't know what my father did to get the attention of God or his angels. Until the end of his days, I knew him as a seeming kind man, above-average honest, slow to a fault to show his feelings, and just as quick to accept what the world put on him. The only thing I could ever hold against him is that he learned too late that he couldn't be enough for me, nor I for him. But perhaps that's enough to pass for righteousness in our age.

Whatever visions we'd once conjured of a life in Nördlingen, the next months made it clear enough we wouldn't be staying. For one thing, my illness had exposed our ruse, which meant that there was no longer work for me at Baker Ruppel's, and without me working for him, the good baker could not justify his hospitality much longer.

For another, word of what had happened with Eleonore had begun to spread, accompanied by inescapable gossip about my mother's death. To this day, I don't know how the townspeople came by that knowledge.

Thereafter, I was forbidden from having any interaction with Eleonore. I saw her from time to time, walking the street in her father's shadow. She noticed me, once or twice, but her father was always there to shepherd her away before either of us could speak.

Come spring, there was little to keep me and my father in the city. Folk who'd once been happy enough to employ him for a day now shook their heads with exaggerated regret. We'd scraped together a purse full of gulden, but not enough to keep us sheltered and fed. My father had applied to the town council to open his own tannery, but that March they rejected the petition on account of his being Catholic.

I was sure it was the deacon's doing that so many people had suddenly turned cold to us, and I told my father as much.

"I doubt it," he said. "But if it's true, what are we to do about that, *Häschen*? He holds the strings."

"It's unfair," I protested, although by then I knew well enough that you might just as soon ask an out-of-tune instrument to carry a melody as to ask fairness from the world. "I didn't push his daughter in the river."

"No, you didn't. But that's not how people see it."

My throat grew tight.

"Come here." He pulled me onto his lap. "My God," he laughed. "You're almost too big. When did you do all this growing?"

"Here and there," I said, looping my arm around his neck.

"You're right. What happened to Eleonore wasn't your fault. You and I both know that. I'd wager her father knows it as well. But it's not a thing people readily accept, that bad things happen and no one's to blame for it."

I thought about the lightning strike in the field and about Albrecht and Anne, my friends, dangling on the gallows. I thought about farmer Holhansen's cows and old Barbara Rüfin. I thought about my mother. A bitter lump formed in my throat.

We'd arrived in Nördlingen at summer's end, 1618, and we left the next year, at the start of the spring planting season, shaking the dust of the city from our boots. I was nearly a year older and certainly the wiser for it. I no longer trembled at the road stretched out before me, with its unknown dangers, for the degradations of the road were well-known to me by then.

Instead, I ached. My mind was clouded by daydreams of Eleonore and me, crouched together in the choir of St. George's, stifling giggles lest her father hear us. Of her taking out her comb and running its tines through my hair, causing my scalp to prickle—a strange and pleasant feeling. Not memories, these—just idle daydreams of what might-have-been, the kind that sting like nettles.

As a balm, I tried to teach myself to hate her, but I found I could no more hate her than I could hate my own foot for stepping wrong and causing me to stumble. I suppose that's how it's always been between us.

As my father and I followed the lane to the city gates for the last time, my stormy thoughts turned once more to all those good, caring people we'd known in Nördlingen. Baker Ruppel with his round red face and thundering laugh. The nurse who'd called me *Liebchen* and held my hand in hers as I slipped in and out of life. Her nephew, who'd run to the next town in search of a priest. And of course, Eleonore's father, the deacon. How easily we'd reached the limits of their care, how narrow a country goodness turned out to be.

I wished then that my heart would turn to stone and cease its painful beating. But it wasn't possible. The indifference of all those good people wound itself around my insides like a barbed cord. The wound it left festers still.

My father must have seen the dark look that crossed my face as we passed through the gate because he laid a hand on my shoulder and said, "You mustn't let it devour you, *Häschen*."

Ah, but Father, you never told me how.

4

Ploughshares into Swords

1619

It was a bitter and rainy October day some six months after we'd left Nördlingen when we first saw the men rounding up recruits for the Catholic League army. By that time, my father had taken up leatherworking, and we would travel the villages of Bavaria selling his wares.

The recruiters had set up their table in a village square near Würzburg. Every now and again, a young man would approach the table, and after a few words, they'd record his name and where he was from in the register and hand him a purse full of coins from the lockbox.

All that summer, my father and I had worked our way across Swabia and Bavaria, planting and harvesting, trapping and fishing, skinning and sewing, while others far away had been busy bargaining away our peace, bit by bit. Here, at last, was the evidence of their labors.

What can I say now about the origins of this war? We were all such innocent babes then. When the Bohemian Protestants took up the defense of their religion and tossed the Emperor's representatives from the castle window, they could hardly have dreamt they were dragging all of Germany into war with them. Who could have envisioned that decades on this war would still be going, and that religion would be the farthest thing from anyone's mind?

What faith is left in Germany these days is stained with blood; it stinks of gun smoke. All our prayers, Protestant and Catholic alike, die in the rooms where they are spoken.

If the Bohemian lords had kept their fight within their own borders, perhaps we might all have been spared. Instead, they looked to Germany for an ally. On the banks of the Rhine, they found the one Protestant prince reckless enough to defy the Emperor and claim the Bohemian crown. Friedrich was his name, and if there was ever a fool in Christendom, it was him. He was, by all accounts, a pretty young man, and he might well have lived out his pretty little life in wealth and comfort in Mannheim with his equally pretty wife and children. Instead, he rode to Prague to take up the Protestant cause—to his ruin and our own.

In response, Friedrich's cousin Maximilian, duke of Bavaria and head of the Catholic League, pledged to raise an army in defense of the Empire and the Catholic faith. To what extent piety mattered to Duke Max, I don't know. Perhaps he was simply jealous of his cousin's newfound crown.

For my part, I've given up trying to understand the thinking of princes. What matters is, there were soon recruiters in near every town in Bavaria, raising an army to join the Bohemian War.

As we passed through the village square on that rain-soaked October day, one of those recruiters took my father by the arm. "What about you, sir? No man who fights for Maximilian and Our Lady shall go hungry."

A laugh sprang from deep in my father's belly. "Me, a soldier?" he said, disbelieving.

He looked at me, the corners of his eyes creased with amusement. He couldn't have been thirty-five years on this earth, but he appeared much older, his hair gray, his body reduced to bone and sinew.

We went on our way. We didn't speak of the offer. In fact, we near forgot it entirely.

A few nights later, we met a pair of priests on the road.

They approached with guarded looks, their hands tucked into the folds of their cassocks. They relaxed when my father made the sign of the cross and invited us to make camp with them.

The older of the two was a ready conversationalist and a storyteller by nature. He kept us up into the night with tales of their misadventures, some which seemed true, others almost certainly fantastical.

His younger companion hardly spoke a word. He had the look of the grave about him, his lips sealed tight as a coffin's lid. A dark and mangled scar snaked its way around his neck and peeked out of his low collar, and he made only the briefest of eye contact with us as we sat down by their fire. The priests' black robes marked them as Jesuits.

While we supped, the older told us they'd recently been near Augsburg, where they'd been seeking Protestants to convert.

"There's no shortage of them that way," my father remarked, adjusting the kettle on the fire. I huddled close to him for warmth.

"They're a plague. A boil to be lanced and cut away." These were the first words the younger priest had spoken all evening. He sat with his back toward both us and the fire, gaze fixed on the road a few yards away.

The older sighed. "The child, brother. Temper yourself." Then, turning to my father: "Misfortune befell us some while back—"

"Not misfortune," the younger corrected. "Calvinists."

The old priest nodded. "Yes, Calvinists. They set upon us some months ago and tried to hang us. Brother Patrick here took the worst of it. But it's the spiritual wounds that take longest to heal."

The other let out a sharp, bitter laugh, but he didn't say another word. Nor did he once look away from the road.

"Do you know the Calvinists?" the old priest asked my father.

"Can't say I do."

"Rowdy, rebellious lot. Worse than Lutherans. Lutherans at least want to keep some semblance of a church. They understand the need for authority to guide God's flock, even if they're terribly misguided on other points. Calvinists—they have it all topsy-turvy. Their elders answer to their congregations. They believe that a man's salvation is predestined. If so, what is the role of the church at all?"

"Don't ask me to make sense of it," my father said.

"The Bohemian pretender is a Calvinist," said the old priest, meaning Friedrich, the pretty little prince. "They're zealots, the lot of them."

That night, I struggled to sleep, and I saw that the young priest was still awake also. He'd moved closer to the fire, but he continued to watch the road. In his lap, he cleaned a small pistol. When he noticed me watching him, he smiled a thin, joyless smile that caused my skin to prickle.

He beckoned me over, and as I approached, he drew a knife from the sleeve of his cassock. The blade was no longer than the length of my hand from my wrist to the tip of my forefinger. My heart beat in my throat as he offered it to me, grip first.

"Put on the whole armor of God, my child," he said then. "That you may be able to stand against the wiles of the devil."

He fixed me with his wide, unblinking eyes and made the sign of the cross. I took the weapon—more out of fear of refusing him than anything—and returned to my bed, eager to be away from his disquieting stare.

The next morning, the priests went north, and we went east, and we never saw them again.

My father had been selling his leatherwork all summer, and by October we had scraped together a small savings. We made plans to go to Bamberg for the winter and put the money into a new tannery. How hopeful we were then!

But we never did reach Bamberg. What happened was this: just a few days after we met the priests, we stopped to hawk our goods in Neustadt an der Aisch, a reasonable-sized trading post halfway between Würzburg and Nuremberg. We did a brisk business there and added to our savings.

But a leatherworker from that town took exception to my father's practicing the leather trade, as he wasn't part of any guild or trade organization. The leatherworker took him before the local magistrate, but the magistrate couldn't order my father to stop his work, only forbid him from selling in Neustadt.

My father complied, and we moved on, but that didn't stop people from that town seeking out his craftsmanship. My father was not one to turn away honest trade, so he took the business, thinking he was breaking no rule.

But late one evening we were woken by a hammering at the door of the house where we were staying. The leatherworker had gathered a group of men, and he demanded that my father come outside. The men had all been in their cups, it was plain, for they stank and slurred their words.

When my father realized why they were there, he offered to pay them a share of his profits, if only they'd leave him alone. "Please," he said. "It's my only livelihood, and I have the child to think of."

"You might have given that more consideration before you went about stealing another man's trade. You're worse than a common thief."

My father saw the violence in their eyes then, and he made to run, but the men lunged for him, and two of them grabbed him by the arms and dragged him out of the house. My father struggled like he had the devil in him, but it was useless. The men were as frothing dogs, stirred into a rage by the leatherworker's slanders and rendered insensitive by drink. My father kicked and clawed at them, but they twisted his arms behind his back until he cried out in pain.

All the while, what use was I? I stood fixed in one spot, slack-jawed and dumb. When I'd recovered my senses, I ran out after them, hurling curses and shouting at them to let my father go. The runt too growled and snapped at the men, but they gave him a swift, hard kick that sent him tumbling in the dirt.

When curses had no effect, I took to pummeling the nearest man with my small fists, but he yanked me by the hair and twisted until my eyes burned with tears.

The others tore the shirt off my father's back and pinned him to the ground. He'd never been a large man, but his exposed flesh was a sorry sight indeed. Each heavy fearful breath revealed the shape of his ribs beneath his sunken skin. That's when I noticed that they'd brought a bucket of pine tar with them, along with a sack of goose feathers.

In my memory, there are two sounds forever melded, one to the other. The first is the wail my father gave when he found my mother dangling from the rafters of his tannery. The second is his cry when the first of the warm sticky tar was poured across his chest. If a breaking heart makes any sound, I am sure it must be a cousin to these.

My father's cries turned my blood sour. My scalp throbbed with pain. The runt let out a yowl. The men laughed.

I was past thinking. I drew the priest's knife, hidden in my boot. Then I charged at the leatherworker and stuck him in the back, just below the kidney.

I confess a feeling of terrible triumph in that moment, a giddy, soaring sensation in my breast as the leatherworker cried out and dropped the bucket of tar at his feet. Then the blood seeped through his shirt, and my stomach grew weak.

"Whore-child, bitch, rotten, flea-ridden—" He let up his cursing only long enough to gasp for breath. Meanwhile, he contorted himself, trying to pull the knife from his back. "You've killed me! You've killed me, you devil-begotten bastard!"

The other men all released my father at once. One of them pulled the knife out, while another grabbed me and wrapped his arm around my neck, cutting off my air. Bursts of color pulsed in front of my eyes. I heard my father calling to me, but his voice was distant and muffled, as if through cloth.

I was certain then that we would both die that day. Had the runt not buried his teeth in my attacker's leg, I am sure we would have.

The man released me and fell to the ground, gripping his bloodied limb. During the chaos, my father got to his feet, gathered the scraps of his ruined shirt, and ran towards me. He gripped me by the arm and dragged me along, urging me to run. I stumbled behind him, tripping over my own feet as I tried to keep pace. The runt ran after.

We must have run at least a mile, stopping only when our legs gave out underneath us, and we collapsed breathless and sore in a stretch of woods far away. So far as we could tell, no one had followed us. Likely they'd been preoccupied tending to the wounded men.

As the warming fire of our terror faded and the autumn air pressed in against our flesh, we came to understand how truly dire our situation was. My father had nothing more than the tatters of a shirt to keep away the cold, and he didn't dare put it on, lest it cling to the tar on his chest. We'd no shelter for the night. Our savings, although meager, had been left in the house we'd been staying in. My father's tanning and leatherworking tools, too.

I spent the next hours scraping the tar from my father's skin with a rock, a task that grew more difficult as the cold air caused it to set. He gritted his teeth and did his best to choke down his cries, but it was slow, strenuous work that left my arms aching and his chest raw and scarified.

The worst of it was that twice I broke down, unable to keep back my own tears, and he was compelled to hold and comfort me, so that I could continue to rub and claw at his excoriated flesh.

For all my certainty that we would die that day, we did not. For good or ill, we were too stubborn for it. The morning after our flight, half-frozen and having hardly slept, my father and I set out again, aiming to put as much distance as we could between us and that terrible village. On the road, we ran into a family of Jews, who were kind enough to provide a fresh shirt for my father and warm blankets for the both of us.

As for the leatherworker, we never heard from him again. I don't know whether he lived or died, or whether I should count murder among my sins. For a year after, his blood haunted my dreams. But in time those dreams faded.

In the next town, we encountered the Catholic League recruiters once more. My father patted me on the shoulder and bade me wait for him, then walked with slow, dragging steps toward the desk where an officious young clerk marked down his name in the rolls and handed him the mustering money. Eight gulden a month was his wage when he joined, plus rations.

In the old story, when Job's friends learned of his hardship, they asked him what sins he'd committed to earn his misery. But Job wouldn't stand for their questioning. He knew himself to be a righteous man, so he called God to account. God answered him: *Where were you when I laid the foundation of the earth? Tell me, if you have understanding. Shall a faultfinder contend with the Almighty? He who argues with God, let him answer it.*

It is futile to argue with God, I know this. We each receive our lot according to his design, and his design is not known to us. But what a rotten design it is, that beats ploughshares into swords and makes soldiers out of tanners.

5

Little Warrior

1620

An army is a living, traveling city. Its bastions are built of human bodies—pikemen arranged, as stone upon stone, in neat squares. All the things a human body needs must follow behind: sutlers selling bread, meat, and beer; iron- and leather-workers, cloth-sellers, bootmakers, slingers of tonics, surgeons to cut the body apart and sew it back up again, seamstresses, tailors, and craftsmen of all kinds. Priests, as well, to assuage the soul, to pray over the battles to come, to remind the soldiers of why they are fighting: for Our Lady, presently under siege by the faithless Protestant.

A soldier must have his family with him, too. A wife to cook his meals and patch his coat and to prevent him whoring and spreading disease. His children close by, so that he doesn't start longing for home, so it's harder for him to imagine deserting.

However many soldiers one counted in the army's ranks, it was reliable that the number following was as many and sometimes more. The Tross, we were called, the baggage train. We marched behind the army, and when they camped, spending long days drilling and digging ditches and constructing whatever other defenses the position required, we bargained and bartered, washed and sewed, dug pits for our cookfires and fetched water for our kettles, pitched the tents and shook the dead leaves of the last camp from our bedrolls.

We waited, as well: for newly recruited regiments to join us, for knowledge of the enemy's location, for the commanders to decide when we should march and where. I'd not given much thought to war before I was in one, but I'm sure I'd never imagined it to involve so much waiting. That first year, we waited for winter to thaw and the army to assemble and did not march until summer.

I was on my own most of that time, hardly seeing my father except at meals, at night when he lay down to rest, and at the end of each month when he returned from the paymaster.

He trusted the money to me, and I made what I could of it, haggling over the price of bread, bartering for offal to supplement our ration, scavenging for the scraps of cloth and leather that others tossed aside in their carelessness, in their naïve belief that there would always be more. By then I knew well enough how quickly good fortune spoils.

What a lonely time that was! More than a full year had passed since Eleonore and I sneaked outside of the city gates to eat and laugh and pour out our hearts to each other in the way of children. There were others my age in the Tross, but I found few friends among them.

The other children were not to blame. They ran about, gamboling and making mischief and laughing among themselves—the happy little fools—while I grew sour, sullen, and hot-tempered. Their play was innocent enough, and it was that same innocence that I resented down to my teeth.

I thought myself wise; I thought that since I knew misfortune and cruelty, I knew the whole measure of the world. I'd known so little kindness that I convinced myself it did not exist, except as a means to an end. So, day after day, I hauled my kettle to and from the water until my hands blistered and grew callused and my mood grew bitter and resentful with only the runt for company.

Early in the new year, a young woman of about nineteen years set up her tent not far from the one my father and I shared. She gave her name as Katharina Ingolstadt. She was a seamstress, and she claimed to be the wife of a musketeer in the regiment, but it was widely held that she was not married at all, and indeed, from month to month, it was often a different musketeer that appeared at her tent.

Folks murmured that she had something of the Greek or the Turk in her, on account of her black hair and sun-kissed skin. But if any had bothered to ask her, she would've told them she was born on a river barge on the Danube, just outside the city from which she took her name.

From the first, my father warned me off having any dealings with her. "That's a woman without honor," he said, by which he meant a whore. "Be wary."

That was ever my father's trouble. He believed the world to be a certain way, and little could shake him of his conviction, no matter how often the world itself conspired to contradict him. If the priests said the army's cause was just, it was just. A whore could not be virtuous, and God would never forget a pious man.

That winter, I spent the long nights quaking with cold by our fire with only a threadbare blanket to warm me. One evening, I returned to my tent to find a freshly sewn blanket of loden cloth folded inside. I guessed right away it was Katharina's doing. I'd seen her working with a heavy cloth in the same shade earlier that day.

I didn't know how to accept such a gift, needed yet unasked for. So, I gathered it up and left it in her tent when she was away. The next night, I woke shivering and found the blanket laid once more just inside the tent. I pulled it over me and let its warmth lull me to sleep.

In the days after, I cast about for a way to repay her without disobeying my father's instructions. One afternoon, I managed to haggle for an additional ration of salt beef at a good price, so I left a portion wrapped in burlap beside Katharina's firepit.

Around that time, a boy named Gerhard started causing trouble among the lower ranks. He was a cuirassier's boy, which meant it was his job to help his cavalryman don his armor and get in his saddle. He had other responsibilities as well, but he was an idle, lazy boy, and he shirked them in favor of wandering the Tross, pulling up tent stakes and tipping over kettles.

The other children admired him, for he boasted that his soldier let him fire his weapon and sharpen his sword. Further, his father was secretary to the Oberst, the regimental commander, and he preened about like a little prince, never once letting anyone forget it.

For my part, I paid Gerhard as little mind as I could. I had enough troubles in a day without getting myself tangled up in his childish games.

My indifference pricked at him to no end. He wasn't used to being anything less than loved; he couldn't stand it. He took to needling me, stepping into my path as I went about my errands, and once plucking my washing from the fire where it hung to dry and tossing it in the dirt.

In those days, as I've said, I was a bitter, hot-tempered child, though few would have guessed it at first look. I carried my anger close and prayed to God to make me its master. Each time Gerhard called me flea-ridden or a whore-child, I held my tongue and dreamed of ripping out his. I knew it would ill serve us for my father to be kicked out of the army on my account. My jaw ached from gritting my teeth morning to night, day after day.

One day, I spied Gerhard skulking outside of Katharina's tent. He held a small drawstring pouch in one hand, and when Katharina went out to fetch bread and fill her kettle, he slipped inside. I could mind myself no longer.

"What have you done?" I demanded of him when he emerged.

He startled. "Stands to reason you'd be friends with the whore. You and your mongrel dog." He sneered at the runt, but the dog, who was a ways off lazing in a sunbeam, paid him no mind.

"What have you done?" I repeated.

The boy shrugged. "Just some itching powder in her sheets. She's probably so riddled with disease she won't even notice it."

He started to walk off, but I blocked his way. "Have you nothing better to do than to sow trouble in other folks' fields? She'll know it was you."

His laugh was mocking. "Why do you care? Was your mother a whore as well? Must have been some kind of rotting cunt birthed you."

"At least my father doesn't spend all his time rutting with prostitutes," I spat, unthinking.

His brow lowered. "Liar."

"I am not. Half the Tross can confirm it. He was over yonder the other night, his ass hanging out in the moonlight as he fucked. What's the matter? Can't he afford a proper whore, or can't he keep one?" It was a stupid, reckless thing to say, but my tongue had gone ahead of my good sense.

With a screech, the boy lunged at me, and I fell back against the cold earth with a painful impact. He pinned me there and started to throttle me.

The pouch filled with itching powder lay fallen in the grass. I reached for it, coaxing it towards my hand with the tips of my fingers, until at last it was in my grasp. Then I pried it open and emptied it into Gerhard's breeches.

The boy stumbled backward, shouting and clawing at his nethers. "How could you?" he squeaked with disbelief. "Oh, God, it itches. It itches terribly. How could you? My father will know about this. He'll have you kicked out of the regiment." He hobbled off then, hand between his legs, still squealing.

Katharina returned a short while later, and I warned her of Gerhard's trick. She thanked me with a kind smile, then invited me to join her at her soup. I refused her and hurried back to my tent to prepare supper for my father.

My hand shook as I struggled to light the fire. The excitement of my confrontation with Gerhard faded, leaving only a fearful unease about what would come next.

Over supper, I confessed to my father what I'd done to the boy, fully ready for him to chastise me, as he had in Nördlingen. But his shoulders shook in silent laughter.

"You're not angry?" I asked, confused.

"Well," he reflected, scooping up his meal with a crust of bread, "I don't see that there was any harm in it. Children being children. They'll hardly kick me out of the army on account of some itching powder."

For the next few days, Gerhard was scarce, and we had our peace. My father was on the night watch all the next week, so I saw little of him. If Gerhard told anyone what had happened, nothing seemed to have come of it. I returned to my routine and gave little thought to the boy.

Ah, but *they have sown the wind and shall reap the whirlwind*. I was a fool for thinking Gerhard would forget the indignity I'd done to him.

Trouble came week's end. The runt had free range of the camp while I went about my chores during the day, but he always returned to the tent by nightfall to curl up with his spine against mine. But that evening, I saw no sign of him.

I didn't worry at first. But when the sky turned that pale and sickly violet that portends night, I began searching for him in earnest. My father was gone to his post on the night watch by then. I passed by Katharina's tent. She was at her fire, and she waved at me, as was her way.

"Have you seen my dog?" I asked her.

She shook her head. "Not of late. He was bathing in the stream earlier. Around mid-afternoon, I suppose it was."

I thanked her and went down toward the water.

The runt's yelps greeted me first, followed by shouts and cruel laughter. Gerhard's laugh stood out amongst the rest, loud and jeering. My heart hammered against my ribs when I heard the sounds, and I broke into a run, chasing the noises in the waning half-light, stumbling over the uneven earth.

By the river's bank, I found Gerhard and four or five others all in a circle around the runt, who was cowering in their midst, tied to a stake. Each took his turn to throw stones at the dog and mock the sounds he made when they struck. The runt wailed pitifully, blood glistening on his snout and by his left eye.

The bitter cord that wended its way around my insides when I left Nördlingen dug its barbs into my heart. For months, I'd tried to tamp down on my anger, but it only grew, a debt that could never be repaid.

When I'd stabbed the leatherworker the previous year, my only thought had been to save my father. When I charged Gerhard and tackled him to the ground, I was determined to kill him.

Gerhard was older than me, but I'd grown mightily in the previous months, so that I was easily the taller of the two of us. I pinned him on his back and drove my fist into his jaw. The force of the impact shuddered back up through my knuckles and into my wrist and forearm. I gritted my teeth against the pain and kept right on thrashing him, even as his nose and mouth grew wet with blood.

Once his companions recovered from their shock, they dragged me off him, throwing me into the dirt and raining blows on my body. I curled myself into a ball to protect my face and belly.

Katharina saved me. Brandishing a kettle and a wooden spoon, she rushed into their midst. "Get back to your mothers, you scoundrels," she snapped, and I heard the beating of footsteps as the whole group retreated.

I remained where I'd fallen, curled up and trembling.

"Still breathing, girl?" she asked, giving my shoulder a nudge.

"I think so."

She laughed. "Aye, you are. Can you move?"

I was uncertain. My bruised body ached in protest, but with some effort, I managed to turn over onto my back, and with the help of Katharina's outstretched hand, I raised myself up to a sitting position.

"Look here," she said, kneeling in the grass beside me. "I won't say that little wretch didn't deserve it, but that wasn't very wise of you, was it?"

I gave her no answer. The runt was still tied to the stake, panting heavily. I crawled toward him on one hand. He growled low as I drew close, and when I reached out to stroke him, he snapped at me in warning. One of his eyes was swollen and bloodied, and his left hind leg sprawled, limp, behind him. The fur on his neck was matted with blood where he'd strained against the rope.

"Hush," I said. "Hush now. It's me." I extended my hand again and received another flash of teeth for my troubles.

"No, runt, don't do that," I pleaded with him. "I'll not hurt you. You know I'll not hurt you."

It took more long minutes of soft words and gentle coaxing, but finally the runt let up his growling long enough for me to fumble with the knot. My right hand was badly swollen, and I couldn't move my fingers to manage such a delicate task.

Katharina saw my difficulty. The runt growled as she approached, but I took his head in my lap and stroked his neck till he quieted again. Katharina knelt in front of us and untied him.

The runt tried to get to his feet, but his hind leg wouldn't support him, and he collapsed again with a yelp.

"I'm sorry," I said, burying my face in the runt's fur. "I'm so, so sorry."

Katharina looked the pair of us over, her mouth set in a thin, straight line. "You should have that checked," she said, meaning my hand. The limb was stained dark red and engorged, though I was sure the blood on it was mostly Gerhard's. A searing ache thrummed through the fingers and into my arm.

"I'll not leave him," I said, clutching the runt close.

She looked about her. "Where's your father?"

"On the watch."

"Damn. Very well. Wait here."

She marched away, the hem of her skirt brushing through the grass. The evening light was gone by then, leaving only the three-quarters moon and the distant campfires to see by. While we waited, the runt whined and panted without ceasing. I did my best to soothe him, speaking to him in hushed words and rubbing his belly. He lapped at my injured hand.

When Katharina returned, she was joined by a tall, heavyset man with a wiry black beard. He puffed and strained as he walked, burdened by a large leather case that he let drop at my feet. I'd never seen him before, and I watched him anxiously as he approached.

"Well, well." The man crouched in front of me and set his lantern on the ground. "Who do we have here?"

Katharina nodded at me in encouragement.

"Josefine Dorn, sir, and this is the runt."

"Wounded in battle, or so I'm told." He chuckled as he undid the buckles on his case. He gave his name as Salomon ben Judah of Frankfurt, a Jew. He was the Oberst's physician as well as a surgeon.

Now there are those who teach that the Jews are a wicked people, who kidnap children and force them to converting, alongside all manner of other slanders and falsifications. At that time, I was still young, and such stories easily impressed themselves on my imagination.

So when the physician asked to see my wrist, I confess, to my shame, I hesitated.

"Go on, then." It was Katharina. At her urging, I held out my hand.

Salomon's own hands were soft and gentle, and he spoke in such a pleasant and digressive manner, telling tales of his early life in Frankfurt and of his travels in France and Spain and the Muslim lands, that I was well-entranced and quickly forgot my fears. Then he squeezed my wrist, and I cried out.

"That hurts then, does it?" he asked. He gestured to Katharina to hold the lantern close. The light revealed flesh so purpled, I might have taken it for rotten.

He took my fore- and middle fingers and gave them a tug and then a twist, reducing the bones into place. I cried out again, as the pain ripped through my arm up to the shoulder. If you haven't felt such a thing, you might imagine a spearpoint being driven up the length of your arm.

"There now," said Salomon. "I know it's painful, but if you want the use of this hand again, you'll just have to endure it, you understand."

I nodded, but the tears slid down my face anyway.

"That's a brave girl. You remind me of my sister Judith. Fearless woman, that. An absolute nightmare if you crossed her, even as a child. She hided me more often than my own parents. *Salomon,* she said, *we'll make something of you. God did not give us much to work with, but we'll make something of you anyhow.* She runs the family business now and writes me twice yearly to ask why I haven't been home to visit. I tell her I'm very busy, but—" he leaned in close "—just between you and me, I'm afraid of her."

I laughed, and he chose that moment to reduce the bones of my wrist. I gasped, and the world around me wobbled.

Katharina laid her hands on my shoulders to keep me from toppling over. "Damn it, man," I heard her say. "You're going to make her pass out."

"It can't be avoided. The bones must be set in place, or they'll grow together all wrong. Do you want the child to have one arm shorter than the other or crooked fingers? No, that won't do. That won't do at all. Now, kindly allow me to do the job you fetched me for."

I couldn't see Katharina's face, but she held me close.

"All's well," I assured her. "I'm fine."

She relaxed but did not leave my side. All told, I'd broken two fingers and my wrist on Gerhard's jaw. Salomon bandaged them three times over with bandages soaked in vinegar and water.

He did praiseworthy work that night. I can write and cut and stitch and separate the stems from my herbs and any other delicate use you might think of without so much as a tremor to remind me of the injury. But rarely still a numbness spreads through that hand that renders it all but useless. It's no fault of Salomon's; I've only my own reckless bad temper to blame for it.

When he'd done setting my bones, the physician turned his attention to the runt. This was the harder work, and in the end the only way he could manage to set the runt's leg was if Katharina and I both laid our weight on the dog's body to hold him down.

The eye was a lost cause. "I'm afraid I'm going to need you to tie off his snout," Salomon said. He reached into his case and produced a needle and thread, a bottle of brandy, a rag, and a spoon.

He took a sip of brandy and passed the bottle to me and Katharina. "Drink up. It'll steel your stomach." I'd never before tasted its like, burning through my throat and belly. I broke into a fit of coughing.

I was certain the runt wouldn't forgive me as I tied the rope around his snout or as Katharina and I held him in place while the physician scooped out the remains of his ruined eye. But dogs are a better sort than all of us, quick to forgive, slow to form grudges, and free with their affection.

After the work was done, Salomon left me with instructions to find his tent by daylight, so he could check his work, change the bandages, and be sure everything was healing as it should. Then he and Katharina stepped a few paces away and exchanged words in voices too quiet for me to hear.

The runt made to stand, whimpering at first when his broken leg touched the earth, but soon enough he discovered the secret to hobbling about on three legs, and his tail began to wag. He hopped alongside me all the way back to our tent.

Katharina entered shortly after with an armful of blankets. "I think it best if I joined you tonight."

"You don't have to—" I protested.

"Hush. I don't want to hear it. You'll not spend the night alone."

"But your…" I faltered. I didn't know what to call the soldier who currently took up nightly residence in Katharina's tent. "…husband."

She laughed. "We both know I have no husband. But you let me worry about that."

Rest taunted me that night. The incessant, thrumming pain in my wrist startled me back to wakefulness the moment I started to drift on sleep's waters. But Katharina stayed by my side, soothing me when I cried out and running her fingertips through my hair until at last I slept.

6

The Many Uses of Flowering Plants

1620

My father returned a short while after sunrise the next morning. I woke with a groan, feeling still more knocked-about after a night's rest than I'd felt just after the blows struck my body. When I saw my father's silhouetted form ducking through the tent's opening, I hid my bandaged arm beneath the blanket, fearful of what he would say.

But my father hadn't noticed my arm or any of my other injuries. He was staring at Katharina, slumbering in his place beside me. "*You,*" he said, giving her arm a shove. "You are in the wrong tent."

"Hm?" The young woman turned over, blinking sleep from her eyes. "Oh. Mr. Dorn. Begging your pardon. Your daughter had a little misadventure last night. Better if she explains it. I was just looking after her welfare."

"My daughter doesn't need the likes of you looking after her welfare."

"Father," I protested.

It was Katharina who interrupted me. "No, Josefine." She gathered up her blanket and her garments, and now she bent forward to pull on her boots. "It's a father's right to look out for his daughter's honor. It's his responsibility to protect her from sinful influences." Still clothed only in her thin shift, she slunk toward the opening of the tent. There she paused, addressing my father with a direct gaze: "But who will look out for the rest of her, I wonder?"

His jaw tensed. "Are you saying I don't know how to take care of my daughter?"

"Oh, no," said the woman. "I'd not dare say any such thing. But even virgins need to eat—or so I'm told. What happens when you're not there? What happens when she doesn't have your eight gulden a month, and the young men turn up regardless with their tongues a-wagging?"

"It will be her husband's responsibility to look after her."

"Right. Of course. My father had the same idea. Only—" she bit her lower lip "—he couldn't manage the dowry. The boy promised he'd marry me anyhow. But wouldn't you know, he was gone as soon as he had what he wanted. I suppose you have that all worked out, though. You'll give her your pike for a dowry, maybe. Or your stinking boots."

"Get out!" my father shouted. A dab of spit bubbled on his lower lip. His chest heaved.

Katharina fixed him with a serious look. "Of course, Mr. Dorn. You're her father. You know what's best."

When she'd left, my father arranged his bedding with quick, jerking movements. I sat up, straining against the soreness in my ribs and back, and lifted the hem of my dress to inspect my side. The skin was mottled with purple-and-black bruises, a mass of discolored flesh that ached at a touch.

The runt also shifted beside me, making one and a half awkward, hopping turns in the narrow space, until he rested his chin on my lap. A crust had formed over his closed eye, and I resolved to ask the physician Salomon about it later that day. I held my bandaged arm, warm and throbbing, close to my belly.

My father took note of our injuries for the first time. "What the devil...?"

Then I told him all what Gerhard had done to the runt and what I had done to Gerhard.

I waited for him to holler at me, but he didn't, not at first. He ran his finger along his mustache; he shook his head; he cleared his throat of phlegm and spat in the dirt.

"What were you thinking?" he said at last.

I stared at the space between my feet. "I know it was ill-judged. I'm sorry."

"Raging like a wild animal. Like you didn't have a proper upbringing. Your mother would be ashamed."

The hairs on my neck stood on end. "Don't you bring her into this," I muttered.

"What did you say?"

"I said, don't bring her into this. She left us, and now here we are. If she didn't wish me wild, she should have lived."

"You have no idea what you're talking about." My father's voice cracked. "Do you think the people of that wicked town wouldn't have tortured and killed us all? She gave everything for you."

"You were proud enough when I put itching powder down that boy's breeches."

"Itching powder is a child's game. You could've been killed! Are you so bound and determined to make everything your mother sacrificed, everything I've sacrificed, worthless?"

"What should I have done? Let them kill the runt? Let them kick me about as well? I'd rather die than roll over in the dirt for the likes of them."

He sighed. "I'm angry too, *Häschen*. But you can't let it rule you."

I nodded, staring down at my fingers.

"What if this boy comes back while I'm gone, looking to settle accounts? What will you do then?"

I didn't think Gerhard would dare. "I can defend myself."

"No."

"Get me a knife, and I'll slice off his nose."

He took me by the shoulders, his eyes wide. At the time I thought it was anger I saw blazing in them, but now I'm sure it was fear. "Josefine. Listen to me. Under no circumstances will you fight back, do you understand? You will go and you will find me, wherever I am, you will find me—"

"But—"

"Don't interrupt me. If you can't find me, you look for one of the other soldiers. Bachmann, he's trustworthy, or the Italian, Stefano. One of them will know where I am. Is that clear?"

"Yes, Father."

He nodded, satisfied. But long after I'd left the tent to go about the day's chores, I heard him tossing this way and that on his bed and moaning to himself in his sleep.

Now I'm older and have a daughter of my own, I think I understand my father better. To be parent to a child is to make eyes at a kind of madness, to lie down beside lunacy. To have a child is to pour all one's hopes and fears into the most fragile of vessels in the certain knowledge that one way or another you will lose them, one way or another your child will leave and take those hopes and fears with them, into the grave or into the unwritten future, and who can say which is worse? Some take one look at that madness and retreat; some lash out at what they know they cannot control; and some, like my father, are swallowed up by it.

A few months shy of twelve years old, I had little understanding of such things and even less sympathy for them. I judged my father an unimaginative fool, who'd made his misery and mine worse with his naïve hoping.

For months, I'd been aware of a swelling in my breasts and of hair growing where it hadn't before. Even now, the child he'd known was fading away, and no matter how much he hoped, he couldn't keep her. I wanted to shake him awake and shout at him: *How could you be such a fool?*

But in truth I was no less a fool than he. After joining the army, we'd given up on making plans for the future; we could no longer imagine ever arriving in such a place. To survive the day in front of us took all we had. Yet the future had gone on making plans for us anyhow. If my hand never healed, if my father died, what then? There were only so many possibilities for a girl like me, one without a pfennig to bring to her husband for a dowry.

I trudged down to the river that morning with my kettle, unable to see through the storm of my thoughts. My right arm ached powerfully at my side, useless to so much as lift the vessel. Halfway back to my tent, the strength of my good arm gave out, and the kettle toppled to the ground, splashing its contents at my feet.

I wondered if my father wouldn't have been better off ridding himself of me after my mother's death. I'd heard of such fathers, who left their children to wander the woods when they could no longer feed them, or else abandoned them to the church. If only mine had done the same, he might have been free. One less hungry belly to fill, one less body to worry after. He was young enough to find himself a new wife, make himself a new family. If he lived long enough, he could forget about us entirely, my cursed mother and I, as if we were nothing more than a nightmare, a troubled night's sleep.

I was lost in the darkness of those thoughts when the runt hopped up to me, tongue lolling from his mouth, which hung open in a wide animal rictus.

"What do you have to grin about, you half-blind cripple?" I said, bending to stroke his neck. He tried to lick my mouth, but missed, lapping at my ear with his wet tongue.

I laughed, and the storm in my mind dissipated. "All right, mongrel. Come on."

I went to check on Katharina, but she'd gone back to sleep. Instead of waking her, I set out to pay the physician a visit.

Though we had yet to leave Bavaria, let alone meet the enemy, there was no shortage of work for the surgeons and physicians that accompanied the regiment.

The physicians were of respectable and educated rank, overseeing the treatment of internal ailments and diseases—smallpox, typhus, and typhoid, as well as the general health and good humor of the officers. They prescribed medicines and offered dietary advice according to the ancient and time-tested precepts of medical philosophy.

The surgeons were a more motley lot. They treated the body itself when it was broken, bruised, wounded, or inflamed. They applied medicines to the surface; they cut and bound and operated. Many of them had little education in medical philosophy at all. And when there were no injuries to treat, they trimmed the men's beards and cut their hair.

Salomon was that rare practitioner who was both physician and surgeon. As he gave it, after traveling to Padua to study medical philosophy at fifteen, he'd come away unsatisfied and had spent the next years traveling in Italy, Spain, and the Muslim lands before returning to his birth-city of Frankfurt to marry and start his practice. In that time, he'd concluded that the best way to grow one's understanding of the body's workings was to study the body directly, using as many of the senses as was reasonable. He'd begun by observing autopsies and had ended by taking up the surgeon's art.

His work-tent lay between the officers' barracks and the rank-and-file. When I arrived that morning, I found him deep in conversation with Gerhard's father.

Though I'd never before seen the man's face, I knew him right away. The father's resemblance to his son was unmissable, particularly in the mouth, the corners of which were pulled ever downward in the same petulant frown.

Gerhard himself was seated on a bench close by, his lower lip swollen, his jaw purpled with bruises. Some sort of device had been fastened over his nose and bound with leather straps around his head, and he kept his gaze fixed on his feet, digging a rut into the ground with the toe of his boot.

My stomach roiled, sick with the certainty that Salomon was telling Gerhard's father of my part in his son's injuries. I ducked behind the physician's cart, grateful that neither Gerhard nor his father had yet noticed me.

"Come now, boy," I heard his father say in a thin, papery voice. Footsteps followed, brushing grass and crunching earth.

Heart thrumming, I dropped down and crawled under the cart's carriage. The bruises on my body pulsed angrily as I dragged my belly across the rocky earth. A fierce shock of pain raced along my injured arm, filling my mouth with bile. I forced it, burning, down my throat. The runt peered at me and whimpered. I patted the ground, urging him to follow me, but he only cocked his head in confusion.

Gerhard paused beside the cart, staring at the runt.

"Hurry, boy, and don't sulk," said his father. "I've wasted enough time on your reckless brawling."

Gerhard took off at a trot, tracking a wide path around the dog.

A moment later, there came three swift knocks on the cart above me. I near jumped out of my skin at the sound.

"It's safe to come out now, little warrior," Salomon called to me. "Or perhaps you were planning to stay there until Elijah's return?"

I crawled out and the physician helped me to my feet.

"So," he said. "Am I to understand that that was the boy whose face you cracked your hand on? Not bad, not bad. I daresay you might have done him a favor. Oh, his nose will likely heal crooked, but he'll be the wiser for it hereafter."

"I wasn't trying to do him any favors."

The runt hobbled up to Salomon, sniffing at the hem of his robes.

"No, no, that was clear enough," the physician said, bending down to inspect the dog's eye. "But perhaps in the future he'll think better of attacking a creature weaker than himself. All men could stand to be reminded of such a lesson, I think. Good dog. Now, I'll need your help holding him still." I wrapped my arms around the runt's middle as the doctor moved his hand along his ribs, his belly, and his joints, pressing into the soft flesh with two firm fingers. The runt's anxious breaths reverberated against my side, and he whined and lapped at my face with his tongue.

"Lucky fellow," Salomon said when the examination was done. "Some bruising, but nothing seems broken. Now, let's have a look at that hand of yours. Does it hurt much?"

"Only sometimes," I lied.

He took my right wrist and applied a gentle pressure, causing me to flinch and cry out.

"I thought as much. Never lie to a physician. We hear too many lies. We can always tell. I can't treat what you won't admit is wrong. Now, let's try again. How is your hand today?"

"It hurts like Christ on the cross," I confessed. "I can't lift a thing with it. And when I let it drop, I think I might faint."

"Best keep it raised, then. I'll fashion you a sling. As for lifting things, you might avoid that for a while."

"It's a mite easier to fill my kettle with two hands," I complained.

"You might have thought of that before you broke that boy's nose and split his lip. You're very fortunate he was too embarrassed by the whole affair to tell anyone who did it, or you could add a flogging to the list of your complaints." He turned to the row of cabinets mounted in his cart, pulled open a small drawer full of vials and thumbed through them, lifting them one by one and squinting. "Useless illegible labels. Let's see about changing your bandages and applying something for the pain."

As he searched, my gaze strayed over his work area. On a sturdy table, he'd laid out his surgical tools and some sort of distilling apparatus. The tools fascinated me with their peculiar and gruesome shapes, which inspired me to imagine their uses.

Beside the tools, a book lay propped open on a wooden lectern, alongside a metal hand with mechanical joints. On the book's pages were meticulous drawings of a human hand, just as it might appear if all the skin and muscle were stripped away, leaving naked bone. The letters on the page were familiar to me, but the words were not. I tested their sounds out loud, but they were nonsense to my ears.

"*Prima Figura Earum*," Salomon corrected me. He pointed at the page. "Latin. The first figure, the second, the third, the fourth, the fifth and the sixth. Now, I can't say for certain without cutting your hand open, but..." he pointed to the third bone of the first and second fingers on the rightmost figure, "I'd say you broke these two, and one of the bones in here, in the wrist. Those were some punches you threw, in other words."

My gaze fell on the mechanical hand. "And what's that for?"

"It's a prosthetic. For when the limb can't be saved."

Anxious bile bubbled up once more in my stomach. "Will I lose my hand?"

He frowned. "Well, that remains to be seen."

"No, I can't," I pleaded. "Please, I can't lose my hand. My father has no one else to look after him, and I—"

Salomon's body shook with silent laughter. "I'm teasing you, little warrior. Your hand will heal just fine."

"You're not half as funny as you think, old man."

"Old? I'll have you know I'm not yet thirty. My great-grandfather of blessed memory lived to be one hundred and two."

"Thirty is more than twice twelve. You're an old man."

He shook his head, still smiling. "Well, far be it from me to argue with such precise mathematics." Then he set to unraveling a fresh bandage and dipping it in the mixture of vinegar water. "So, tell me. You're not one of the officers' children. Your father is…"

"A pikeman. Karl-Josef Dorn."

Salomon nodded. "And your mother?"

"Dead, two years now."

"Ah, I'm sorry to hear it. May peace be upon her. And did you go to school? Where did you learn your letters?"

"My mother taught me."

"Good woman. Hold out your hand." Piece by piece, he undid the previous night's bandages. Then he tipped an ointment from a small jar and rubbed it into the skin. It prickled, but the pain soon subsided.

I sniffed the air. "Roses, and something else. Cinnamon?"

"Indeed. Good nose. I should be careful, or you'll sniff out all my secrets. It's a special mixture of mine, it should ease the pain and stop the bandages from rubbing the skin raw. I can send you away with more for a few kreuzer. I should like to charge less, but cinnamon, as you know, is dear, especially here."

I felt heat on my cheeks and neck. It was the first I'd thought of money, and I had no gulden to give him, not for the ointment, nor for any of the other help he'd rendered me. "I'm sorry. I didn't bring any money," I lied. "But if you tell me what I owe you for today and for last night, I'll bring it to you when my father gets paid next."

He shook his head. "You don't owe me anything for last night or today. The young woman settled matters. But if you change your mind about the ointment—if that arm takes to hurting like Christ on the cross again—do come back."

I nodded, bitter with myself for not realizing that when Salomon and Katharina had conferred with each other the night before, they'd been talking about money. I was now in Katharina's debt twice over, and I didn't know how I'd begin to repay her.

"Wait here," Salomon said when he'd finished wrapping my hand in the fresh bandage. "I'll fetch a sling for your arm."

He shuffled around to the back of his cart and climbed inside.

The pain in my wrist was already beginning to ease. I noticed then that he'd left the jar of ointment sitting out. Such a medicament was an extravagance my father and I could ill afford, even with his army pay. He already had need of better shoes for marching, and I, useless child, was outgrowing my clothes faster than I could sew new ones.

God help me, I slipped the jar into my pocket.

Salomon came back with the sling, which he folded over and tied around my neck, looping it around my injured arm so as to keep it bent at the elbow. Then he warned me not to let my hand drop, lest the humors sink down and collect in the injured part. I thanked him again and hurried on my away before he could notice the jar was missing.

When I returned to my tent, I found my firepit filled with fresh wood, and the kettle standing upright next to it, full of water, ready for cooking. Katharina was in conversation with her soldier, but she broke off when she saw me and strolled over, the soldier's coat draped over her bare shoulders, her hair hanging down.

I noticed the shape of her for the first time, how her hips swayed as she walked, how they curved beneath her skirts. I felt frail and boney and still very much a child beside her.

"I'm going to pay you back," I said. "Somehow, I'll manage it. Write me out a bill of credit if you must, but I'll repay you."

She tilted her head. "What are you talking about?"

"I'm grateful for all your help, but I'm not a beggar. I don't need your alms."

"I still don't know what you're on about, child. Sit down and have some dinner."

At the mention of dinner, my stomach burbled. "Thank you."

Katharina dismissed the soldier. He slunk away with a dejected look on his face, and she returned to me with a savory-smelling pot and a basket slung on her arm. I rinsed out a pair of clay cups and bowls, and we made our meal in the grass: boiled beef, brown bread, and beer.

"I meant it, though," I said, as I filled my mouth with food. "I know you paid the physician on my behalf. It must have been dear. I'll find a way to pay you back."

"That's not necessary."

"It is. I won't be in anyone's debt."

"It's not necessary because I didn't pay him. I offered, but he wouldn't take it."

My stomach turned. I would have to go back. I would have to confess to stealing the ointment. My appetite vanished.

"How is your hand?" Katharina asked, taking a long draught from her cup.

"Better."

"Good." And then: "That boy's father came by, looking for witnesses. The boy won't tell who beat him, but his father's determined to find out."

I swallowed my food with difficulty and set my plate aside for the runt to eat from.

"Don't worry," Katharina continued. "None of the other children dared confess their part in it. I told him it was one of the boys from among the new recruits. He seemed to believe me."

"I'm sorry you had to lie for me."

"It's nothing. The little wretch deserved what he got."

We ate in quiet for a while. But my thoughts wandered back to what Katharina had said to my father that morning. It's a father's right to protect his daughter's honor, she'd said. And what if mine couldn't? And what if he died and left me with nothing?

"Does it hurt?" I asked her then.

She swallowed a bite of bread. "What?"

"Fucking."

Her cheeks turned pink, and she lowered her head. "That's a filthy word coming from a child's mouth. Did your father teach you that?"

I shook my head. "I've been in the Tross nearly five months. I've heard enough soldier's talk. Well, does it?"

She blushed again and bit her lip, considering her answer. "It depends on, well, a lot of things."

"Such as?"

She sighed. "Let's just say many women take pleasure in the marriage bed and leave it at that. You're too young to be worrying about such things."

"That isn't what you told my father this morning."

Katharina dragged a crust of bread along the edges of her bowl, shaking her head. "Your father just needed some sense talked into him. That's all."

"Why did you give the boy what he wanted, if you weren't married to him?"

"What boy?"

"The one you were supposed to marry, only your father couldn't raise the dowry."

"Oh. That boy. Look, I told your father what he needed to hear. Truth is, my father owns a fleet of river barges on the Danube, as well as warehouses in Ingolstadt and Regensburg. He had no trouble raising the dowry. But I didn't care for his choice of husband, and when I refused to marry, he struck me and ordered me out of the house. I didn't know where to go, so I ran away." She chuckled. "I traded my honor for passage out of the city on one of his own ships."

"When was that?"

"About eight months ago." She leaned back on one arm, plucking idly at a blade of grass. "I made my choices. They don't have to be yours."

"And if my father forces me to marry a man I don't like?"

"He won't do that."

"How can you know?"

"Because he loves you."

After the meal was done, Katharina went back to her soldier, and I went back to my tent. Just before sundown, my father stirred, took food, and left for the watch. As the noise and bustle of the camp was replaced by the low spit and crackle of fires, I settled in for sleep. But my dreams were guilty and gave me no rest.

A hand shook me awake the next morning before dawn. I blinked into the dark tent, thinking it was my father. But the man in front of me was too large. Still, the runt bounded and leapt on him in eager greeting.

"Get up, little warrior." I recognized the voice. It was Salomon. "There's something I'd like to show you. Dress yourself and come with me."

My mind was still fogged with sleep, but I did as told. Then I remembered the ointment.

"I'm sorry," I cried out. "It was me. I stole the medicine. I meant to pay for it, I swear it, just as soon as I had the money."

Salomon laughed. "Of course you stole it. You're about as sneaky as your three-legged dog."

"You can have it back. I didn't use a drop. Please don't hurt me."

"Hurt you? Child, if I wanted to hurt you, I'd turn you in for thieving. Now, get up."

"Where are we going?"

"We're leaving the camp for a little bit. Don't worry, I'll have you back before your father returns."

"And if I refuse to go?"

"That's your choice, but I'll need my ointment back."

I considered for a moment, then dressed myself to follow him. He took big strides, and I had to jog to keep pace as we crossed the Tross, leaving behind the rank-and-file tents and the horse stables and finally crossing the ditch that bordered the camp.

When we reached the main road, he handed me a leather glove and instructed me to put it on. It dwarfed my small fingers, but I did as I was told. Then he led me to a thicket that grew alongside the road, and held his lantern near one of the shrubs, so that the light dappled the leaves.

"What plant is this?" he asked.

I ventured a guess.

"No," he said. "Try again. Smell if you must. Touch, if you dare. Use your senses. But only taste if you're sure. If you poison yourself, you kill me as well. They'll not hesitate to blame the Jew for your stupidity."

So we went. Salomon pointed to a plant; I guessed its name. Some I knew from when my mother would take me into the woods outside of Ellwangen. Some she had only told me to stay away from and not to bother with.

When I was right, the physician listed off the plant's properties, what it could be used to treat, how it could be applied. When I was wrong, he asked me to close my eyes and describe it to him from memory—the sight, the smell, the touch—until I knew its characteristics by heart, and only then did he tell me the plant's name and what it was for.

When the sun was high enough that we no longer needed the light of the lantern, we retraced our path back to the camp. He pointed to each of the plants again as we passed them, and this time, it fell to me to describe the uses of each.

I was weary when we returned. My head felt thick and overgrown with leaves and stems and roots. I was relieved to see that my father hadn't yet returned from his night on the watch, so I wouldn't have to explain where I'd been and why. I reached under my bed for the ointment I'd stolen the day before.

I offered it to Salomon, but he waved it away. "Keep it. It was a gift."

"No, it wasn't. I took it."

"Oh, fine." He took the jar with a quick, impatient gesture, and tossed it back to me. I trapped it against my chest. "There. Now it's a gift. And close your mouth, don't gape, unless you wish to swallow flies. That's better."

He continued: "Now, if you have the time and inclination, you are welcome to pay me another visit. There are more things I can teach you."

I opened my mouth to speak, but he stopped me short.

"Wait. I wasn't finished. I have certain conditions. First, no more talk of repayment. You come because you want to learn what I have to teach, or not at all. Second, I'll always deal with you honestly, and I expect the same from you. If I catch you stealing from me again, I'll not hesitate to hand you over to the officers. Are we clear?"

I stared at him without answering. It was beyond my imagination why Salomon would offer to teach me anything, or what use his knowledge could be to me, half-educated and a girl at that.

"Are we clear?" he asked again. "If we are, you can indicate it by saying 'Yes, sir' or simply nodding."

"Yes, sir," I said.

Then he looked me over once more, reflective and, it seemed to me, sorrowful. "Good. You are too clever a child for picking fights and stealing potions. Yes, God help me, we will make something of you yet."

7

Blood and Plunder

1620

That summer, at last, we marched. The signal came at dawn, and we rose to the murmuring sounds of camp being broken. Cloth tents were beaten and folded, fires sputtered as they were doused, and the half-awake muttered their greetings one to the other.

As a young child, rising with the first light had come as easy and natural to me as drawing breath, but more and more, I longed for sleep, and each new morning pressed down on me like a pile of stones. Katharina likewise slept like the grave, and more often than not it fell to me to jostle her awake, so we could pack our tents and march.

"Whose grand idea was it for the sun to rise so damned early?" she complained.

"God's, I suppose."

"Well, God has a lot to answer for."

I could find no grounds to disagree with her.

My father marched with the soldiers, so I saw him only when we stopped to make camp. Katharina purchased a handcart in one of the first villages we passed, and we packed it with our things and took turns pulling it. When my feet grew weary, I rode for a spell in Salomon's wagon.

We crossed into Austria at the end of July, just a few weeks after I turned twelve. It struck me as strange, how little our surroundings seemed to change, how imperceptible was the difference between one country and the other. Yet gradually, the nature of that new land became apparent.

There are those that say that Hell is a cold place, eternally cut off from the warmth of God's love. If so, then Austria must not be far from the devil's own country. As we left Bavaria, the summer gave up its heat, and turbulent winds bore in heavy storms, soaking the roads and trapping wagon wheels halfway to the hub in unyielding mud. Axles cracked and had to be repaired, and if that could not be managed, we all had to do our part unloading the goods and clearing the road. Sickness, too, spread through the camp, rendering strong bodies frail and feverish.

By now, all Germany knows the sight of an army on the march. I needn't describe it in any great detail. It is a beast with many thousands of legs, dragging its stomach across the earth, maw open wide. It devours whatever comes before and shits out desolation on the other end. Wherever we went, the people who lived in those lands fled, taking with them whatever they could manage in their haste. What they left behind, the army took, sometimes burning the village for spite afterward.

How many such silent villages did we pass through? In one place, the villagers had left nearly all their doors and windows open as they fled. The wind moaned through those abandoned buildings like a restless spirit. So unsettled were the commanders at the sound that they ordered the priests to go through the whole place, praying over every building and sprinkling holy water on the thresholds. It was the one place we didn't plunder.

On another day, as the Tross came up behind the army, we found the road littered with the carcasses of cows and swine. As far as we could see, for a mile or more, lay dead animals. The meat appeared freshly slaughtered, and fights broke out between the butchers over who would have the privilege of the best cuts. Others refused to touch the meat, fearful that some terrible blight had killed the animals off.

But soon spear-points and musket balls were discovered embedded in the carcasses, and it became clear that it was our own army that had done the killing. We gathered up as much as we could, but in the end, much of it was wasted. We couldn't fit so much in our stomachs, and without time to salt and preserve it, it soon spoiled.

We marched through northern Austria unopposed, and talk spread of an easy war. We were thirty thousand strong with twelve great guns, each named after one of the apostles, and we marched under the banner of Our Lady, the Mother of God. So intimidating was the Catholic League army, it was said, that the enemy evacuated his bowels and flung himself on the mercy of the Emperor at first sight of our pikes breaking the horizon.

But easy is a matter of where you stand. I still think of the unnatural peace of those abandoned villages, the freshly chopped wood stacked neatly in anticipation of winter, the ax left in the stoop, the clothing drying on the line. How quiet it all was, just before the officers ordered the soldiers to fire the buildings.

During that time, I continued my education with Salomon. When we camped, I hurried through my morning chores, joining him by mid-afternoon. When we marched, he drilled me as we rode together. He was an exacting instructor, but a patient one—all the more remarkable for having me for a student.

He had a mind not only to teach me herbology, but to finish my instruction in reading and writing and to add Latin besides. I disliked this work intensely and complained often. It would have gone easier for me if he'd had more than medical books for me to learn from. The reading was ponderous, and my mind would often wander, so that an hour would pass without my having read even three pages.

Twice I declared my intention to quit, and twice he waved his hand at me dismissively and said, "Very well, then. I have enough work to do without playing schoolmaster to a lazy and unwilling student."

Thus, he played me very cleverly, knowing I was too proud and too willful to prove him right.

A month or so into my learning, an injured soldier was brought to Salomon. The soldier had fallen into a ditch and broken his leg. The bone was bent at an unnatural angle, sticking out through a wound in the flesh.

Salomon called on me to be his assistant, tying the man down to a chair and holding his leg extended while he opened the wound far enough to re-insert the bone. The physician warned me to look away, but I watched the whole while he worked, entranced. The patient moaned and blubbered as if on point of death, but I spoke to him with the same firm and compassionate tone Salomon had shown me, not once taking my eyes off the injured leg.

The priests teach that we should fix our minds on spiritual things above all else. But I was never blessed with so light a soul. For as long as I can recall, I've been made of flesh and bone and humors. When my flesh aches, my soul suffers in sympathy; when I go without food, my belly is racked with hunger-pangs and my mind turns to bitterness. All my greatest mistakes and all my greatest triumphs have had their origin in my gut.

The shard of shattered yellow bone sticking out from that soldier's leg pointed to a world within a world, more real to me than all the philosophy in all of Salomon's medical books or all the religion recorded in the Scriptures. I told myself I would read a thousand such books and memorize the whole of the Bible and the Torah alike, if I only I could learn to set a bone or stitch a wound as Salomon did.

Convincing Salomon to teach me was the first difficulty. In the first place, he objected, I was a girl, and men often come to their surgeons with complaints that would be unseemly for a girl to know of, let alone treat. In the second place, he was certain my father wouldn't agree to it. But by and by, I wore him down until at last, he agreed to reconsider the first point, so long as I had my father's permission.

It took me some time longer to work up the courage to ask my father.

In early August the army reached Linz. We quartered in the city while waiting for the Emperor's army to join us. My father and I were given the upper room of a house belonging to one of the city's bakers. It was no storeroom floor, but in a strange way, it felt as if we had unwound the past two years and returned to Baker Ruppel's shop in Nördlingen.

My father was in good spirits in those days. We were all glad to be out of the chill and the muck and to rest our legs ahead of the march into Bohemia, and he brimmed with a certain confidence that the war would soon be over.

"We'll take my discharge pay back to Bavaria," he said, again and again. "I'll set aside some for your dowry, and in a few years' time, when you're of age, we'll find you a husband."

I nodded, but I was uneasy. There was nothing I would have liked better than to see my father's worries at an end. But when had it ever gone so for us?

It was during that time I finally approached him about my desire to study surgery with Salomon. On the day I'd resolved to do it, I went down to the baker's shop and purchased a sweet egg tart, which I knew he loved, and waited for him to return from drills.

He was later coming back than I expected, and I was a jumble of nerves by the time I heard his laughter in the street as he bade farewell to his companions, Bachmann and the Italian, Stefano.

As he supped, he seemed to be in as bright a mood as ever, making cheerful talk about his day and grousing about the arrogance of the Emperor's soldiers, who'd lately arrived. But when I laid out the egg tart, his gaze darkened.

"This must have cost a pretty penny," he said stiffly.

"It wasn't so dear," I said.

"Do you think we have money to waste?"

"I don't understand."

"Our pay is three months in arrears. You know that."

"I bought it with money I earned from my sewing. It's just been so long since you've had one, and it's your favorite—" My lip trembled; suddenly I felt very stupid. "I'm sorry."

He sighed. "No, I'm sorry. You're right, *Häschen*, it is my favorite. Thank you."

He took spoon in hand and ate through the tart in silence. Once or twice, he offered me a bite, but I refused it. His reaction had left my stomach queasy. I watched him, kneading at my skirts all the while.

"On the matter of money," I began quietly.

He looked up suddenly. "I'm sorry for scolding you. I'd rather not speak any more of it."

"I think I might have found a means to earn some more. Besides sewing, that is. Salomon has said—"

"Salomon? He's the one that's been teaching you your letters, yes?"

"Aye. Salomon has said that he could teach me some things, here and there, of the surgical arts. At first there would be no pay, but if I learn enough to work as his assistant, he would pay me as well as any surgeon's assistant in the army."

He bent over his bowl, scraping the last of the tart from the edges and licking the spoon clean. "No," he said at last. "Absolutely not."

"Why not?"

"Because surgery is no profession for a young woman."

"That's not a reason, is it? Tanning is not a woman's profession either, but Mother worked every day in the shop. It was she who corrected your journeymen when they were doing it wrong, more often than not."

"That's a different matter," he countered.

"How?"

"We were married. A wife helps with her husband's profession. You'll do the same when you're married."

"And if you die before that happens?"

His shoulders tensed. We'd been waiting in Linz for over a month. We'd march into Bohemia soon. We'd meet the enemy there.

"Papa," I said quietly. "I want to do this. I think I could be good at it. I have a strong stomach and a steady hand. I think those are reasons enough to do it, but if you don't agree, at least think on the money. Think on what it could do for us. You wouldn't have to worry about what would happen to me if you were gone. Salomon would take me in his charge. And I'd make enough money that you wouldn't need to worry about my dowry, even if Duke Maximilian never pays you what he owes."

"And if your husband objects to having his wife deal in butchery and men's private business?"

"I'll stop. I'll serve my husband's profession, just as Mother did."

He took his sword from the bedpost and strapped it around his waist.

"Please," I said.

When he looked back at me, his lips were pressed together and his eyes bright with injured pride. "I'll hear no more talk of this," he said. "I'm your father. I'll see that you are cared for. I'll provide your dowry."

Then he marched out the door, letting it fall shut behind him. When he was gone, I fell into the bed and let my tears flow until they soaked the pillow. The runt heard my choked sobs and jumped up, burrowing his nose into the mattress and stroking my cheeks with consoling licks.

In September, we marched at last into Bohemia. A meager creek is all that separates Bohemia and Austria at that point, and we forded it without trouble.

In that new land, we encountered the enemy for the first time, but only in brief skirmishes at the front and back of our lines. Far more devastating was the illness that spread through the ranks, brought on by long, wearying days on the march and frigid, unrelenting autumn rains.

I rode with Salomon, and each day he had a dozen or more men lined up for treatment, feverish and racked with coughing, some spitting up blood. Others showed certain signs of typhus. All along the way, men succumbed and were buried in hasty, shallow graves. The cold seeped into our skin, and both Katharina and I developed chest-racking coughs.

We sighted the enemy's main force a few miles south of Prague, but an argument between the Catholic League and the Emperor's forces brought us to a halt. We remained in that spot, lodged in the sticking mud of our commanders' indecision, until early November.

It was that month that the thing I'd long feared finally came to pass.

I woke with a warm, wet sensation between my legs. I gathered up my skirts around my waist and saw a blushing red stain on my blankets. I hurried to dress and stepped out of my tent into the heavy fog of early morning. The camp was already stirring, packing up to begin the day's march. I ran to Katharina's tent and roused her from her sleep.

"What do I do?"

"What do you mean?"

"I'm bleeding."

"Why are you asking me? Talk to the physician—oh." Then she laughed. "You mean to say, you know what fucking is, but you don't know what to do when you're in flower?"

My face burned bright. "Will you tell me or not?"

"Oh, you poor motherless babe, come on then."

"Where are we going?"

"To find you some rags!"

So, I had my coming-of-age, chasing Katharina through the Tross as she collected old linens. She stitched them together hastily at our tent while I packed both her things and mine, and then she showed me their uses.

As we marched that day, a terrific stabbing pain shot through my gut, and I feared I'd been stricken with some deathly illness. The next the army came to a stop, Katharina took me to Salomon and explained my circumstances. He gave me a potion to help ease my discomfort.

The potion did little good. We marched three more days, giving chase to the Bohemian army, which was not far ahead of us now.

By the end of those days, I wanted nothing more than to curl up and die.

On the fourth day, my sickness continued, but we'd come to a stop at last. The enemy army was positioned atop a nearby hill. I woke once, briefly, when my father left our tent to join the ranks, then slept through till early afternoon.

By then the battle was over. We heard only half-formed reports in the Tross, but it was said that the fighting had lasted less than an hour. With two thousand cavalry, our commander, General Tilly, had charged the enemy's center while the Emperor's forces attacked the flank. The Bohemian army broke ranks. Their king, that foolish German prince, Friedrich, fled back to Prague with our army on his heels, rejoicing with shouts of "Sancta Maria!"

I waited, sick and anxious, for my father's return. News reached us that Prague had fallen, and we were to join the army in the city. Still, he hadn't returned. I stood unsteadily, my legs weak from illness and worry, and packed my things, not knowing whether I was marching to rejoin my father or to learn that I was an orphan.

How can I describe the city we entered? Its defenders had all fled; the king, too. It must have been a grand city in better times, to judge by its boulevards lined with beautiful gabled houses, towering churches, and painted synagogues. But everywhere I turned my head, there were scenes of sorrow. Our soldiers harried the people from their homes, demanding that they pile their valuables in the streets and in the squares. Many of them protested that they had nothing left. The Protestants had already robbed them to fund their now-defeated army.

When at last I found my father, he lifted me off my feet in an excited embrace. He said he hadn't so much as bloodied his pike in the battle before the army had been given orders to march onward to the city.

"Look," he said. He drew a dress from his rucksack. "It's about your size, or it will be soon enough."

I held the dress, running my thumbs over the soft weave of the fabric. There was a faint scent of rosewater on it, and I couldn't help but think of the young woman who'd worn it first. What was she doing? Was she wailing over her fallen city? Had some soldier dragged her from her home to claim her honor? Or had she managed to flee before the army arrived? Yet even as these thoughts raced across my mind, I longed to try it on.

"It's lovely," I said.

"Ah, but there's one more thing." My father smiled wide beneath his whiskers and drew out a silver necklace, set with small garnet stones. He held his head high as he laid the chain in my hand. "Now you needn't worry about bloodying your hands with a surgeon's knife."

My tongue clung to the top of my mouth. "No," I said.

"No?" He stared at me.

"It's too precious. It belongs to someone. I can't." My eyes burned. Tears slipped down my cheek.

"No!" he snapped. "You'll take it. You'll take it, and you'll shed no more tears for traitors and heretics, do you understand me? I didn't march all these miles through rain and stinking mud to have muskets and cannons aimed in my direction, so that you could weep over the people who chose this war. You wanted a dowry; here's your dowry."

He threw the necklace at my feet and stormed away.

He'd become a true soldier, my father. But he was wrong. The people of Prague hadn't chosen this war any more than we had, though they suffered dearly for it in the days and months to come.

Part 2

Woman

8

The Boy Who Believed in Goodness

1622

The winter after Prague fell, we waited for the order to disband the army, but it never came. As that year's snows thawed, my father sold the garnet necklace he'd looted and spent the money on fresh boots and warm coats for the both of us. The remainder he put toward a packhorse, hopeful that the war would soon be over.

Yet on it went. After the Bohemian rebellion's defeat, Duke Maximilian, our master, made his ambitions plain. His cousin, the defeated pretender-king, was an Elector, one of those rare princes who hold the power to vote on Imperial matters. At that time, there were only seven such electors in the whole of the Empire. As it turned out, Duke Max had struck a secret deal with the Emperor—as payment for providing the Catholic League army, Maximilian would receive his cousin's Elector title and his lands besides.

So, after Prague, instead of disbanding, we marched west into Germany, chasing the pretty little prince Friedrich and securing his lands for Maximilian.

The other German princes were incensed. They protested in the name of that vaunted and mysterious concept known as the "German liberties." By this phrase they meant simply that what was theirs was theirs, and no one, not even the Emperor, might take it from them.

Did they not know that that's what princes do? What were the German liberties to the rest of us—to a half-orphaned girl, a whore, and Jew? Where were the German liberties in Ellwangen when witches were discovered left and right, so that their greedy neighbors could take their houses and lands? Where were the German liberties when the cities of the Empire wrote their acts banning the Jews from their gates? To this day, there are towns where a Jew may come and trade, but if he dies within the walls, his property is confiscated by the city and his family receives nothing back. Where were the German liberties when Katharina's father denied her the right to consent to her own marriage? No, the German liberties were not for us; every liberty we had was entailed on others, if it wasn't outlawed entirely.

So, we marched. The pretender-king gathered another army in defense of his titles, his *liberties*, and each time we caught up to his soldiers, we drove them from the field. The days, the months, the battles all ran together like dye in wool.

On a stretch of rocky mountain road, the horse my father had purchased with my dowry tripped and broke its leg. The poor creature lay on the ground, stamping at the dirt with its forelegs, unable to rise. My father took one look at the limb, then walked off. He returned with a pistol.

After he'd put the animal out of its misery, he and Bachmann dragged the carcass from the road. All throughout, my father kept his lips pressed together in a grim, unchanging expression.

That night when we made camp, he told me that if I still wanted to study surgery with Salomon, he thought I'd be wise to do it.

"A young woman can do worse," he said, his voice weary with resignation, "than bringing a little skill in medicine to her marriage."

That was the moment I knew there would be no end to this war—the moment my father stopped believing in it ever ending.

By August 1622, we'd driven the pretender-king to Mannheim on the river Rhine. Between us and Mannheim lay the fortified city of Heidelberg. There we dug in and began our siege. In September, we were joined by a Spanish army. Spain and the Empire are bound together by the blood of their Habsburg rulers, and the Spanish offered us support on their way to the Low Countries.

The months of that siege were uncommonly hot, the kind of heat that brings time to a crawl. The musketeer took half a second longer to load his weapon, the carthorses slowed to a halt and their driver had not the energy to whip them, the very blood in our veins ran sluggish. Even the runt found a spot in the shade, stretched himself out in it, and did not budge except to follow the shadow as it moved.

It was during that unrelenting heatwave that the Spanish cavalryman came to Salomon's surgery, borne by four of his countrymen—three cavalrymen and a Jesuit novice.

The injured man was conscious, but only barely, his eyes lolling in his head, unable to speak for pain. Blood stained his lips—he'd bitten his tongue, but that was not the worst of his injuries. His left leg was twisted sideways, white bone jutting out through the cloth of his breeches, and his hair was matted with blood where his skull had been bashed in.

"How the devil did this happen?" I directed my question at the four men, as they set their comrade in the chair. The soldiers blinked at me without understanding.

The Jesuit novice looked pale and veiny as a fish's innards, but he stammered out an answer in halting German. The men had been racing, with hurdles constructed out of felled tree branches. The injured man had been the race leader when his horse clipped the last and highest hurdle, toppling head-first and throwing him. His head struck a rock when it hit the ground, and the next rider trampled his leg.

"Idiots," I hissed between my teeth.

"Mind your tongue." It was Salomon. He maintained a policy of not speaking ill of the ones in our care, no matter how stupidly they'd come by their injuries.

I addressed the novice: "Tell them to tie him down fast. But remind them to take care about the leg. Don't need them knocking it further out of place."

The novice translated the command, and two of the soldiers took the rope from Salomon and tied the man to the chair, his hands behind his back.

As he finished speaking, the novice swayed, sweat glistening on his blanched skin. "Leave or get yourself a seat," I said to him. "We've got our hands full enough without you flopping over like a dead fish."

There was a stool by one of Salomon's worktables, and the novice shuffled unsteadily over to it and sat down.

Salomon handed me a razor, and I stood behind the cavalryman's head and cut the hair away from his scalp, all around the place where his skull had struck the rock. The wound was a jagged line, red-black and swollen. "May I use the drill this time?"

"What? And drill into the man's brains?" Salomon scolded me. "Are you so eager to kill someone? You should have become a soldier."

"And how should I know how not to drill into a man's brains, if you never let me practice? This one's as good as dead, anyhow."

"Is he still breathing?"

"Yes."

"And his heart—it's still beating?"

"Yes."

"Then I don't care what he's as good as. He's alive, and it's our task to do what we can to keep him that way. To answer your question, you'll get to do the drilling when you stop asking and start listening."

"May I do the stitching then?"

"Yes, you may do the stitching."

I cleared the blood from around the wound and then took my place by the man's head, tilting it back, and holding it in place, lest he jerk and ruin Salomon's work. I craned my neck to see as Salomon sliced open the skin, peeling back the flap, and then lined up the drill.

With his eyes shut and his ear close to the man's head, he turned the crank, one, two, three turns and another half, and when he pulled the drill away, a perfect circle of bone slipped free, and blood pulsed out of the opening. He daubed the fluid away with a rag, revealing a glimpse of clear liquid and brain matter beneath. When he was satisfied that no more fluid was forthcoming, he put the round of bone back in place and then stepped away to prepare the needle and thread, which he gave to me.

I wiped the sweat from my forehead with my sleeve, so as not to let it drip into my eyes. They were good stitches, tight and even. As I was tying off the last of them, I heard the novice empty his stomach. Then Salomon and I bandaged the wound.

The cavalryman was still breathing when the trepanning was done, so we turned to the leg. But his fellows shouted as Salomon began cutting away the man's breeches. The novice walked over to us, wiping bile from his colorless lips, and explained that the soldiers were worried about exposing the man in front of a young woman.

I started to protest that I'd been living in the Tross for near three years and that I'd be very surprised if there was anything in that man's breeches that I'd not already seen, but Salomon interjected. "Josefine, there are blankets in the wagon. Why don't you show the young priest where they are and have him bring one to me?"

I heaved a sigh and did as told. The novice took the blanket from me bashfully, his lips still pale, and motioned for me to wait. By the time Salomon called for me, the leg had been freed from its breeches, the blanket draped over the man's middle, and his modesty and my blushing innocence alike were preserved for another day.

We needed the soldiers' strength to stretch the leg, so that the muscles were extended when we pushed the bone in place. During this procedure, the man thrashed and cried out, but the ropes held fast.

All the while, the novice sat nearby, muttering prayers beneath his breath. Long after the soldiers had gone, he remained, perched by the injured man's side, tapping his fingers on the covers of the prayer book he clutched in his hand.

He was still there when the sun started sinking and I readied to leave.

I'd not taken much care looking at him in the furor of the moment—one priest looked much like the other, and we had no shortage of them—but now I took him in. He was built like a switch, tall and narrow as a spruce tree. Though he'd regained his color, his skin was still white as sand, but it took on a honeyed glow in fading light. He was young, even for a novice; sixteen, perhaps, to my fourteen. His hair, near black, came to his shoulders in gentle waves. A few strands of it clung to his face in sweaty clumps. I tamped down on the urge to brush it out of his eyes.

He noticed me looking, and I tore my eyes away, focusing on the injured soldier. "Who is he to you?" I asked. "Is he your brother or your friend or…"

"No. He's not… I don't know him."

"Then what are you still doing here?"

"It didn't seem right to leave him alone. I thought I should be here in case he wakes up, or in case he…"

He was like an itch, that novice. One you couldn't scratch or soothe. I was irritated by him, and I couldn't say why.

"We have more priests in this army than flies on a cow's carcass," I said. "If anything happens to him, we'll throw a rock, and one will come running. Go back to wherever it is you priests sleep."

But nothing I could say could budge him.

"I'm not a priest yet, but nevertheless, I think I'll stay."

I shrugged. "If you've nothing better to do." Then I left him there.

By that time in the siege, we'd packed away our tents and built a more permanent camp of wooden huts. Humble structures though they were, the huts provided better protection from both sun and rain, and the longer we remained dug in around the city walls, the closer they came to feeling like a home. My father and I shared a hut near the middle of the camp, not far from Salomon's surgery.

My father was in bed when I returned, but he shifted stiffly onto his back when he heard me and sat up. I sat at the foot of the bed and pulled off my shoes. "How was it today?"

"A little soreness, but that's all. Every day's better. Stronger."

In May that year we'd met the enemy at Wimpfen and a musket ball had cracked his hip. Salomon had little trouble dislodging it, but the body takes its own time, and there is little even the most skilled of physicians can do to hurry the knotting together of bone. It was a few weeks before he could sit upright for any length of time without pain, a few weeks more before he was fit to march.

"Have you eaten?" he asked me, reaching into his bag for a ration of bread.

"I ate with Salomon," I lied. Pay was in arrears again. Duke Maximilian preferred to spend his coin on equipment and officers. The common soldier was always last in line for his pay and often found the coffers empty. But neither was desertion a choice—they'd hang my father and then where would I be?

At least while summer lasted there was food to be found, and I nourished myself on fish I pulled up from the river or berries I picked while out gathering herbs for the medicines. Salomon had made good on his promise to pay me an assistant's wage at the start of the campaign, so I had some money set by. Still, even Salomon often found he had to choose between restocking medicines and buying meat, since if the soldiers didn't get paid, neither did anyone else.

"You should eat," my father insisted now. "You're a growing young woman. Put flesh on those bones of yours."

"You're one to talk," I said. His appetite had been poor since his injury. "I reckon I could wrap my thumb and forefinger clean around your wrist." I took him by the arm in demonstration—not quite, but my hands were yet small.

"Don't worry about me," he smiled weakly. "I ate earlier. I promise."

I took the bread and picked off pieces of it from the center, chewing slowly. By and by, I dropped a chunk here and there on the ground for the runt to scoop up with his tongue.

My father laughed. "I think that dog eats better than either of us." A fly buzzed past him, landing for a moment on his lower lip. He batted it away.

All those years, and we were still no better at saying what was on our minds.

"I saw some blackberries down the road, growing along a small pond," I said. "I'll pick some tomorrow and bring them to you."

"Blackberries," he said, with a chuckle. "Your mother hated blackberries."

He talked of her more and more. Once, it had bothered me, but now I didn't feel any one way about it.

"No, she didn't," I said.

He squinted his eyes. "She did," he insisted. "Remember? She'd always give me a double share. She picked them only grudgingly."

"She gave them to you because she knew how much you liked them. She'd eat them off the bush when we went picking, and then she'd say the rest were for you. She made me promise not to tell."

He shook his head and smiled. "You and your mother both. I was always outmatched."

I changed the subject: "They say we'll be in the city soon."

"Aye, I've heard the same. That's good news. I'll get you some meat. You need meat."

"Will you go into the city on your leg?"

"Needs must. We need the plunder. But don't trouble yourself over it. My leg will hold. I've had good rest since we made camp. Soon I'll forget I was ever injured."

I knew he didn't half believe the words he was saying, but I mustered a smile anyway. It was an unspoken agreement we'd had since Prague. We'd speak of these little illusions and pretend to believe in them for each other's sake.

When I returned to Salomon the next day, the novice was just where I'd left him. He must have lain down for at least a spell during the night, for blades of grass clung to the back of his cassock and to the tangles of his hair. I couldn't resist the impulse to brush him down.

"Stubborn," I chided him, plucking a twig from his hair.

"I confess it." That good-natured smile again.

I checked on the cavalryman; his breaths were low and shallow. The novice stood beside me. "Well?" he said. It was always the same question, no matter the patient. Their friends, their family only wanted to know if they would pull through. But surgeons are not prophets. As Salomon was fond of saying, we apply our skill, but God alone decides who lives and dies.

"Did he wake at all in the night?" I asked the novice.

The young man shook his head. Then he asked, "Why didn't you spend the night here with your father?"

"My father? Oh, Salomon's not my father."

"Ah," he said. Nothing more.

All that day, too, he remained in that spot: sitting, praying, watching, occasionally mouthing words as he read to himself from a small leather book.

By midday, the cavalryman had yet to wake. Salomon and I prepared our dinner: bread, cabbage, and cottage cheese. I filled a wooden trencher and brought it to the priest, along with the small basketful of blackberries I'd picked that morning.

"I haven't seen you eat since you arrived," I said.

"Thank you." He scooped up the cheese curds with his bread, and took a bite, followed shortly by another. In little time, he'd cleared the plate. "It was very good," he said.

"You were very hungry." I sat down in the grass beside him with the basket of berries. The runt settled down next to me, pressing his warm back against my side, panting in the summer heat.

"Yes, I was." He rubbed the heel of his palm on his knee. "I'm sorry for making such a fool of myself yesterday."

"I take it you haven't been with the army long."

He shook his head. "Six months. And I still can't keep my stomach at the sight of blood. The first time I heard cannon fire, I thought my heart was going to beat out of my chest."

"Why are you here?" I bit down on a blackberry.

"A Jesuit's call is to go out into the world. *Ad Majorem Dei Gloriam.* I came here looking to do some good."

"Bad luck," I chuckled. "Good dies in this place."

"Do you believe that? Truly?" The whites of his eyes shimmered when he opened them wide, as he did then. I tried to focus on my dinner.

"My father was a tanner. Now he's a pikeman. They used to pay him eight gulden a month to skewer other men. That was when he was a private. Now he's a corporal, so the pay is more, when it comes. The pay often comes late, if it comes at all, but we still need to eat. Where do you suppose the cheese came from? The cabbage? Do you suppose we planted a garden here in this wasteland outside the city walls and grew the vegetables ourselves?

"I don't know how the Spanish manage their armies, but in Germany, if you don't pillage, or spend money you received from someone else who did the pillaging, you starve. So, look around, and you tell me, who here is good? Point them out, and I'll tell you all their sins, and the choices they ran out of a long time ago."

He reached into the basket and came up with a handful of berries. "You take a grim view of things for such a young lady."

"I'm not a lady, and I'm not so young as my age."

"Well, I've not given up hope. God is good, and there is good here. I've seen it. You and that doctor, for example. I see how you fight to save the life of a stranger."

"It's a trade. We charge for it."

"That man won't survive to pay you."

The novice was not so simple-minded as he seemed. "No, he won't," I agreed.

True enough, the cavalryman took fever that afternoon, and by late evening he was gone. Salomon tried every technique he knew to fight the festering in the man's leg, but for nothing.

I wish I could say he didn't suffer, but he moaned and wailed horribly through it. The novice fetched a priest, who performed the last rites, and then he stood beside the dying man, gripping his hand while he screamed out nonsense at the last. To the novice's credit, he didn't flinch or falter or lose his stomach over those terrible sounds. Then he left to inform the man's friends and arrange the funeral.

I thought that was the last I'd see of him, but shortly before nightfall he came back.

"What are you doing back here, priest?" I snapped at him. "The idiot is dead. There's nothing more for you to do." I knew I was being harsh on him, but I was in a sour mood. Death is as common as life, but this death had been more senseless than most.

"I'm not yet a priest," he corrected. "But I thought you might need an ear, someone to talk to. We could pray, if you like."

No, it wasn't the death that made me sour.

"Pray about what?" I snapped.

"We watched a man die today."

"I've seen hundreds of men die," I said. "They die every day. It's nothing new."

He lowered his head, toeing a loose stone in the grass. "I see. I'm sorry to have upset you. I'll go."

No, it wasn't the death that had made me sour. It was the novice, waiting by a stranger's bedside to help him die, even after his friends, the fools whose reckless games had gotten him killed, had made themselves scarce. Six months with the army—how was it that his stomach still turned at the sight of blood? How was it that none of the mess around us seemed to touch him, when it had touched everyone else—my father most of all?

Why did he have to be so damned *pure*?

"Wait," I said. "You did a good thing today, holding that man's hand. It was good he wasn't alone. It was good he had one of his countrymen with him."

He smiled. "*Ad Majorem Dei Gloriam.*"

"What's your name?"

"Isidoro."

"Good-night, Novice Isidoro."

"Good-night, Miss..."

"Dorn. Josefine Dorn."

"Good-night, Miss Dorn. Sleep well." He bowed his head and departed, strolling back to wherever it was he came from with a slow, easy gait. I watched until his black cassock disappeared between the huts.

9

Bathing Day

1622

During those hot months of the siege, Katharina and I took to bathing in the river Neckar with the other camp women. Bathing days were always a happy occasion, and we made a great procession as we walked some miles downstream to find a secluded spot, far from the eyes of the soldiers and the continuous sound of cannon bombarding the city's walls. We were a hodge-podge drawn from every station—children and mothers, whores and officers' wives, orphans and widows. We brought food and drink with us and made it a day.

As the women stripped off their clothes, I was reminded of a certain very old book Salomon had in his possession. It was written on lambskin and the text that was there now was not the original. He'd shown me the pages where the old text had been scraped away to make space for the new one.

Our bodies were like that book, story written over story, in scars, in mangled joints, in sunken breasts, in our sun-seared flesh. Just from a glance you could guess who had meat and who didn't, who'd been ill and who'd been well, who walked the long marches and who rode in a cart. What you couldn't know was what any one woman thought of it all, what she hoped for, what visions crossed her dreams at night, or how all those experiences had rewritten the woman she'd been before the army, before the war.

An uncommon hush always fell over the gathering as we eased ourselves into the gentle current, and the cold water pricked our skin with gooseflesh, making our nipples stand on end. Then someone would laugh and someone else would tell a bawdy story about one of the officers, and before long the river was full of laughter and chatter.

The runt splashed into the water ahead of me and Katharina, his tail slapping the surface. As I waded in, I caught sight of my own reflection in those ripples. I didn't much care for it. By then it was impossible to miss my mother's face looking back at me, only I was not so well-rounded as she had been. No, I was all angry angles, my skin sunken in around my shoulders and collarbone, my breasts plump, but small. My father was right: I didn't eat enough.

I looked on Katharina's soft curves with a feeling I couldn't then name, part envy, part longing.

"So," Katharina said, standing in the shallows and splashing water over her arms and chest. "Are you going to tell me about the priest?"

I waded farther out, bracing as the waters rose up above my waist, and lowered myself in to the shoulders. Once the initial chill passed, what remained was blessed relief from the stifling heat. "What priest?" I asked.

Katharina swam out to me, gliding near the water's surface. "Salomon says there's been a young Jesuit loitering around his surgery all last week. He says you two have been eating together, talking."

"He's not a priest. He's a novice."

"Very well, a novice. Tell me about him."

The novice Isidoro had appeared at Salomon's almost every day since the cavalryman's death. Mostly he prayed over the sick and injured. Usually by the time I arrived, he was already there, kneeling with his head bowed and his mouth moving in soft-spoken prayer—*gratia plenas* and *te benedictuses* dancing gracefully off his tongue. When he was finished praying over one man, he'd move on to the next.

I left him to his duties as I went about mine, but at dinnertime he'd sit down beside me, and we'd talk. He'd been born a bastard in a noble household in Sevilla. In spite of the circumstances of his birth, his father had favored him growing up, which had made his older brother jealous. One day, his brother drew his sword on him and slashed open his chest. Isidoro fled for his life, and while his injury was healing, he'd prayed to God for clarity. A German priest in the hospice where he made his recovery gave him a copy of the writings of Ignatius of Loyola, founder of the Jesuit order, lately sainted. He took it as a sign.

"What's to tell?" I said to Katharina. "He comes to Salomon's surgery from time to time to pray."

"Is that all? I had a very different impression when I saw him the other day." She undid her hair and shook it free.

"When was that?"

"When you were out buying herbs. The young man came looking for you. He seemed very disappointed not to find you."

My face burned. I splashed it with water hurriedly. "Where was this, then? At my campsite? Surely not."

"At Salomon's."

"And what were *you* doing at Salomon's?"

"Oh, you know I've been having that pain in my foot. I asked the doctor to examine it."

I gave her a dubious look. "Your foot seemed fine on the walk here."

She shrugged. "It comes and goes."

"Right. You've been complaining of a great many mysterious pains lately."

"Don't change the subject on me. We were talking about the priest."

"Novice," I corrected. "And you've been away at suppertime too." I tilted my head back to rinse my hair.

"That's my own business."

"Are you fucking him? Salomon? Are you two rutting?"

Katharina slapped cold river water into my face. "I said that's my own business, not yours."

"You are, aren't you?"

"No." Her jaw clenched. "And don't ask me that again. Don't use that word again."

She dipped her head beneath the water, the locks of her dark hair splaying across the surface like tree branches until they too sank beneath. I watched her naked form swim away from me, leaving me to finish my bathing alone.

Later, as we dressed, she said, "We're not fucking. Salomon came to me this past spring when your father was injured. He wanted to be certain how you were coping with it. We started to talk; well, mostly he did. He told some stupid story about a baker and an ass, and… never mind."

"He tells a lot of stupid stories. But why invent injuries? Why not just visit him?"

"No, I couldn't."

"That's not a reason."

"And when he asked me why I was there, what would I tell him? A woman approaching a man like that, no. It's not done. It's just not done."

"You approach men all the time. I've seen you do it."

"That's a different matter entirely."

I understood then that what ailed her lay not in the flesh, but in those invisible places where all our secrets take root. I looked on my friend—her shoulders tense, her face pensive. My heart gave a little ache in sympathy with hers.

By and by, we settled down to eat our dinner and drink our beer in the shade of the trees. The women chattered late into the afternoon, swapping bits of camp gossip, especially regarding the Spanish soldiers. The general agreement was that they were better cultured and less brutish than German men, and at least one widow in the group felt confident in her prospects of finding a new husband among them.

We walked back slowly, sorry to see the day so soon behind us. Outside my father's hut, Katharina turned to me.

"Take care with the priest," she warned. "They are men like any other. No matter how much they may try to deny it to themselves."

Then she wandered off in the direction of Salomon's surgery.

When I arrived at Salomon's the next morning, he had gone out. The novice was in his usual place, attending to the sick. When he saw me, he left his prayers and approached me, grinning.

"Here, I brought you something." He flicked his wrist and a plum dropped from the sleeve of his cassock and into his open palm, followed by a second and a third. With a laugh, he tossed them in the air and took to juggling.

"You missed your true vocation," I teased. "You shouldn't have been a priest. You should have been a fool."

"Not a priest. A novice," he sang out playfully.

"A novice fool," I retorted.

"Therefore, a wise man."

He caught the plums one by one and took a bow. Then he tossed one in my direction. The fruit tasted of pleasant memories, and I had to cup my hand beneath my chin to catch the juices.

A shriek from Salomon's hut pierced our levity. I turned, cheek full of plum flesh, to see Katharina run out. Her hair was down, and she covered her face with her hands as she made her retreat. I jumped up and chased after her, the runt following close behind.

"I've no wish to talk about it," she said.

"What did he do?" I demanded.

"I said I don't wish to talk about it."

"Did he hurt you?" I persisted. "If he hurt you, I'll geld him. I swear it."

She spun on me. I could see streaks where her tears had run their courses. "You'll do no such thing. He's your teacher. I won't let you ruin that on account of my stupidity."

"Tell me what happened."

She exhaled a shaking breath, then beckoned me to walk with her. "We got to talking again last night, Salomon and I. He had a wooden flute, and I told him that I'd played as a girl. So, he asked me to play him a tune, and as I played, he started to sing. The words were Yiddish or Hebrew. I don't know. I didn't understand them."

I wrapped my arm around her waist as we walked.

She continued: "It was the music—or no, in truth, it was the way that round stomach of his puffed up with each deep breath as he sang. I forgot myself in a way I... I don't forget myself with men, ever. I kissed him. I didn't want anything else. I just wanted to kiss him. And he kissed me, and once we'd started kissing, I... we..." She paused, lingering in the memory, and a small smile crossed her face. "He didn't hurt me. Quite the opposite."

"What's the trouble then?"

"This morning, when I woke up, I found a handful of gulden beside my pillow." Her lip trembled.

"He paid you."

"Don't blame Salomon," she said. "I was stupid. I should be wiser by now. I'm not the sort of woman a man loves. I'm the sort of woman he keeps for a time—if he can afford it."

We'd reached Katharina's hut. Her words settled in me like spoiled milk. I told her I'd stay with her, but she refused. "Go back to your work and forget all about this. I will, after a few nights' rest," she said.

But even as she said it, I knew it wasn't true. Even then, I thought of Eleonore, a girl I'd not seen in years, with such immediacy I could hear her voice calling me "Not-a-boy." Such wounds always take the longest to heal, if they ever heal at all.

Katharina insisted I return to Salomon's, so I went. But by the time I arrived, I was in ill-humor.

"Miss Dorn." It was the novice. "What happened? Is everything well with your friend?"

I brushed past him, irritably. "Go back to your prayers, priest."

His mouth hung open, and he didn't bother to correct me when I called him "priest."

To make my mood worse, the day was a quiet one, without a maiming or a mauling or an outbreak to liven the hours or distract me. I tried to pick up my studies, but I could ill focus on them.

An hour or more went by and Salomon returned. He saw me at my reading and endeavored to be a good teacher by questioning me on what I'd read. I answered him dutifully at first, but soon my patience ran out.

"What does it matter?" I cried at last, slamming the book shut.

"Oh, are we to do this again?" Salomon sighed. "It will do you no service to cut into men without an ounce of theory in that empty head of yours."

"How is it you're so clever and also so stupid?"

He pressed his lips together. "What devil has gotten into you?"

"Katharina ran from your hut while you were out. She was in tears, and you must know whose fault that is."

He blinked at me, baffled. "Me? What did I do?"

I saw then that he genuinely had no understanding.

"You paid her."

"I paid—? My goodness! I am not going to talk about such matters with a child, and Katharina should know better as well."

"I'm fourteen, which makes me a woman by any measure."

"All the same. If I had a daughter, I'd certainly not be discussing these things with her."

"Lucky I'm not your daughter."

He groaned. "That makes it worse."

"But you did pay her."

"Of course. What's the trouble? Was she not content with the amount? Then she should say so. I thought it was generous, though I admit I don't have much experience in such matters. I'm not the sort of man… since my wife of blessed memory died, I've kept to myself."

"She didn't want you to pay her."

"What do you mean?"

"She loves you, you lackwit! Why do you think she's here all the time? You're a doctor. You know there's nothing wrong with her foot, or her head, or her ankle, or her wrist. She gave herself to you, and you treated her like a whore."

His eyes grew wide. "No, that can't be," he muttered. "That simply can't be."

"Why? Is she too sullied for you?"

"Certainly not."

"Then what?"

"Isn't it obvious? She's a Gentile and I'm a Jew! It's bad enough that what happened… happened. But love? It's foolishness. It's impossible. It's absolutely impossible." He rose from his chair and started to pace.

And then he kept on pacing.

A patient came to us, complaining of fever, and still Salomon remained, treading that same spot while twisting the curls of his beard into tight knots. Now and again, he'd stop, mutter something, then shake his head and resume his course.

I tended to the patient to the best of my ability and sent him off with one of Salomon's potions. Still, Salomon paced back and forth.

"What's the matter with him?" Isidoro asked. The bleeding light of the setting sun caught on his cheekbones and the rounded curve of his lips.

I looked away from him. "He's a smart man. He'll figure it out."

"Perhaps I should stay the night here, just in case," he offered.

I shrugged. "If you've nothing better to do with your time."

Katharina was already in bed when I returned, her day's sewing untouched in a basket in front of her hut. I took an armful of it and settled by my own campfire to work. My father stepped out and sat down beside me, stretching his hip.

"Did you love my mother?" I asked him.

He chuckled. "Aye. As meat loves salt."

"How did you know that you loved her?"

He tilted his head, his eyes drifting toward the stars. Then a smile spread on his lips, and he told me the story. It's one of my most treasured possessions. Perhaps someday, I'll even tell it.

10

The Wildflowers of May

1623

On the day my mother died, my parents spoke to each other in hushed voices, hoping I wouldn't hear. Then my father brought me a leather bag and told me to gather my things. He gave me no explanation, so I went to the trunk where I had my clothes, my comb, my grammar book, and a few playthings, and I sifted through it all, not knowing what to bring and what to leave. I didn't know yet that my friends, Anne and Albrecht, were dead, but I had a foreboding. I knew, without knowing it, that a terrible thing had happened.

The day my father died, there was sun. It was a year after the fall of Heidelberg. The pretty little pretender-king had fled yet again, and we'd spent the next year's campaign chasing the remnants of his army out of Lower Saxony and Westphalia.

We caught up to them just a few miles from the border to the United Provinces, where we halted our march. I left the Tross early in the morning to find my father among the ranks and bring him his ration. The runt, as ever, loped alongside me.

I'd turned fifteen the previous month, and if any question remained that I was now a woman, the leering looks of the soldiers put that question to rest. One of them grabbed me by the elbow as I walked past.

"Marry me," he pleaded, to the laughter of his friends.

I looked him over—he was a pimpled boy of no more than eighteen, with thin wisps of hair that passed for a mustache on his upper lip. "God be praised!" I exclaimed. "You've finally come to your senses." Then I brought my hands to rest on my belly. "And here I thought my child would be damned to grow up a fatherless bastard."

He released me right quick, to the renewed laughter of his comrades.

My father's eyes glinted with amusement when I reached him. "You have a wicked tongue. I waver between wishing your mother was here to see it and relief that she's not." Concern flickered across his features then, and as he bent down to scratch the runt's ear, he said, "You're not really...?"

"No, not a chance!" I was yet a maiden.

My father handed his pike to the man beside him, and we walked a few paces from the lines. There was a hitch in his step as he favored his old injury.

"I heard we have them cornered," I said, handing him his bread and sausage.

My father prayed over the food and then ate it readily, the crumbs catching in his beard. "Appears so," he said. And then, looking at the clear, pale blue above us: "Fair weather for fighting at least. No wind, should keep the cannon smoke out of our eyes."

"What about your leg?" I asked.

"It's fine. Better than it's been in months," he lied.

I took a sip of beer and handed it to him. I was parched just then, but not on account of the sun or any exertion. I looked at my father, shifting his weight from one leg to the other and licking his fingers.

"You might not go," I said.

"Josefine—" my father sighed.

I didn't let him continue. "Your leg still troubles you. Everyone knows it. You could go to Salomon to have it looked at. He'd keep you out of the battle."

"My leg's not so bad as all that."

"You can't lie to me. I know you too well."

He shook his head. "Every soldier in the army has complaints. I can stand. I can march. I can fight."

"But you don't have to."

"And if I don't, I'll not be paid."

"They hardly remember to pay you anyhow. Salomon pays me well enough now to make up the difference."

"It's my duty to fight."

"Is it your duty to die, too?"

A vast quiet settled between us. We never spoke of the possibility of his death. That was also part of our understanding, our shared illusion. He would live forever. But this day, I'd awakened with a sick foreboding in my stomach after a night of restless dark dreams.

"If I must," he said at last.

"Then you're a coward," I snapped.

"What did you say?"

"Nothing. Never you mind it," I backtracked.

"You'd call your father a coward?"

"I just don't understand why you won't go to Salomon!"

"You think I'm a coward because I won't run and hide in a doctor's tent while every fit man in the regiment fights, is that it?"

I held my tongue. All through the campaign, I'd seen him shuffle along, shoulders bent and weary, a husk, a man who had accepted the inevitable and was just waiting, marking time.

"Is that it?" my father repeated. "Tell me the truth."

"Very well then, yes. You're a coward. You've been ready to die for a long while. Since you got your injury, at least. I think you're more afraid of living than you are of dying. You're no better than Mother in that respect."

He struck me. My cheek burned hot. Tears filled my eyes, blinding me. Disbelieving, I touched my fingertips to the tender flesh.

"Disrespect me all you like, but do not disrespect your mother's memory in that way," he growled. "She knew what tortures awaited her if she was arrested. And don't forget they wanted to arrest you as well. I am sure she only thought of you when she died."

"I'm sorry." My voice was small. "You're my father. I need you. What good are you to me dead?"

"I've no intention of dying," he said. He touched my cheek tenderly and brushed the tears from my eyes with his thumb.

"But you're still going to fight?" I asked him.

"Yes," he said. "I'm still going to fight."

It was useless. He'd made up his mind long before that afternoon. He'd march and fight until he died, and there was nothing I could do or say by then to persuade him otherwise. Perhaps if I'd found a way to talk to him sooner—but that was not our way.

I resumed our unspoken agreement as we ate the remainder of the ration. Then he returned to the ranks.

Afterward, I went to Salomon's to prepare for the expected battle, clearing away all who were well enough to walk and making ready the instruments and poultices.

The novice Isidoro was there already when I arrived. For reasons unknown to me, he'd chosen to remain with our army instead of continuing with the Spanish one. I found him deep in prayer, clutching his little book. When he looked up, his cheeks were pale and his mouth an anxious grimace, as they always were before a battle.

"If you can't keep your stomach, best leave," I said. "The injured don't need their priest looking like a vision of the grave." I knew he wouldn't leave; he never did, no matter how many times I told him to.

Katharina was there, too, laying out rags and bandages.

In the end, Salomon had apologized to her for the misunderstanding. And then he'd gone on to explain that there was no sense in her loving him, since there could be no end in it. Though he cared for her a great deal, he had no intention of ever being one of those Jews who converted to Christianity and then slandered his former faith, though he'd wrestled mightily with the question, for her sake. For her part, Katharina said that was just as well, since she'd never said anything about him converting, and she didn't think she'd like him half as much if he did.

So, they'd gone on, cautiously and in secret, with only me and the novice knowing anything about it, and I made the novice swear an oath on his little prayer book not to breathe a word to anyone.

The battle was joined in the afternoon. Though we were some distance from the fighting, we could still make out its discordant strains—the pop of the muskets, the crack of cannon, the hammering of horses' hooves, and beneath it all, a sustained, high-pitched hum—the shouts of the men, urging each other onward amid the clash of blades. In short enough time, the Protestant army threw down their arms, while the victors let loose a roar, a deafening sound, as from a ten-thousand-throated lion. Only the dead were silent.

The injured came to us throughout, first our own men and later in the day, soldiers from the Protestant army who'd been taken captive. We treated them all, the gunshot wounds, the sword cuts, the contusions, and broken bones. We performed three amputations that day, and the novice had to leave us during them, so terrible was the screaming. Salomon let me practice tying off the ligatures, which he preferred to cauterizing. The only good I could say of any of it was that while there were injuries to be treated, I had little time to worry about my father.

But in time the procession of the wounded slowed, and I began to pace and rub my hands together.

"Go back to your tent," Salomon said. "Find your father, before you wear a ditch in the middle of my surgery with your pacing."

"He's not there," I said. I can't say how I knew it, except that I had that same foreboding feeling as I'd had the day my mother died—knowing without knowing. "He would have found me. He would have come here."

"Come now, you can't know that." It was Isidoro. "I'll go with you, if you're worried about going alone."

I nodded and we went, but my father was not at our tent.

"He's most likely celebrating with his companions," Isidoro said.

"No, he's not. I can feel it in my stomach. He would have found me."

"Don't give up hope," said the novice.

"What good is hope?" I snapped at him. "Why do you want me to suffer, hoping he's alive, when I know he must be dead? No, priest, bury your hope."

He hung his head and said nothing more.

When we returned, Salomon was packing away his instruments as Katharina warmed bread over the fire. She ran to embrace me. "I'm sorry, Josefine. I'm so terribly sorry."

"No one else came while we were gone?" the novice asked.

"Not a soul since the two of you left," Salomon answered. "Anyone who could not make it back from the field under their own power by this point has been left, may God have mercy on them."

I was still clinging to Katharina, my head resting on her shoulder. "I have to go find him," I said.

Katharina looked skyward. The late afternoon sun loomed just above the treetops. Soon would follow that shadowy fore-darkness that marks the passage of day into night. I sucked in a breath, expecting her to refuse me. But she said, "We'd better move quickly then."

She climbed onto the wheel of Salomon's cart, taking a shovel down from the roof.

"Just a minute." It was Salomon. "If you intend what I think you intend—"

"We intend to find Josefine's father and bury him if need be."

"Käthe, my love, it's almost nightfall. Are you sure that's wise?"

"Salomon ben Judah, why are you talking about wisdom at a time like this? The woman wants to find her father, and I'll not have her go alone, nor will I see the man thrown in a mass grave."

"A battlefield is no place for—" Salomon started to object.

"Are you going to help us, or are you going to let the womenfolk handle matters alone?"

The doctor chuckled. "Those are my only choices, eh?"

Katharina handed him the shovel, then took me by the elbow and marched toward the field.

"Well, I'll bring my bag, just in case," Salomon muttered behind us, and I heard him shut up his cupboards and turn the keys in the locks.

"Wait, I'm coming too," called the novice, and he trotted up beside us. The runt ran ahead, eager for an adventure and insensible to the nature of our errand.

By now, I've seen too many battlefields, but till that point, I'd only known the aftermath of the battles through wounds and graves. To see that field strewn with bodies while the carrion birds alighted on them, it racked my body with shivers.

The first part of the fighting had taken place in a ditch, and there the dead had fallen on each other in piles, the one side indistinguishable from the other. Then, further up the hill, where the cavalry had broken through, the corpses of man and horse pocked the ground like unnatural grain springing up out of the earth. My heart turned to lead and sank into my belly. Had I picked a rare stone and thrown it into a creek bed, I should have stood a better chance of finding where it landed than I did finding my father in this dry riverbed of dead men.

No less unsettling than the sights were the sounds. I'd expected the silence of the grave, but that was far from the case. Even hours after the battle, it was still possible to pick out the moans of the half-living. Somewhere in the distance a man screamed, "Kill me! Kill me! Kill me!" without end or reprieve. Buzzards squawked at the crows, and both fought with each other over the pickings, although it seemed to me there was plenty to go around. Here and there, others moved among the bodies, collecting armor and other valuables for sale.

I strained to picture what my father had told me about the regiments and where his was likely to have stood when the fight began. And then I waded in among the dead. The runt whimpered, but followed at a slow prowl, his head lowered defensively.

Behind us, Isidoro gave a fearful shout. I spun around, ready to reproach the novice for his cowardice, but then I saw a hand reaching out from a pile of bodies and clinging to his cassock. Salomon hurried to him and cleared away the dead. I recognized the soldier—my father's friend, Bachmann. Blood bubbled up from his lips, and his chest had bloomed crimson, with a bullet hole the center of those delicate petals. I asked him if he'd seen my father, and he pointed a weak finger ahead, further on.

The doctor gave the shovel to the novice and knelt to cut the soldier's shirt open and tend to his wound. "Go on," Salomon said to Katharina. "I'll be right behind you."

We walked onward, pushing bodies away from bodies and dodging the rats that ran out from beneath the dead. The screaming man was close, but his cries were growing weaker. Meanwhile, from the camp came fresh sounds of celebration—shouts and songs, flutes being piped and drums beaten.

I turned to Isidoro: "Do you still expect to find goodness in this place?"

"I suspect they're simply glad they aren't here," he said, stepping over a body.

"A pitiful cause for celebration," I muttered.

Ahead of us another pair of figures moved among the dead. They were covered up to their knees in the mud of the field, and their hair hung down around their ears in stringy clumps. Even in the warmth of the summer evening, they wore layer upon layer of clothing, a motley of doublets, jerkins, breeches and hose. A Spanish helmet rested on one's head, and on that same one's shoulders a Bavarian pauldron. They carried a sack with them and were filling it with items taken off the dead.

The runt stopped in front of them, growling. One of the men drew a sword and waved it in warning. Katharina put a protective hand on my arm.

"What's this?" they asked. "A pair of women and a skinny little priest? What happened? Did you get lost?"

"We're looking for her father," Katharina said. "And you best hope you haven't looted him, or you'll have more than your souls to answer for."

The one with the sword looked from her to the blade. Then he smiled and gave a slight bow of his head. "Best get on with your search then. The light's fading, and there are rough sorts out there. My condolences for your father, young lady."

I called the runt back to me, and we pressed on. By and by, Salomon caught up to us, and a grim shake of his head was enough to tell us that Bachmann hadn't survived.

We found my father at the edge of a small indentation in the earth, displaced by errant cannon-shot. He was on his back. He'd lost his helmet, and there was a deep sword-gash in his head. The blood had congealed around the wound and matted down his hair. His eyes were wide open. My eyes, blue as the summer sky.

The novice prayed a quick prayer. Then he said, "I'm sorry, Miss Dorn."

Katharina knelt to lower my father's eyelids. The runt lay down beside him, nudging him with his snout before letting out a wailing howl. For my part, I was fixed in place, unable to turn away from the sight and unable to stop myself imagining how he'd died. The impact of the cannonball striking the earth had toppled him, that was clear enough, knocking his helmet away at the same time. And then some enemy soldier had delivered the final blow. But had he fought? Had he given his all to make it back to me, or had he simply surrendered to fate? Nothing about the scene offered any answers.

I found a Bavarian helmet on the ground nearby and put it on his head, covering the ghastly wound. Then I reached into his belt pouch and retrieved his rosary beads and the few coins he carried on him. The beads were made of amber, and they caught the light of the setting sun.

"Come, young priest," said Salomon. He removed a blanket from his bag and laid it on the ground. "Help me lift him onto the blanket."

Isidoro looked to be on the verge of being sick, but he nodded and took my father by the boots while Salomon lifted his shoulders.

Once they'd wrapped him in the blanket, the doctor turned to me. "Where shall we take him?"

Ellwangen, I wanted to say. *Load him on a wagon and ride until you reach Ellwangen, however long the journey takes. Take him far from this ditch, from this war, and lay him in the yard behind the tannery next to his wife, my mother.* But instead, I scanned our surroundings until my eyes fell on the tree line. "To the trees," I said.

The novice and the doctor huffed and strained to carry him across the field, stepping over the dead who were strewn across their path. The screams of the dying man had finally stopped, but the sounds of the celebrations had grown louder and more boisterous.

We each took turns with the shovel, piling up the earth in the shadow of a knotted oak tree, and when the hole was near ready, Isidoro ran back to camp to fetch a proper priest.

I can't say what it felt like to dig that grave. For a long while after, I thought that it was I who went to sleep that day for the last time, went to sleep and started dreaming and didn't wake up.

The priest prayed over him as we laid him in the ground, but I wasn't listening. I ran the rosary beads through my fingers over and over without praying. When the time came, I scooped up the first handful of dirt and sprinkled it over his body. I didn't cry, not then. The tears would come later.

After the burial, Katharina and Salomon invited me to stay with them for the night, but their kindness felt like pity, so I turned them down.

Isidoro insisted on accompanying me back to my tent. There, I went about gathering wood and building my fire. The novice remained, helping me pile the sticks and light the kindling.

"Why are you still here?" I demanded, as the first embers glowed beneath the stacked wood.

"I'm worried about you."

"Why? Nothing's changed." I took bread and meat from my pack while he stoked the flame. "I was alone most of the time before, and now I'm still alone. The sun will rise tomorrow, and I'll get by, as I always have."

"Your father died. That's not a small thing." He sat on the ground, and I sat down beside him.

"He was a soldier. It was bound to happen sooner or later. Bread?"

"Thank you. There's a vast difference between knowing something's likely to happen and it happening."

"What do you want? Are you hoping I'll break down in tears so you can comfort me? I'll ask you again: what are you doing here? You are about to become a priest, and yet you spend all your free time with a Jewish doctor and his whore and—"

"You," he filled in. "I spend all my free time with you."

"Why?"

"Because I... care about you."

I nearly choked on breadcrumbs. "You care about me. You're about to take your vows."

He chewed slowly. "That's true. But don't you think it's possible for a man to love both God and a woman?"

"You sound like a Protestant."

He shrugged. "So do you, sometimes."

"I don't know what I am."

His face was toward the flame, and the light dappled his skin in brilliant oranges, reds, and yellows.

"You care about me," I whispered.

"Yes, I think so," he said.

He inclined his face toward mine, and I heard his breath hitch. "Miss Dorn, I—"

I didn't let him finish. I leaned in and kissed him.

I'd never once kissed a person in that way, but as soon as his lips touched mine, a warming feeling spread through my center. I'm sure he hadn't had any more experience with kissing than I did, for the longer we kissed, the more he seemed to search for something to do with his hands. At first, he reached for my waist, then he explored my cheek and my hair before settling at last on the back of my neck.

My father was dead and buried in an unmarked grave under a tired old oak tree above a stinking river of dead men, but Isidoro was there, and his breath was warm, his skin was soft, and he tasted like sweat and prayer.

I pressed myself closer to him and reached into his lap, feeling through folds of his cassock for his hardening member. His eyes grew wide then, and he broke away, scrambling backward with a hand between his legs.

Blood rushed to my cheeks. "What's wrong?"

"This isn't right."

"Don't start acting like a priest again. Not now."

"Your father just died. You're in mourning. I can't—"

"Horseshit. You think I don't know what I want?"

"I can't marry you. I have no money. No profession."

"I'm not asking you to marry me."

He shook his head, his cheeks fluttering as he tensed and untensed his jaw. "You need to get some sleep. I need to get some sleep. We can talk about this in the morning. I promise we'll talk about this in the morning."

"I don't want to talk. I want you to fuck me."

"I can't. Not tonight."

"Then to Hell with you."

"Josefine." He reached for my arm, but I swatted his hand away.

"You heard me." I stood. "To Hell with you. Go, take your vows. I don't need you to care for me, whatever that means. I didn't ask you to, and I don't need you to."

I should've gone directly into my tent then. I should've laid my head on the bedroll next to where my father used to sleep and let the cord around my heart unwind itself and dissolve into tears.

Instead, I marched toward the bright light of the bonfire where the soldiers were gathered, drinking the beer and wine they'd plundered from the town in the battle's wake. They perched on chairs, on logs, on empty barrels, or else they danced around the fire with their wives and whores. The musicians struck up a bright tune, then, and a chorus of voices, hoarse from the day's shouting, started to sing:

> *No more beautiful death in the world*
> *Than they that are slain before the foe*
> *On the green heath, in the open field*
> *Let them hear no cries of woe.*
>
> *They that die in narrow bed*
> *Must lie alone in the grave.*
> *But here they find good company,*
> *Fallen like wildflowers in May.*

I sidled up to a dark-haired soldier, took the beer from his hand, and downed the contents. Then I touched his shoulder, just as I'd seen Katharina do many times before, and told him to bring me another.

The world around me was liquid by the time I stumbled back to my tent on the soldier's arm. Even so, I was clear-headed enough to notice that Isidoro had gone, and that I felt some way about it—relieved, yes, but also angry. If he'd cared for me, he should have stayed—so went my drunk and bitter reasoning.

My soldier and I had barely crawled inside the tent when he started to cover me in greedy, drunken kisses. His stubble-covered cheeks were rough against my face, but his hands knew exactly what they wanted to do. He freed my breasts from my blouse, pausing to fondle them before lifting my skirts and parting my legs. He wasted no time then in spearing me. The pain was rending, but he was quickly done, and then he was on his way.

After he'd gone, I checked my skirts for signs of blood and spotted the bedroll clean with a damp rag. Then the tears I'd been storing up for my father finally came.

II

A Place of Open Arms

1623-1624

In the Bible, Job's story ends with God repaying everything the poor man lost. Job receives new sons and new daughters, more houses, more fields, and more flocks than before.

But I often wonder about poor Job. What was it like in that second life, with that second family? Did it ever feel like home? Or did he ever pass through a familiar doorway into a once desolate room, only to find himself a stranger in a place now filled with the shouts and laughter of children? Did his heart ever fly from his chest in retreat, seeking the comfortable familiarity of grief? How could he ever again chance to leave a part of himself out in the open where God or the devil could reach in and take it? I don't know. The Bible doesn't say. The story was never about Job after all.

As for me, the weeks that followed my father's death were an epoch, and Grief was that devil in the Bible that calls himself Legion. It possessed me in all its thousand forms. Most mornings the air felt as thick as mud, and the face the demon wore was Lethargy, so I didn't stir from my tent until mid-afternoon or later, rousing only when Katharina came to force me out of bed. Then Spite took hold of me, and I told Katharina she was no family of mine, so she needn't concern herself with me. But she refused to listen to such talk, coming each day when the sun was high to pull my blanket off me. She once poured a bucket of water over my head since I'd also neglected my baths. I kicked my feet at her in Obduracy then, but when she threatened at last to leave, Loneliness appeared and begged her to stay.

During that time, the pretty little prince signed an armistice with the Emperor. Again the war was over, and again it didn't end, for it's not in war's nature to end. It justifies itself perpetually; so long as there are princes ready to do its bidding, to wager blood that is not their own in the name of religion or ambition or the German liberties, it goes on, and if it runs out of reasons, war itself is its own reason. The dead must be avenged, what was lost in one battle must be regained in the next, the soldiers must have new towns to plunder, and so on, till the end of time.

A few evenings after my father's death, I found the novice waiting outside my tent. Such a relief it was to see him again, I ran to greet him. But he held up his hand, as if to say *come this far and no further*. Then he stammered out an apology for his behavior that night.

He said he never should've kissed me, that it had been a moment of sinful weakness, and that he'd likely always care about me, but it wasn't good for him just then to be around me, and he was ashamed for dragging me into his sin.

When I found my words again, I told him if that was how he felt, then we had nothing more to say to each other. But when he'd gone, I crawled onto my bedroll and buried my face in the runt's fur until he squirmed away from me.

At times I wonder what might have happened if I'd not taken him so plainly at his word, if I'd instead asked him to stay and eat and to forget for a few moments more about being such a blessed priest. Would it have changed the paths our lives took? Would it have given us more time?

It's useless to wonder. The past is fixed as it is, by fate or by choice, and if I'm still not certain which it's because choices are not arrows or even bullets. They are rocks in a landslide that strike each other and bounce away on another course entirely until the intentions behind them are no longer visible in their effects.

Katharina and I were at our sewing a few days later when she told me that she and Salomon had decided to leave the Tross. The needle in my hand slipped, pricking the tip of my finger, but drawing no blood.

"Oh, and where will you go?" It took all my will to stop my voice from wavering.

"Öttingen. The counts there are more or less welcoming to Jews—or to their taxes in any case. Salomon knows a family in one of the villages, a place called Pflaumloch, on the outskirts of—"

She didn't need to finish her sentence. I was familiar with both the village and its nearest city.

"—Nördlingen," I said.

How quickly it all returned to me: the sweet, roasted scent of rye left to bake overnight in the ovens; the reek of straw- and sand-covered manure in the city streets; the clamor of dogs, cats, and swine running this way and that in the shadow of the grain houses; and the sticky, floral taste of honey, sweet honey, sticking to bread.

"You know the city?" Katharina asked.

"My father and I wintered there once. Öttingen is good country. Fertile land, open skies. The people... well, they're the same as anywhere, I suppose. Some are kind, some are cruel. Whatever the world makes of them. All in all, you could pick a worse place to found a family."

Her hand strayed to her lightly swelling stomach. "How did you know?"

"You give yourself away, always stroking your belly."

She looked down, chewing on her lip as she so often did when something was weighing on her mind. "I suppose it's not a secret I could keep forever."

Then she took my hand and squeezed it. "Come with us."

"I couldn't. I'd only be trouble to you. An extra belly to fill."

"No, I'll not hear that kind of talk."

"You'll have your hands full enough with your own family."

"All the more reason for you to come. We'll need the help, and you should continue your learning with Salomon. Besides which... I'd miss you." She leaned on me, resting her head against mine.

"I'll think it over," I said.

As if there were any thinking to do. I had little wish to trail behind Katharina and Salomon, little wish to be the baggage to their growing family, but where else could I go? I couldn't soon see myself taking a soldier for a husband.

Katharina fell quiet, twisting her thread around her thumb with nervous energy. "There's another thing," she said, lowering her voice to barely more than a whisper.

I waited for her to continue.

"Salomon and I are getting married."

I searched her face for signs of a jest but found none. "How? He didn't decide to convert, did he?"

"No," she said. "I did." And before I could say a word either good or bad about it, she continued, "Josefine, I know this must seem rash, but trust me. I've given it a lot of thought."

"Rash? They'll burn you *both* if it gets known!" I whispered.

"I know," she said, shaking her head. "I know. Salomon said the same thing. He said no one in their right mind would choose to become a Jew and certainly not in the Empire. He said all it will bring me is misery."

"Then why? Because of the child?"

"Partly. Salomon assured me he would support us either way, but it didn't sit right with me, that he should take all the risk of acknowledging the child, yet it would never be a Jew."

"But that's not the only reason?"

"No, it's not. I..." She seemed to wander deep into her own mind. "I don't expect you or anyone to understand it. I'm not even sure Salomon does."

"Tell me."

"I know it will be hard," she continued in a low voice. "But I also know hardship can't be all there is. I know, because for all his talk of misery, Salomon would never give it up, not even to save his own life. I know because wherever we march, if Salomon learns of a Jew living nearby, he seeks them out to see if they need anything, and when he does, it doesn't matter if the family is rich or poor, they welcome him with food and drink as if he were a dear friend or brother. I know because when I hear him pray, every night and every morning, I find myself wanting to pray with him. I've prayed plenty in my life, but I've never before *wanted* to, not in that way. I would risk so much more than death to be a part of that, to have my children be a part of it too. Do you understand?"

She kneaded her cloth anxiously, watching for my reaction.

What was there to understand? All the bishops and all the priests in the world couldn't have made sense of it, but what does that prove? Only how little all their learning amounts to. But I'd lived a rough and rootless life for long enough that I had little trouble recognizing the lilt of yearning in her voice. To put it plain, what Katharina had found in Salomon was a home, and Salomon's home was among the Jews. So like Ruth the Moabitess, she would make his people her people and his God her God.

"When do we depart?" I asked.

Katharina smiled wide. "Soon. In a week if we can manage it. Two at the latest. Our hope is to leave early enough to take care of matters and get settled before the winter months."

We left three weeks after. I'll not write of where Katharina's conversion took place, whether it was within the borders of the Empire or without, in case wicked eyes should find this account. Neither will I write the names of those involved, not the rabbi, nor the women who instructed her in the commandments and immersed her in the water, for they may yet be living.

I will say they were not the first community Salomon approached with the question. Two others before them declined, fearing the penalty if they were caught. The elders in that place also refused at first, but the women caught wind of it, and knowing Katharina's condition, they prevailed on the men to take the chance.

Salomon and Katharina stayed a month in that community, while Katharina received her instruction in the law and the commandments. In their generosity, the Jews of that town also provided for me to stay among them.

At her conversion, Katharina took the Hebrew name Rachel, which is how she has been known ever since, though Salomon still calls her Käthe from time to time in their private, affectionate conversation. If any ask, they tell folks that she came from Ottoman lands, which is why she has no family or community in Germany and why Yiddish is a second tongue.

It was late autumn when we rode into Öttingen, our wagon wheels juddering across frost-hardened land. A bright ache filled my chest at first sight of the blue-green tips of the spruce trees brushing the pale sky. They were almost exactly as I remembered them, except they were the wrong height, somehow shorter than before.

It wasn't the trees that had changed, of course. The last time I'd crossed those lands, my father had been alive, and we still believed in all those many pleasant fables we'd told ourselves about the future. I kept expecting my father to step out from between the trunks and call me *Häschen*.

The village of Pflaumloch was a lively little settlement just an hour's journey from Nördlingen. The Jews there had a bathhouse, but no synagogue, so they had to travel elsewhere to worship.

As it happened, so did the Christians. Ownership of the village lands was divided between Nördlingen's Spital and the Catholic Count of Öttingen-Wallerstein. Each landlord had at one time or other tried to appoint their own clergy to the town, only to have the adherents of the other faith drive the poor clergymen off. As a consequence, the village church had been sitting vacant for decades.

Salomon and Rachel, as everyone then knew her, spent the remainder of that autumn and winter settling in. Salomon had the rent of a small house from the Count with rooms enough for the two of them and their growing family and a small plot of land for an herb garden. Rachel stayed with another Jewish family until the wedding.

Salomon treated me as his ward and arranged for me to stay in the home of an elderly Catholic couple, the Bauers, who saw to it that I attended Mass with them each Sunday. Everyone agreed that it was very virtuous of the young Jewish family to show so much care for a Christian orphan.

The wedding was set for early March. Salomon's sister Judith came down from Frankfurt-am-Main two weeks beforehand. She was just as Salomon had described her, a woman of robust stomach and unyielding judgments, who filled near every room with her voice as soon as she entered it. On first laying eyes on Rachel, she threw her arms around her.

"What a lovely creature you are!" she exclaimed. "I see why my brother is so impatient for marriage. There are just two things you must know about being his wife. First, he's the most intelligent fool you will ever meet. If it's not in a book, he doesn't know it, so it falls to you to bring the wisdom to the marriage. Second, he will sicken himself to the grave with worry if you let him. It's his pride, you see. He thinks that since he's a doctor with a university education everything rests on his shoulders. But it's God alone who sets the beginning and end of our days, and don't you let him forget it. I give you this advice as your soon-to-be sister."

"Thank you, Judith," said Salomon, guiding her to the room they'd prepared for her. "Please try not to frighten my bride before the wedding."

By the time he returned, Rachel and I had given over to fits of giggling.

"I don't see what's so funny. She's a busybody and always has been. None of it's true, my love."

"Oh, but Salomon," Rachel said, gasping for breath. "It is. She has you exact."

But it wasn't long after Judith's arrival I found Rachel curled up in the larder, clutching her belly and shaking with quiet sobs.

"What's the trouble? Are you unwell? Has something happened to the baby? Should I get Salomon?"

Rachel rubbed the tears from her eyes. "No, no, the baby is fine. All is well. I'm well."

"Then why the devil are you in here sniveling? You scared me witless."

"I'm not worthy of him," she said then.

"Stop talking drivel. Where did you get this idea?"

"Judith."

I blinked at her, uncomprehending. "Judith adores you."

"Aye, she speaks nothing but honeyed words to me. But she lays out her real mind to Salomon in Yiddish. She knows I don't speak it well, so she thinks I don't understand it either. He could have had a match with any respectable woman in Frankfurt or Hamburg or Hildesheim, she says, with a dowry of five hundred gulden at least. His first wife was a rabbi's daughter."

"And what does Salomon say to her?"

"He says she's a busybody, and she should keep her judgments to herself."

"There you have it. What's the worry? In two weeks, you'll be married, and Judith will be in Frankfurt."

"She's right, though," Rachel sniffled. Even large with child, she looked frail and diminished beneath the wavering shadows of the larder. "He's a respected, educated physician. It's foolishness for him to marry a woman like me. A Tross whore with nothing to offer. Not even a proper Jew."

"The devil take her for suggesting it, and the devil take you too if you believe it. Give me ten minutes with her and I'll make her see straight."

I rose to make good on my word, but Rachel reached out to stay me. "No, you mustn't."

"And why not? I talked sense into Salomon, didn't I? If Judith knew the half of what you've risked to marry him…"

"If she knew, she'd be even more set against it, I'm sure. No, Josefine, she's to be my sister, whether she likes it or not. It'll do me no good to have you charging in all hot-tempered in my defense. I must learn to handle her myself."

"If Salomon had wanted a five-hundred-gulden bride, he had plenty of time to find one," I told her. "He chose you. Don't forget it."

She smiled, and the last of her tears slipped from her eye and came to rest on her lip. She brushed it away, and I helped her to her feet.

The wedding took place on a Friday, and it seemed as if every Jewish family in the county was in attendance. Those from farther afield started arriving a few days before, and soon the village was overrun with wedding guests.

I don't know if Rachel ever spoke her mind direct to Judith, but on the day of the wedding, they bickered like sisters. Judith flitted around Rachel, fretting over her dress and her shroud, until Rachel swatted her away, exclaiming that the woman was making her far more anxious than the wedding itself.

Thursday morning, Judith and I rode to Bopfingen in Salomon's cart to pick up the wedding belt Rachel had purchased for him from a silver merchant there. The merchant had a nephew, a young man about my age who they all called Unsinkable Chayim. The story was that a few years back he'd been on a ferry that capsized, and he was the only one on board who did not drown.

Unsinkable's uncle sent him to ride with us and make sure the belt was to the bride's liking. He was reasonable company, neither too talkative nor too quiet. He asked me where I was from and how a Gentile had become so close to a pair of Jews. He was sorry to learn of my father's death. He had ambitions to follow his uncle into the silver business, but he'd also begun to deal in pearls from the coast.

"But I shouldn't start talking about the pearls," he said. "Or I'm apt to talk your ear off."

"Is it true they grow inside of a creature?"

"Oysters, yes. God's creation is full of wonders."

The morning of the ceremony we all went up to Baldern by Bopfingen, where there was a small synagogue that served the Jews of the nearby villages. Salomon was in an unusually quiet mood the whole day; never before had I seen the man so tongue-tied.

Besides me, there were a handful of Christians in attendance; mostly high-ranking acquaintances Salomon had made while doctoring, the sort of folk it's wise to invite to a wedding, if one wants to be thought well-of. The Count of Öttingen-Wallerstein was invited and sent a representative in his place.

The feast that followed the ceremony was as big a meal as I could remember having. I ate myself into a stupor on goose, bread dumplings, seasoned beef both boiled and roasted, and beer and wine enough to souse the whole village three times over.

After the feasting came the dancing. It was the obligation of every man in attendance to dance with the bride, who gamely joined in. The men wore gloves while dancing, and the young unmarried women were encouraged to get to know them, so long as their skin did not touch.

I danced twice with Unsinkable Chayim. He was a fine dancer, light on his feet, and patient with my clumsy movements. Afterwards, when we were sweaty and breathless, his hand slipped down to my waist, and we ducked away from the party. We let ourselves into a nearby barn, where I stripped off his gloves and a fair more besides and let him touch me as he pleased, skin included.

I returned to the party afterward, and there I found the bride, resting on a chair with a dreamlike look in her eye. Her belly was large by then, close to the time when most women would begin their lying-in.

I embraced her and rested my cheek on her head. "Are you happy?" I asked, though the answer was plain on her face.

"Ecstatic," she said, beaming. "But so, so tired."

The festivity lasted till nightfall and on the next day, the Sabbath, everyone gathered at the synagogue once more to hear the wedding proclamation. Then a group of Christian musicians they'd hired for the occasion started to play, and the celebrations began afresh. After that we returned to Pflaumloch, where the feasting and dancing continued at Salomon and Rachel's house, five more days.

Rachel's labors began almost a month to the day after the wedding. Salomon had taken the cart the night before on a house call, so it fell to me to fetch the Jewish midwife from Bopfingen on foot.

I was huffing and puffing by the time I arrived at her home, but I'd made the two-hour journey in an hour and a half. I left word with Unsinkable Chayim to fetch Salomon and rode back to Pflaumloch with the midwife, who, thankfully, had a horse and cart at her disposal.

The child hadn't yet come by the time I returned, and though the village women had taken good care of Rachel, she'd made little progress. The midwife took one look at her and started preparing medicines to help things along. I spent the afternoon running this way and that, drawing and boiling water, grinding up herbs, and applying damp rags to Rachel's hot and sweat-soaked body.

Salomon arrived in the evening, and though he wasn't permitted in the room, I think it did her some good to hear his voice through the door, for matters progressed soon after. In the middle of that night, the child finally came. She was a pink and wrinkled little girl, who announced herself to the world with full-throated screams.

Rachel was pale and exhausted by the end, and when the midwife asked her what her daughter was to be called, she muttered, "God-damn-it, do I have to do everything?"

On the day they were meant to announce the child's name at the synagogue, she was still nameless. It was three weeks before they finally agreed to call her Hannah.

12

The Sweet Taste of Honey

1625

That first year in Pflaumloch we lived in a world apart from the war. Life in the village ground on much as it always had—fields were sown and ploughed, the stone turned in the mill, and the baker fired his ovens, untroubled by the armies.

Yet I was ill at ease with peace. Every morning I woke and threw open my window to see the same broad oak standing immovable outside it. Season by season, it budded, grew leafy, and changed hue, before shedding its dress entirely. I watched it warily, marking time until… I didn't know what. I only knew that I was restless down to my bones.

Salomon and Rachel fretted about what to do with me. They'd be carrying on an animated conversation in Yiddish, and I'd hear my name dropped into the middle. I gleaned that Salomon wanted me married, but Rachel had her own reasons for not wanting to push me into it.

If I'd cared to marry, I would've had little difficulty finding a husband. There were enough ready young men of all religions in the village—the youthful schoolmaster with his ink-stained fingers; the field hand whose skin smelled of sweat and sunshine; the journeyman blacksmith with burns up and down his body and soot in his hair. I was reckless with their affections but not my own. It pleased me to let them kiss and touch me, but my heart I kept locked away in a quiet, desolate place that I visited only in solitude.

I continued my training with Salomon, joining him on his rounds. By then, I was more than passing good at identifying herbs, naming symptoms, and specifying cures, but my true skill lay in cutting and cauterizing, drilling and stitching. As ever, the bodies themselves were my favorite texts, their sentences written in gristle, blood, and bone.

Nearby Nördlingen remained what it had always been, remote and impassive, the white-walled city with its imposing black church tower. Its walls held the rest of the world at bay, sheltering the goings-on of the city from the ungoverned wilds of the country outside.

Several times I accompanied Salomon through the arch of the city gates on house calls. Each time, I rode tense and alert through the streets, expecting to see her—to see Eleonore.

Once, I caught sight of her father, the deacon, on the steps of St. George's. He looked directly at me, but there was neither twitch nor glimmer of recognition in his expression.

I found the city both malign and alluring. It was a place I missed, even as I couldn't wait to leave.

In summer 1625, the first reports of the armies' approach reached us, followed swiftly by hoofbeats and the snapping of banners on the wind.

We weren't taken entirely by surprise. We'd followed the progress of the war closely in the pamphlets and the one-sheets, so we knew that Friedrich, the pretender-king, had found himself a new champion. This time it was the king of Denmark who'd taken up the cause of German liberties. He hoped to secure a bishopric for his son as well.

On hearing that the armies were close, Rachel, Salomon, and I wandered the rooms of their house, taking it all in. Our minds were blanks, for there was too much to consider all at once: blankets and tablecloths, kettles, pans, and water basins. The was larder full of meat, herbs, beans, and flour, the plinth piled high with firewood, and that was only the kitchen.

Upstairs were their beds and belongings. Salomon collected books like a magpie collects shiny baubles. Rachel started to mount the stairs but collapsed onto the bottom step, burying her head in her hands.

Husband and wife debated whether to stay or flee. They were in the valley of the shadow, for it seemed either way they were damned. They might gather their daughter and their valuables and seek shelter within Nördlingen's walls, but there was no certainty the city would admit them as Jews, nor could they be sure that the house would still be there when they returned. If they stayed, they must take their chances with the soldiers.

In the end, after consulting with the other Jewish families, they made preparations to flee. We spent a long afternoon going through the house, packing the most necessary items, and sewing valuables into clothing.

Salomon looked up at the Sabbath lamp, hanging from the ceiling. "Should we take it down?"

"Whatever for?" Rachel snapped.

"For safekeeping."

"And what will we do for light on the Sabbath? It stays until we have no other choice."

I returned to the house of my hosts, the elderly Catholic couple, after sundown. The inventory there was more overwhelming still—decade upon decade of memories in the house where they'd raised their children and their grandchildren and earned their rest. By the time I passed through their door, they'd already made up their minds to stay put.

A few weeks later, the first pikes of the Protestant army were spotted in the north, and I left with Salomon and Rachel for the city.

Nördlingen that summer was hot and rank as the inside of a sheep's guts. People trudged in, not just from Pflaumloch but from all the surrounding villages, seeking the protection of those white walls.

Not even during the height of the Pentecost Fair, when the city teemed with merchants, had I seen the place so overpeopled. Refugees crammed into every open space, sleeping head-to-toe on the floors of the inns, in the church, and along the streets among the wild dogs, pigs, and horses. Their carts, piled high with their possessions, blocked the roads.

The city council granted the Jews temporary permission to stay, but only until the danger had passed. The families were given lodgings separate from the rest of the fleeing masses, which the council claimed was for their own protection. As a Christian, I was permitted to lay out my bed in St. George's among the widows and orphans. As ever, the runt slept beside me.

That first night I slept poorly. From the moment I entered the gates, Eleonore was at the fore of my mind. I didn't even know if she yet lived, but I felt a certainty that if she did, I wouldn't escape the city without seeing her again. The thought tormented me. I longed to see her, and I dreaded it.

Come morning, I'd made up my mind not to wait for fate or chance to decide. I dressed, tied my valuables to my person, and with the runt following me, I strode up to the deacon's house. At the doorstep, I hesitated. *This is foolish*, I thought. *She'll have no memory of you.* I pushed the thought away and knocked.

I can't begin to describe all the knotted ways I felt when that door opened, and she appeared standing in front of me, her eyes wide with recognition. First came the bitter ache of the cord had that wound itself around my heart all those years before, followed by the roiling grief of my father's death. Both were washed away by the pleasant memories of lazy days spent wasting time in each other's company—the fondness, the warmth, the longing for some indefinable contentment I'd long ago lost. I looked at her and tasted honey on my lips.

Till that point, in all my imaginings of our reunion, we were still children. But she wasn't a child anymore, and neither was I. She was a woman, with all that that entailed. I sucked in a breath and tried to remember what I'd come to say.

"Eleonore," I said, failing.

"Not-a-boy." She took two steps and embraced me.

My heart sped up in my chest.

"I can't believe it," she said. "I almost didn't recognize you. I need to know everything. How you are, where you've been—but not here. My father and stepmother are home, and I want us to be able to speak openly."

She took my hand then and led me to the market, weaving in and out of the throngs of refugees that clogged the lanes. People greeted her by name, and she smiled back at them, as light and airy as I remembered. But her grip on my hand was iron-tight, as if fearing I'd slip through her fingers.

"I thought I'd never see you again," she said, stopping at a food stall. The goods were picked-over, with only a pair of sorry-looking tarts remaining. She moved on. Each stall we went to was much the same; those that still had wares to sell were surrounded by people, pushing and jostling and shouting their orders.

"I looked for you every day after you left, hoping you'd return. When did you get back to Nördlingen? Where have you been?"

"Here and there," I said.

Suddenly she cried out, "Cherries!" and rushed to a nearby stand. There indeed were cherries, fresh and baked into tarts and turned into cordial. She picked a cherry out and fed it to me. "Well?"

I nodded as the sour-sweet juice hit my tongue. She looked very pleased with herself and bartered for two handfuls' worth. We split them between us, eating as we walked and spitting out the pits.

"'Here and there' is no answer, Fi."

It wasn't, but what could I tell her? I didn't fully know what I'd expected when I came to her door. At one time, I'd wanted to blame her for all that happened, but I'd never been able to. The moment I saw her, the moment she embraced me, it was as if not a second had passed since that winter day on the banks of the Eger, her fingers in my hair. It was a pleasing illusion—one I couldn't bear to spoil with talk of war.

A warm, inviting scent filled my nostrils. "Mortar cakes," I said, pointing. There were only a few remaining. We chose a pair of savory cakes, but Eleonore's face fell when the seller named the price. She chewed on the inside of her cheek as she felt the weight of her purse diminishing. I brought out my own money and paid for the cakes and a bottle of wine besides.

"You didn't have to—"

"It's no trouble."

"You're full of mysteries, aren't you?"

We searched the city for a place to retreat to, but every corner we searched was overstuffed with people hiding from the war. She talked to fill the silence left by my reticence.

"I'm afraid I'm not half so mysterious as you are. I've been here, just here. Well, not exactly. I did finally leave the city, if you can believe it. Guess where I went?"

"Don't tell me," I teased. "Flanders? Spain? Italy?"

"Nuremberg."

It was unfair of me to laugh, but I couldn't help myself. Nuremberg is a fair city, though by now it's seen the same hardships as the rest.

"It's not Paris, is it?" she acknowledged. "My father decided to remarry the year after you left. A cloth-seller's widow. Her family is in Nuremberg, so she visits them from time to time and takes me with her."

Indeed, her years had been quiet compared to mine. The fainting spell she'd had in the tree returned once or twice yearly. The doctors had no remedy for her, but neither did it cause her much trouble.

Her father's remarriage had been a matter of convenience rather than affection. The woman had money and a business from her previous marriage, but no children to pass it on to. Her father's wages as a deacon were meager. The widow's income would keep them in house while he continued his work for the church, and Eleonore would learn the cloth-selling trade into the bargain.

She spoke of her stepmother Margarethe with fondness, but her voice sank a register whenever she mentioned her father, much alike to the way some priests speak of sin and the devil. Her whole body tensed.

Apart from working with her stepmother, she'd also been enrolled for a time at the Lutheran school. She'd been a good student but had fit in poorly with the other girls there. "All they talked about, even then, was marrying and rearing children."

How familiar she was and how strange. There were times she seemed every bit the fairy-like girl I remembered, only inhabiting a woman's body. But then a cloud would pass over, her gaze would fall, and she'd appear entirely changed.

I took her hand and led her away from the crowds, toward the city walls.

"Where are we going?"

"Someplace quiet."

"We can't leave the city," she protested.

"We don't need to."

I led her to a watchtower, one of the places she used to hide to escape her chores when we were children. "Do you remember how to get in?"

She grinned and plucked a pin from her hair.

The lower level of the tower was unoccupied, set aside for storage. Inside was cool and still, the morning light only barely slipping through the windows slitted into the door. The runt flopped over onto his side in the narrow beam of sunshine, and Eleonore and I collapsed with our backs to the outward-facing wall.

At last, we were alone, apart from the watchmen who passed above us, patrolling the walls. I uncorked the wine and drank direct from the bottle, and Eleonore leaned her head on my shoulder.

"I can't believe you're here. After all these years. I keep touching you to make sure you're real. Stop being so mysterious. Tell me what happened. Tell me where you've been."

"Give me one of those cakes," I said. "I'm famished."

She passed me a cake. "I hate him, you know. My father. I've never forgiven him for what he did to you and your father. Spreading all those terrible rumors. The lies about you and your mother being involved in witchcraft. I swear he didn't hear it from me. I told him it was all untrue. He wouldn't listen. He went on and on about protecting me from devilish influences. If I could've run away, I would've."

"Wise you didn't." I stuffed my mouth with mortar cake and washed it down with wine. "Here, try some."

She broke off a piece and took a desultory nibble. "It wasn't wisdom. It was fear."

"They don't have to be different," I said.

"Why won't you tell me where you've been?"

I exhaled deeply. "If you must know, we were with the army. Until about a year and a half ago."

"Oh. Are there tanners in the Tross then?"

"My father wasn't in the Tross."

"Oh," she said, understanding dawning.

"The day he died, I begged him not to go into battle. But he wouldn't be a coward, so he died a brave man."

"Fi, I'm sorry."

She was full of questions for me, then: about life in the army, about what I'd been doing since my father's death, and how it was that I'd returned to Nördlingen after all this time. I told her everything as far as I dared, leaving out only those details which might incriminate Salomon and Rachel.

She asked too about the runt and his missing eye. "Oh, you poor creature!" she exclaimed when I'd told her the story. He raised his head to look at her and wagged his tail, uncomprehending.

All the while I talked, her attention was unwavering. Now and again, she'd lay a hand on my shoulder, or on my hand, or on my knee, in that same careless manner with which she'd once reached out and stroked my hair, as if insensible to the effect it had on me. Insensible to how it made my blood run hot.

The runt's sunbeam moved as the morning turned to afternoon, and he curled up next to Eleonore, resting his chin on her lap. She fed him the last piece of cake.

"It should've been my father that died. Not yours. I wish it had been him."

"You don't mean that."

"What if I do?"

I offered her the last drops of wine, which she drank eagerly. The dark liquid stained her lips.

"I can't believe you've been living not three miles from here for over a year now, and this is the first time I've seen you," she said then, resting her body against mine. My heart stuttered. "Why didn't you come to the city before now?"

"I did. Many times. With Salomon."

"But you didn't look for me before today?"

"I looked for you every time," I confessed. "How could I not? For years I've wondered where you were or what you were doing or if you even remembered me."

I found her hand and traced idle circles around her knuckles with my fingertip.

"But you didn't come to my door. You didn't knock."

The air between us vibrated. It hummed.

"I didn't know if I should."

Had she been a man, I would've known what to do next—the way to move, to tilt my head, to part my lips ever so slightly in invitation.

She was watching me intently. "I'm glad you did."

A wisp of hair escaped her braids, and I brushed it away from her face. She inhaled sharply as my fingertips grazed her skin. Then she jumped to her feet.

"What is it?" I asked.

"Nothing. I thought I heard someone coming."

I stood. "I didn't hear anyone."

"I'm sure I heard something."

She made for the door, but with two quick strides, I caught up to her and stopped her. "Wait," I said. "Listen."

I put my ear to the door. "I don't hear anything. It must've been the changing of the guard above us. No one's there now."

My hands found her waist. Her breath fluttered when I touched her. She stood almost an inch taller than me, and I had to incline my head slightly to meet her eyes.

"Fi," she said. "Josefine."

"What?"

"You're not a boy."

"No, I'm not." I stepped forward, pressing her body between me and the wall, and waited for her to push me away. Then I leaned in and found her lips with mine. "But I know what I'd do, if I was," I whispered.

"This is a sin," she said, looking back at me wide-eyed. But she made no effort to free herself.

"What's sin?" I asked. It's wrong to kill, and it's wrong to steal, and it's wrong to covet your neighbor's cow. Except if you are a prince and raise an army, or a soldier living by plunder, or a magistrate and you condemn your neighbor's family to the pyre for being witches. *Except, except, except.* "We're hurting no one, taking from no one."

Her lips hovered close to mine. When next I kissed her, she kissed me back.

The more of her I tasted, the more I wanted to taste. I knew I wouldn't be satisfied with her lips alone. They were crumbs, and I was ravenous. It was sinful, and I didn't care. I'd been sinning from the moment I closed the tower door.

13

Waiting

1625-1626

Imperial recruits arrived to reinforce the garrison, and the restless and greedy violence of soldiers was added to our woes. The townspeople clashed with their defenders, and both soldier and burgher alike held the gutter-dwelling refugees in contempt.

A mercenary army in the service of the pretender-king arrived outside the gates shortly after, setting up camp right up against the walls, and for the next week the gates were closed, sealing us all in together.

Life as a refugee had a familiar cadence. As in the Tross, we rose every day with survival on our minds. The women busied themselves with sewing and washing, repairing pots and baskets, and other useful chores. The men hired themselves out where they could. The children ran errands and begged in the streets.

I at least had Salomon, who found a brisk business in physician's cures in that overcrowded city. We were on the move from morning to dusk, and by the time I returned to the church in the evening, I was weary and hungry. Most nights I ate my bread and fell asleep directly on the floor of the church.

The day after our kiss, I returned to Eleonore's, but she wasn't home. So, I went on to her stepmother's shop near the weavers. Though it'd only been a single day, it had been time enough for doubt to eat into my gut like a burning poison. What if she'd thought better of kissing me after we left? What if she'd come to her senses?

When I entered the shop, Eleonore was folding cloth at a table in the back, surrounded by shelves of wool and linen. She gave me only the briefest of glances as the door swung closed behind me.

"Margarethe, a customer," she called to her stepmother.

A round, fleshy woman of some forty-five years emerged from behind a shelf and greeted me with a genial smile. "And how may I be of service?"

I mumbled a response, a lie about needing wool for a Sunday dress. The woman stepped out from behind the counter and planted two of her fingers at the base of my chin, tilting my head upward.

"Come now, let's see you. Yes, good. Sunny complexion. A little thin overall." My cheeks burned. "Oh, but those eyes. Lovely eyes, like the North Sea after a storm. I'll find you something to bring out their color, and you'll have young men lining up all down the street to propose to you."

In the back, there was a clatter of metal against wood. Eleonore bent down to pick her shears up from the floor.

"Careful, girl," her stepmother chided. "You'll dull the edge."

"I'm off to Mrs. Spandl," Eleonore said then, replacing the shears and tying off a bundle of fabric.

The older woman nodded. "Take care that she inspects the cloth before you go. I'll not have her coming back to us tomorrow with dubious complaints about moths. It's her own fault if she lets them lay eggs in her sewing room."

Eleonore's shoulder brushed mine as she passed, but she kept her head bowed and her eyes fixed in front of her. I placed a hurried order for a length of slate-colored wool at a price far higher than I could rightly afford, and then I rushed out the door to follow her.

"Whatever it is I did to anger you, I'm sorry," I said when I'd caught up to her. "I'll not kiss you again if you don't want it. I'll hate every moment I'm not kissing you, but I'll do it. I may be well and truly damned, but I can stop myself dragging you into Hell with me, I promise."

She rounded a corner into a narrow alley between the buildings. There, engulfed in the shadow of that passage, she stopped, turned to me, and put her mouth on mine. Yes, I was well and truly damned.

"Don't be stupid," she said.

"I don't understand. Why wouldn't you speak to me? Why wouldn't you look at me?"

"How could I look at you? Margarethe would have seen everything. I could not have kept it hidden. I only just found you. I can't risk being separated from you again."

"Still, you might have given me some sign."

She lingered with her cheek next to mine. "Is this not sign enough for you?"

"So where can we go? When can I see you? I can't stand it, being ignored by you," I whispered.

"Not here. Not in the city. It's too crowded. Someone will see."

"Where then? The gates are sealed. The towers are full of soldiers."

"We must wait until they open them again."

I groaned. "Don't say that."

"I hate it as much as you do."

"I don't believe that's possible," I said.

"Yesterday I had never kissed anyone. Today I cannot think."

"Then give me one more kiss. Something to live on until the siege is over."

She looked this way and that, waiting for several passers-by to clear the passage. Then she gave me a quick, soft kiss on the lips.

She turned then, smoothing her skirts and her bodice, adjusting her blouse at the shoulder. I watched her go, stepping into the warm light of the open lane. I counted to a hundred under my shaking breath, and then I did the same.

The waiting was unbearable. It is one thing to wait in anticipation of a long-expected event, counting down the days until it arrives, but to wait for something without deadline or hope of an end is to labor under a curse. Every day the army remained outside the walls, my soul slipped closer and closer to Hell.

It was during that time I first met the cabinetmaker. I didn't know his name yet, only his profession. He was a young man, as yet unmarried, at the end of his *Wanderjahre*. He'd been on his way back to Augsburg to take the title of master cabinetmaker when the armies arrived, and Nördlingen's gates closed.

Rather than bemoan his bad luck, he'd gone to the deacon, Eleonore's father, and offered to assist with the refugees in the church. Each day at midday and again in the evening, he walked up and down the nave, handing out the bread ration.

I will try to recount my first impression of him as I saw him then, without coloring it with what came after. He was an uncommonly tall man, standing at least a head above most others, and when he rolled up his sleeves, his forearms looked as if they'd been carved from oak. But for all his size and apparent strength, there was something sensitive about him, retreating. He withdrew from eye contact and spoke so quietly as a rule that I had to strain to hear him. Several of the widows flirted with him relentlessly. He accepted their attentions politely, but, I thought, without real interest.

Now, a few hundred strangers wedged into one space is bound to stir trouble. No less so when those strangers have traveled from who-knows-where, carrying all that they could take with them, not to mention a heap of cares and worries. Even in the house of God, there were tussles and feuds aplenty.

Besides the widows and orphans, the church was also shelter to several young families and a few older men. Each group accused the others of encroaching on their space or rifling through their things. There were long arguments over who deserved priority of place in line for the daily bread donation.

During these times, the cabinetmaker's sensitivity seemed to strain against the heat and the clamor and the press of greedy hands clawing at the ration, but I never once heard him shout or lose patience. Afterward, he'd retreat to some quiet corner of the church, though there were hardly any such spaces left, to sit and ponder the woodwork.

We were none of us our best selves in that time. The circumstances made us naturally ornery, and every day, kindness was a choice we fought hunger and exhaustion and overcrowding to make.

Early one morning, I woke to shrieking. One of the widows was pinned beneath one of the men, a known drunkard, who was busy making rutting motions with his hips. I tried to push him off her, but even inebriated he was stubbornly anchored to the spot. The cabinetmaker joined me, heaving the man off with grunt.

The man was indeed drunk. He'd not even managed to unfasten his breeches before he took to humping the sleeping woman. Now he tripped over himself in confusion before rising to take a swing at the cabinetmaker.

The cabinetmaker was built like the church tower, and he grappled the man with ease, throwing him to the ground with such force, the cross on the altar wobbled. Then he pinned him, pressing his left forearm against the drunkard's windpipe. The man opened his mouth in a soundless gasp.

"Let him go! You're choking him!" I cried.

The cabinetmaker sat up, a stricken look on his face. The women encircled the drunk, keeping him in place until the watch arrived. After that, the cabinetmaker left.

We didn't see him again for days after. The deacon handed out the bread ration, and folk took to speculating and spreading rumors. Some guessed that the drunkard's friends had gone after the cabinetmaker in revenge. Others supposed he'd finally grown tired of the church rabble and left of his own accord. One old man even claimed he'd been pinching items all week and selling them in secret, and now he'd been arrested.

A few days later, I saw him coming out of one of the woodworkers' shops. I considered the mystery solved, thinking he'd simply gone and found work practicing his trade.

I didn't know the half of it. At the end of the next week, he returned to the church with the deacon and several other craftsmen, bearing a set of eight-foot oak-wood paneled screens, which they stood upright in the middle of the nave, separating the men from the families, orphans, and widows.

They were breathtaking creations, those panels. The knotted branches of oak and chestnut trees stretched the length of them. Birds with soft plumage perched on nests of dried grass, each blade and twig coaxed from the wood in precise strokes. A deer peered out from between the tree trunks, catching the light in its varnished eyes.

"They're beautifully done and much needed," I told him.

"I could've used more time, but they will do," he said. It was perhaps the first time I'd seen him smile.

The deacon was well pleased too. He drew special attention to the screens in the next Sunday's sermon. The cabinetmaker, however, hardly seemed to note the compliment. He went right back to his daily labor, distributing bread.

That's how I remember him then: quiet, self-effacing, strong, with an artist's eye and an artist's sensitivity. Perhaps too sensitive, in the end. This war demands numbness; it's most destructive to those that feel it most keenly.

It was our good fortune and the city's that that first siege didn't last long. It wasn't even properly a siege. The mercenary army that had camped outside the walls was a poor force—ragged, threadbare peasants to a man, underfed, under drilled, and underpaid. Most of them were Englishmen, red-headed and freckled foreigners with sickly complexions dragged thousands of miles from home on the promise of fortune and the chance to fight for God and the German liberties. They were too few to fully encircle the city and neither did they have sufficient guns to bombard the walls. After a number of fruitless weeks, they moved on, seeking fresh fields to plunder.

When the siege was done, I rode back to Pflaumloch with Salomon and Rachel, their daughter Hannah perched on my lap. The mood was celebratory. We were all greatly relieved to be in the open air and out of the city once more. But as we drew closer to the village, we fell into anxious quiet, anticipating what destruction we might find.

The house was a sorry sight. The blankets had been stripped from the beds, the dishware was gone, but for a few broken shards. Salomon had hidden his books beneath the floorboards before he left, and the boards had been torn up in the ransacking, the books scattered around the room while the soldiers searched for objects of more evident worth. The Sabbath lamp remained in its place, hanging reassuringly from the living room ceiling.

A few days later, my and Eleonore's long season of waiting came to an end. She chose the meeting-place—the ruin of an old church outside the city walls, not far from the leaning oak where she'd fallen into the river all those years before.

There was hardly a church left in that spot to bear the name. Only one wall remained, and that not even high enough to enclose the frame of the window. Here and there, it was still possible to make out the cruciform shape of the building, marked by mounds of crumbling stone, peeking out from beneath their coverings of moss and ivy. So long had it been since there'd been a roof that a spruce tree had sprung up in the center where the altar once stood, and the floor of the nave was a soft bed of wet needles and pinecones.

Eleonore was seated on the low wall when I arrived, her hair dappled by the sun's rays as they slipped through the tree branches. She jumped down when she saw me, laughing and half tackling me with her embrace. We toppled onto the bed of pine needles.

I'd made a dress from the cloth I'd bought at her stepmother's shop, and now I wore it. As she ran her fingers along the seams, she said, "Margarethe was right. The color does bring out your eyes."

We spent a long while just looking on one another, tracing the shapes of each other's faces with delicate, modest touches.

Then she kissed me. I'd been kissed plenty of times by then, but not in the way Eleonore kissed me. She kissed me like she was afraid my lips would disappear. She kissed me till she was breathless, till we were both breathless, and then she went on, stirring me up. A whimper escaped my throat.

I pulled away, and her eyes widened. "Did I do something wrong?"

I touched a finger to her lips. "Hush."

Shaking, I undid the strings of my bodice, slipped my blouse down over my shoulders, and guided her hand to my naked breast.

Her cheeks bloomed pink, and her lips parted in surprise, but she did not withdraw.

Bit by bit, we shed our clothes, until our naked bellies were pressed together. I traced the curve of her thigh to the soft, hot place between her legs, and she gasped and writhed beneath me.

After, we lay in the grass, the sweat cooling on our naked skin as the tree branches swayed above us. I turned my head and took in the whole of her naked form for the first time, the tender swell of her belly, the round, inviting softness of her thighs, the pale pink of her breasts as they rose and fell with her breathing.

Did I love her already then? At the time, I would have said without hesitation that I did. In truth, I didn't yet know even half of what it takes to love another person. Of desire and being desired, I knew plenty. When we were together, I was on fire. When we were apart, I thought I would perish for want of her. I couldn't imagine there was anything more to love than that.

But of bearing all things, believing all things, hoping all things, enduring all things, I yet knew nothing.

14

What a Woman May Choose

1626-1628

We tumbled through the seasons in the memory of that old church, spending the hours like profligates, as if they would never run out. The last of summer's heat faded, and in the chill of autumn, I dug a fire pit and built a fire. We drank hot wine, and she shoved me up against the cold stone of the ruined church wall and slipped her fingers inside me.

In winter, the frost kept us away, but that only made us bolder; I visited St. George's of a Sunday, just so I could stand near her as she prayed. After, when the congregation had all gone and the church sat cold and dark and quiet, she led me up into the organ loft, and I dropped to my knees and buried my face in her skirts. In spring, we found ourselves in the ruin again, rolling among the pine needles and licking rainwater from each other's skin.

It's a symptom of youth to believe that you are immune to time, to believe that you will be the first person in all of history to sprout wings and fly. We lived in those moments as if they would never pass.

But one evening as Salomon and I finished our rounds through the villages, he parked his wagon by the roadside and rubbed his hands together, as he always did when he had something very important he meant to say.

"Listen to me, Josefine," he said. "Käthe and I have been discussing it, and we both agree it's time you started looking for a husband. You're the right age for it. My first wife was sixteen when our parents made the marriage contract. I was seventeen."

My stomach turned to a leaden lump as I listened.

"You needn't worry about the dowry. I took charge of that when I took you in after your father's death. There's money set aside. Three hundred gulden. Not a princely sum, but it should be enough to set you and your husband on your way."

"I..." The objection formed and died on my tongue. "Thank you."

"The Bauer family have agreed to help find and vouchsafe the match. But of course Käthe insists that you will have your say. We do not want to force your hand."

I picked at a fleck of dirt that had lodged itself beneath my nail.

"Tell me the truth," he said then. "I will not judge you. I have seen how distracted you are of late. And I know you've told the Bauers you were making rounds with me when you were not. Is there someone already? A young man you're besotted with."

"No, there's no young man."

"Very well. If you say so, then I believe it. But take care all the same. You can take it from me: a man does not think when it comes to these matters. He is all impulse and desire. And when he can't control himself, he'll look to control the rest of the world instead.

"I wish it weren't so," he went on. "But it is. Think how many men take mistresses, get bastards on them, and shame them for it, all while expecting their wives to be chaste. Young men, old men, it hardly matters the age. Don't let your heart deceive you into carrying the burden of some careless man's consequences, do you understand me? If there is someone, bring him to me, and I'll see he does right by you."

It seemed to me that as he lectured me, he was being hardest on himself.

"Are we agreed, then?" he asked.

"Aye," I said, but my throat burned.

On our return to Pflaumloch, I must have worn a sullen look, for Rachel said to me, "We just want you to be safe and happy. Both Salomon and I."

How I suffered for love in those days. I knew it was love because I suffered. When Eleonore and I were apart, I drove myself to distraction thinking of her smell, her laugh, and the bright mischief in her eyes.

I was only ever at peace when were together, when I could lie in the shade of that tree, my head on her breast, listening as she confided her quiet, secret thoughts in me.

"I wish you really *were* a boy," she said. "I would marry you. I'd follow you wherever you went."

"If I were a man, I'd not go anywhere. I'd have my own surgery. I'd become a Protestant and buy us a house on the square."

"No, not here. Too close to my father."

"Where then?"

"Nuremberg, so Margarethe could visit. Or somewhere west. Across the Rhine and away from the fighting."

"Very well, then Nuremberg. And how many children should we have?"

"Must we have children?"

"Oh, yes," I said, rolling on top of her and pinning her arms above her head. "I'm afraid I won't be able to keep my hands off you."

She squirmed in my grasp, but her struggle was feigned. With a smile to make the devil blush, she pressed her fingers into my scalp and guided my head down her belly and between her thighs: "Then it's a good thing you're not a man."

In our fantasies, we roamed all of Germany—to Nuremberg, to Frankfurt, and then we went farther still, across the Rhine to France, Spain, and onward to the edge of the world.

And then our fantasies ended, and we went our own ways, returning to Nördlingen, to Pflaumloch.

How I chafed at those partings! The trouble was that Eleonore had her whole life in Nördlingen, but I had only her. There were weeks at a time when she was unable to make it to the ruin for one reason or another. I tried not to let it make me jealous, but the longer our separation, the easier it was for bitter thoughts to plant themselves, take root, and grow.

In spring of 1626, Eleonore left for Augsburg with her father. She told me ahead of time, tearfully, and though we both protested at the thought of being parted, neither of us had any say in the matter. She was gone for that whole season and into summer.

In her absence I dragged myself through the days, weighed down by a burden only I could see. Salomon and Rachel both grew more concerned and redoubled their efforts to ease my soul by providing me a husband.

The Bauers introduced me to a succession of young men they thought would make fit matches. Martin, Johann, Friedrich, they were called. Each of them was well set up or soon-to-be, and none of them were so poorly made that I wouldn't have once given them a tumble. The flaw was mine and mine only: I looked in their eyes and found them dull compared to hers.

Eleonore wrote to me from Augsburg. I've long since lost those letters, but there was little of interest in them anyhow. She didn't dare write anything of significance, lest her father read them. But midway through summer, she told me she'd be returning the second week of August.

The start of that week came and went, and I waited for her in the church ruin, day after day, while that old and bitter wound on my heart pulsed, and I grew more impatient, more agitated.

For nine days straight I came to the ruin and saw no sign of her. I read and re-read her letter only to realize that she'd said nothing of meeting me on her return. I felt a fool, but what else could I do but wait?

Ten days after her promised return, I went up to that crumbling old church in a flinty mood, ripe to twist the nose off any person who so much as looked at me askance. But she was there ahead of me, seated on the broken wall, and as ever, she jumped down to greet me.

"A fine thing, leaving me waiting all this time," I snapped.

She stopped short. "What's got into you? I told you I had no choice about going to Augsburg. My father as much as commanded it."

I snorted. "Right. You always do what your father tells you. I remember."

"Fi." She said only that: "Fi."

"Go on, then. Tell me it's otherwise."

"We talked about this. Why don't you believe me?"

"How can I?"

"Don't you trust me?"

"I trusted you before, and you know well what happened then. I nearly died of fever. And when I came out of it, you wouldn't speak to me. You wouldn't look at me. You let them drive me and my father out of the city. You talk about running away, but you don't have the first notion what life outside those walls is like. It's not this. It's not taking your pleasure and then running back to safety. To Augsburg, with your father."

There was a tremor in her voice when she spoke again. "Why must you continue punishing me for something that happened seven years ago?"

"Because I can't sleep for thinking of you, all the while you make me beg for scraps of your attention, as if I'm nothing more than a dog."

She buried her fingers in my hair then and pulled me into a rough, strong kiss. Her lips tasted of salt, of tears. Still, she continued to kiss me: grasping, needing kisses.

"Stop it. Stop being so stupid. You know I think about you always," she said, breaking away at last. "I don't know how to make you believe me. I don't know why you can't see it. Everyone else can. Why do you think my father insisted I go with him? He knows. He doesn't know it's you. He doesn't even remember your name. He thinks it must be one of the young men in the city that's driving me to distraction."

"Is that why you made me wait *ten days* to see you again after you came back?"

"Ten days? I just arrived yesterday. I told you in my letter…"

"Yes, you said the fourteenth. That was ten days ago."

"I said the fourteenth. Today."

Each of us realized the mistake at once. My face grew warm with shame. Eleonore laughed.

"Damned Papists," she groused. "It's not enough for your Pope to control the gates to Heaven, is it? He has to make a muddle of the calendar, too."

"Well, if you Lutherans didn't have to be so contrary all the time…" Nördlingen, like all the Protestant cities in Germany, still holds to the old calendar. "I'm sorry," I said. "I've been a—"

"A right ass? Yes, you have. But here—" She pulled a small packet out of her waistband, wrapped in paper and tied with string. "I brought you a gift. Open it, and I'll forgive you."

The parcel fit in the palm of my hand. I tugged at the string and the paper fell away, revealing an ivory comb. The shaft was adorned with beautifully carved pinecones, each one rendered in minute detail by the craftsman's patient hand. I ran my finger along the teeth, while willing the lump in my throat to dissolve.

"I *am* an ass," I whispered.

"I gather you like it, then." She didn't wait for my answer. One by one, she unfastened the pins in my hair. Then she took the comb and ran it through each lock with firm, tender strokes.

What she neglected to tell me that day in the ruin was that she was engaged. I discovered it by accident, the next year at the annual Pentecost Fair.

That was where I first saw the two of them together: Eleonore and the cabinetmaker.

They stood by a flower stall in the market square, and he took a sprig of lavender and put it in her hair. She blushed and lowered her head.

My blood ran hot. I stalked toward them, and if Eleonore hadn't spotted me first and looped her arm through mine to take me aside, I'd have raged like the possessed right there in the middle of the crowd. She led me to that same tower where we'd first kissed and told me everything.

"How long?" I demanded, once we were alone.

"Since last year. Augsburg," she confessed.

The cabinetmaker's name was Konrad Lehmann. Her father got to know him during the siege—he made a beautiful screen for the church, surely I'd seen it? The deacon took her to Augsburg in the spring to meet him, and both of their fathers arranged the contract.

"Do you even know him?"

"We spent some time together when I was in Augsburg. He's shy, quiet. He takes time to warm up to people."

"Do you love him then?"

"No," she insisted. "And please stop shouting."

How could she say she didn't love him when I'd seen how she looked at him? Why didn't she tell me about him before? Round and round we went: my questions, her denials. Of course she'd agreed to the engagement: he was a gentle young man from a good family with good prospects for the future.

"What about us?" I demanded.

"I don't know what you mean."

"What about me? Am I nothing to you?"

"For the last time, please stop shouting!"

I wasn't even aware I'd been shouting. I couldn't hear myself over the pulsing of my heart in my ears. I slammed my fist into the wall with such force that it awakened my old injury and caused my fingers to seize up and go numb. I wished I could do the same for my heart, to stop it cracking apart.

When I turned back to Eleonore, she'd collapsed to the floor, clutching her knees to her chest. Her face was buried in her arms, and her shoulders rose and fell with arrhythmic sobs.

"I'm sorry," I said, massaging the feeling back into my fingers. My throat was dry from shouting and mortar dust. "I'm sorry."

"You know if I had the choice—"

"What do you mean, if you had the choice? Your father can't force you. How long were you planning to keep it a secret from me? Would you have told me before the wedding or after?"

"It wasn't a secret. We were waiting for him to finish his masterpiece, so he could open his shop in Nördlingen and purchase his citizenship. He just arrived in town. I would have told you. I meant to tell you."

"Swear to me you don't love him."

"I've already said so." She rose.

"Swear to me you won't marry him."

"You know I can't—"

"Why not?"

She walked toward the door, shaking her head. "You know very well why not. Josefine, I love you. I think... I'm quite certain I've loved you since we were children. Whether I'm married or not doesn't change that. But I don't know how to make you believe me, and I can't talk to you like this. It hurts too much."

She lifted the latch and left. I stood in the dark of the tower a while longer, listening to the hammering of my heart.

It was a week before Eleonore returned to the ruin. I came every day in hopefulness that she'd forgive my jealous stupidity. Finally, I heard the soft and familiar brush of her skirts in the grass, and then she appeared alongside the low wall. She stopped short when she saw me, in the spot where the doorway once stood.

I was seated with my back against the spruce tree. "Eleonore, I—"

"I've no wish to be shouted at again," she said.

"I didn't come to shout," I said.

"Good." And then: "I'm sorry for not telling you about Konrad sooner."

I offered her my hand, and she took it, settling into the roots beside me. The warmth passed through the wool of her dress into mine, but I couldn't help a shiver passing through me, nor the gooseflesh from rising on my skin as I wrapped my arm around her. She let her head fall on my shoulder.

"He was in Augsburg, and I was here," she explained. "It was easy to, well, not forget exactly. But to push it off. It didn't seem quite real, in any case. Rather like a very vivid dream that fades away once a person wakes. I didn't know how to tell you."

"I'm sorry for shouting. My mind gets all muddled around you. I feel everything more intensely."

"I'm glad you kissed me that day in the tower. I couldn't have imagined it. I never would have dared. I didn't realize until you did it just how much I wanted you to."

"I didn't know either."

She ran her fingertips over the knuckles of my right hand, which were still slightly discolored from striking the tower wall. "I never set out to hurt you. But what choice did I have? A woman, a good, Protestant woman has only one path that's open to her. To be a wife and a mother. A Catholic woman might at least choose the church, but for a deacon's daughter? If it hadn't been Konrad, it would have been some other man my father chose for me."

"I know. I know." I clutched her hand to my center. "Rachel and Salomon want me to find a husband."

She stifled a laugh.

"What's funny?"

"Nothing. I'm sorry. Somehow, I can't imagine you married. But that's good news, isn't it? If you find a husband nearby, you can stay, and we can still see each other."

"You know I'll not be content, just seeing you. Never touching you. Never kissing you."

With a gentle touch, she turned my face toward hers. "I meant it when I said it made no difference whether I'm married or not." She kissed me, and the kiss was the opposite of her touch, desperate and needful. "We'll find a way."

I once asked my priest what the purpose of hope was, except to be the packhorse for despair. He told me that every seed ever planted, every child ever birthed, every lover ever kissed was done in hope.

Eleonore and I spent the rest of that year hoping. When we kissed each other, we did so with the hope that there would be another. When we held each other, the same. When we confided in each other, we did so in the hope that whatever happened, wherever we went in the world, there would always be someone else who knew us whole and unconcealed.

Ever since the Protestant mercenaries had first laid siege to the city, armies had begun passing through the lands around Nördlingen, quartering from time to time within the walls. The city grew restless with soldiers in their midst. The burghers were torn between their Imperial loyalties and their Protestant faith and indignant at being forced to quarter ravenous and undisciplined men in their homes and shops.

In February 1628, a builder named Dollmann was shot dead by a pair of unknown men outside the city walls. Just a few days later, a rider from one of the Imperial regiments killed a farmer, Kaspar Mahler, with his saber. Mahler's killer was arrested and hanged for his crimes, but Dollmann's murderers were never found.

After years of quiet discontent, the cord that had been holding back their anger snapped, and the citizens of Nördlingen took to surreptitiously dropping rocks, bricks, and clay pots out of upper-story windows at the soldiers as they walked the streets.

In March that year, the Imperial commander summoned Salomon to remove a shard of clay that had lodged itself in the cheek of one of his men. Salomon gave the patient a perfunctory examination and then nodded to me.

I looked the man over. The fragment had lodged itself just below his right eye, and as his face twitched in pain, it had started to drift higher. I laid my surgical tools out on the table and asked the commander for a basin of water and a candle.

The commander was young, perhaps in his late twenties. He pursed his lips at my request and waited for Salomon to speak.

"You heard the young woman," the physician said.

The young officer coughed. "Are you not Salomon Frankfurt, the Jewish surgeon?"

"You sent for me by that name," Salomon replied. "So it would be very strange indeed if I weren't."

"I sent for you so you could remove this piece of pottery from my man's face."

"Aye," I interjected. "And that's what I mean to do, if you'll bring me what I asked for."

"If I may, Miss Dorn." Salomon looked the commander over. "You are a cavalryman, aren't you?"

The man nodded.

"Are you a good shot?"

"Passing good."

"But you're a fine rider, I'm sure. I'd certainly not challenge you to race on horseback. Any more than you would challenge your finest marksman to a duel, am I right?"

"What are you getting at?"

"I'm an excellent doctor, but I'm only a passing good surgeon. If you want your soldier to keep his eye, you'll give the young woman what she asks for."

The commander barked a reluctant order, and I received my basin and candle. Then he took his place at my side, watching me hawk-like as I wiped the blood from the man's face to get a closer look at the wound. The officer leaned forward when I leaned forward, close enough that I could have grabbed him by the cock without taking a step.

I fixed him with a stare. "You'll get a better view from across the table."

He cleared his throat and moved to the other side.

Surgery's delicate work, no matter what they may say. It's not like mashing herbs with mortar and pestle. If the hand shakes, if the angle is wrong, if the grip on the forceps slips or the vision falters, the shard moves a quarter inch, and a man loses his eye.

Imagine running headlong through the woods with a pack of hounds close on your heels. The tree branches whip past you, while their roots spring up beneath you. Think quick or take a branch to the eye. Stop and the hounds will get you. There is no time for doubt or indecision. There is your own body and the body in front of you, and all else is nothing.

I ran my finger along the man's cheek, feeling for the edge of the shard beneath the skin, and made a small cut. Then I took the forceps in my left hand, settled on my angle, and tugged. The soldier convulsed and cried out, but I had a bandage at the ready and pressed it against his cheek.

"Hush your whimpering now," I said. "You're a soldier, and this is no musket ball. Just a bit of women's crockery." Then to the commander: "Hold this."

While he held the bandage to the injured man's face, I prepared the medicament for the wound. Then I stitched it shut. It was quick, clean work, and when I was done, the commander joked that the soldier's vision seemed to have improved.

The next time he needed a surgeon, he sent for me directly.

On the ride back to Pflaumloch, Salomon and I shared a jug of wine and a laugh over the commander and his reaction to learning I was to operate.

"A fine load of shit that was about horse races and duels," I told him.

"Ah, but Josefine, I meant every word of it. I can't say when it happened, exactly, but at some point you went from an impatient, over-eager, thieving little ne'er-do-well who was as apt to drill a man's brains out of his skull as save his life, to an impatient but nevertheless very skilled surgeon."

"I know I'm skilled. I was just worried the patient was going to twitch his own eye out while you prattled on."

"Clearly, I was not remiss in leaving 'humble' off the list."

But as we drained the jug, Salomon grew quiet.

"Tell me the truth, Josefine. I've been patient with you, haven't I? I've been just to you, I hope. Generous. Not expecting anything in return. Only wanting what was best for you, to see you independent. It's *tzedakah*, you understand? It wasn't an obligation. I was glad to do it. The moment this skinny little child, her hand shattered to pieces, arrived at my tent, too poor to pay for herbs, but too clever by half, I like to think I did what any decent person would. I taught you everything I could: reading, writing, medicine, Latin. Even when you didn't care to learn it."

"Aye, you've treated me as a daughter. Have I been ungrateful?"

"No, no. Not at all. But I don't think it's true, that I treated you as a daughter. I think I may have failed you there, somehow. No, looking back on it, I treated you more like a son. Like an apprentice. I was not prepared. I didn't think on what a young woman might need to know."

I followed his thinking easily enough. "You mean, like choosing a husband."

"Yes, like choosing a husband." He paused, running his hand over his beard and kneading at the curls. "I don't want you to think... it's not that we're trying to rid ourselves of you, you understand? Rachel and I will always have a place for you and for your family when you are blessed with one of your own.

"But if a woman wants to be set up in life, she needs a husband. So, you have to choose. It's been almost two years now, and you've had some fair offers. Fine young men. Rachel will not allow me to choose for you, so I'm telling you, by month's end, you have to choose."

I tried. I surely did. I met with all the Johanns and the Martins and the Friedrichs, with the Kaspars and the Jürgens and even a Richard, a tall, broad-shouldered hunter, who spoke not five words our entire meeting, two of which were *Auf Wiedersehen*. But at night when I tried to imagine my future as any of their wives, I couldn't see it.

Choices are not arrows. They do not go where they are aimed. They are cannon fire, lobbed blind and striking the ground with shuddering force. They knock you from your feet and sweep you down the slope, into the ditch, into the bog, and all you can do is scramble to stand up again before the mortal blow finds its mark.

Eleonore made her choice at the start of April. Our ruin was dusted with late snow, and she pulled her coat tight around her body as she waited for me. I could see the muddy tracks in the ground where she'd been pacing.

Their fathers had agreed on a day. The wedding would take place in three weeks' time. She didn't know when she'd be able to see me again.

I nodded when she told me. "I understand," I said. To say more would have been to break down crying, and I'd told myself I'd not cry.

"Is that all?" she said. "You're not going to shout? You're not angry?"

"If I shouted, would it change anything?"

She ignored the question. "I'll write you. And when we're established, when our household is set up, you can come visit."

"And what? Shall I suck your tits in your husband's bed?" She flinched, but I continued. "It's a fable we've been telling ourselves."

"Fi, please. Don't speak like that."

"No, Eleonore. I can't go on with this play-acting. I don't want your letters, and I don't want to marry one of the Martins or the Johanns and sit at sewing with you while our children play together. I want you. Though it means I'm twice damned, both on this earth and hereafter, I can't pretend it's otherwise, and I can't wait here for you to decide that you feel the same."

"But I do feel the same."

"Then run away with me." I'd not planned to say it, but once I started, the words spilled out of me, faster than I could hold them back. "I can make my living at medicine. It'll not be an easy life, but we can be free. We can go someplace no one knows us, Frankfurt or Amsterdam, far from the war, and be together."

Several times she started to speak, then fell silent again.

"Aye, so I thought." I turned to walk away.

I couldn't see them then, the threads that held her in place. Her father's will, her stepmother's, her future husband's. Fear and doubt I saw, written plain on her face, and I assumed the obvious explanation was also the true one—that she would always choose the safety of her father's house and that city's walls over me, no matter how much she protested that she hated him. No matter how much she claimed to want to run away. I didn't think to ask what she feared, what she was unsure of; I didn't think to ask *who*.

"Please," she said. "Don't go."

But I was already lost in my thoughts, imagining her wedding night, dancing with her cabinetmaker, Konrad, with his broad shoulders and long, narrow fingers.

I walked direct from our meeting into Nördlingen and didn't return to Salomon and Rachel's house until after sunset. Supper was laid out on the table when I opened the door and scraped the frost from the soles of my shoes. I ate quietly while the married couple chatted about the day. The big news was that Abraham Hirsch's bitch was large with pups, and folks in the village were sure the runt had done the siring.

"It'd not surprise me one bit," Rachel remarked. "There were always whelps in the Tross that bore a passing resemblance." And then, to me: "You'll need to start tying him down when he's not with you if you don't want the whole village out for his balls."

"I'll take care of it," I muttered, glancing at the runt, who was lying in the corner, chewing on a piece of bone.

When the dishes were cleared and cleaned, they went to lay the children down for bed: Hannah, now four years old, and Daniel, born just five months earlier, in mid-December.

"I've made my decision," I said when they returned.

Rachel embraced me. Salomon sat opposite me, slapping his open palm on the table and smiling broadly. "Great news. Who will it be? Just don't tell me it's that Richard fellow. You need a man who can string at least two sentences together, or else how will you carry on any sort of conversation in your house?"

"Hush, Salomon. You don't know what she wants. So, tell us, who is it?"

"No one," I said. "I'm leaving."

Rachel sat down beside me, taking my hand in hers. "What do you mean?"

Salomon said nothing at all.

"The soldiers have orders to leave the city after the snows," I explained. "I signed a contract to join them as a surgeon. I'll be going with them."

Rachel's face fell. "You're going back to the army? Why?"

How could I explain it? How could I tell them that if I stayed, my heart would shatter?

Salomon had yet to speak, but now he brought his hand down on the table and stood. "No," he said. "I'll not hear this nonsense spoken in my house. You will go back in the morning, and you will tear up that contract. Or I will do it for you. You're a foolish girl; they'll believe me if I tell them it was a mistake."

"It wasn't a mistake. I've thought it over. You said it yourself, I'm as good a surgeon as you ever were. I belong with the army."

"No!" he repeated. "Never in all my life have I heard anything so absurd. You belong here."

"It's just for two years," I said. "And with the progress the Imperial army is making up north, the war will most likely be over before then."

"I can't listen to this any longer. Käthe, talk sense into this foolish girl, will you?" Salomon lumbered to the doorway. Then he turned, and I saw the pain written on his face as plain as if I'd taken a knife and cut him.

"Salomon—" Rachel began.

He said, "If you leave this house, if you go back to the army, I swear, I'll never speak a word to you again."

"Salomon!" Rachel exclaimed, but he'd already gone.

"I'm sorry," I said to her. My voice was no more than a rasp.

She squeezed my hand. "He doesn't mean it, you know. You just took him by surprise. You took both of us by surprise. He's so proud of you. He just wants you to be taken care of."

"What about you? Will you try to talk me out of it?"

"I know better than that, I think. You have a stubborn heart. I'd be a liar if I said I didn't know what that was like."

She stood and took a jar from one of the shelves. It clinked as she carried it to the table. She tipped it over and poured out a heap of coins, some three hundred gulden. "We'd been saving this for you, for when you got married. You should take it now, I think."

"I couldn't."

"No, I won't hear that. Take it."

"What will Salomon say?"

"He'll be angry, I'm sure. But in time he'll come to his senses, and when he does, he'll be happy to know you didn't go empty-handed."

I took the money and added it to my own savings. A good sum, in all, and when it came time to stock my surgery, I was glad to have it.

I left Pflaumloch a few days later. It was a misty morning. Salomon, true to his word, had not spoken to me since I told him I was going, and he did not emerge from the house to say goodbye.

But Rachel hugged me, and before I went, she cupped my face in her hands and said, "Come back here, do you understand? Promise me you won't be too stubborn to come back to us."

I gave her my word. But the trouble with promises is, they are far easier to let fly than they are to keep.

15

The Man War Could Not Touch

1628-1629

We marched north later that month, joining Pappenheim's regiment with the Catholic League army in Stade on the river Elbe. On the way I bought a horse and cart and stocked the cart with all the necessaries for my surgery.

What a cracked ribcage of a country that was. Compared to Öttingen, where I'd just come from, the northern lands were rough, swampish, and reluctant to yield their bounty—the very land God had cursed Adam to till when he expelled him from the Garden. The people there lived at the mercy of the soldiers, gleaning the scraps from what was stolen from them. They would have begged for peace if they'd possessed the strength.

My first week back with the army, I treated a bullet wound, a burn, and a compound fracture, not one of those injuries belonging to soldiers.

What baleful spirit was at work in me? Why had I returned to this? When I'd left Pflaumloch, I'd held my purpose clear: to put mile on mile between myself and Eleonore, so that I might forget I ever loved her, so that I might not have to endure the sting of seeing her settled and happy with the cabinetmaker.

But of course I'd been restless long before Eleonore and I reunited, and as I plumbed yet another bullet wound with my finger, searching for the ball buried deep in the flesh, I considered that perhaps there had been another reason, a defect deep in my nature that drew me back to the war. Perhaps I simply wasn't made for peace.

Indeed, no sooner had I arrived among the unruly, ill-fed, ill-shod soldiers—among the grousing craftsmen, chancers, and camp whores—than a feeling like home came over me. Most of the faces were unfamiliar ones, yet I felt just as if I'd known each of them for years.

Not all faces were unfamiliar. On one of my first days back, I encountered the Spanish novice, Isidoro. But of course he was no longer a novice. He'd taken his vows the year I followed Salomon and Rachel to Öttingen. He was a proper Jesuit, a priest. Yet all those years, he'd remained with the Catholic League army.

He was startled to see me after so long, and we had little idea of what to say to each other, given how we'd left things. We muttered a few words each of polite greeting and went on our way.

It wasn't until some weeks later that our paths crossed once more. I'd been called to the tent of one of the camp prostitutes, a young woman no older than fifteen, who was many hours deep into a troublesome labor.

I was in a splenic humor, for no matter how often I'd protested that I was not a midwife, the officers continued to fetch me for the task. I must have aided in the births of some half-dozen children that first month while the other surgeons busied themselves with cutting and stitching and cautery.

It was midday and the tent trapped the sun's heat, rendering the air inside stale and stifling. The priest was kneeling by the girl's bed, moving his lips in silent prayer. But for the mustache and beard he'd grown in the intervening years, I didn't think he'd changed at all. He was still slender as a sapling, and he still wore his black hair down to his shoulders—the lone sign of vanity in the whole of his priestly appearance. He looked more a man and less a boy—that was the only change.

"I hope you're not responsible for this," I said, beginning my examination.

It was no kind of greeting, but he smiled anyway. "No," he said. "Certainly not. Though I'm sorry to see you still have such a low opinion of me after all these years."

I started to ask what he was doing there if he was not the father, but the words withered in my mouth as I felt the contour of the child's head high in the womb, too high. The woman's face was ghostly pale, the purple of her veins visible beneath her translucent skin. Her birthing moans were weak, her eyes half-opened.

"A word with you," I said, retreating from the suffocating heat of that close place. The priest followed.

"She went into labor nearly three days ago," he explained. "Every midwife in the camp has tried to help her along."

"So, you're here…" I began, knowing well enough how the sentence ended.

"They called me here early this morning to administer the sacrament."

"And you're still here because…?"

"She shouldn't be alone."

No, he hadn't changed at all.

"Well, the cause of her troubles is no mystery," I said. "The baby's the wrong way round. But if the midwives have been here to help her, then you know that already. I'm no midwife, so I don't know what you expect I'll be able to do about it."

"She didn't ask for a midwife. She asked for a surgeon."

I sucked in a breath. "She wants someone to cut the child out of her."

He nodded.

"And I suppose all the other surgeons refused to go near it."

Another nod. I cut a track back and forth, pacing. He shuffled alongside me, walking with an uneven, limping gait.

"So," he said. "What will you do?"

"What sort of question is that? It's not done! Oh, now and again, you hear a story. A Dutch cattle-gelder slices open his own wife on their kitchen table and saves both the woman and the child. But it's hardly to be believed; if it were, I don't think anyone would bother telling it. No, I'd be out of my mind to cut her open."

"So, are you?" he asked. What a question! Was I mad enough to butcher a young woman—a girl—to save her child?

"Where's the father?"

He shook his head. "She says she doesn't know who the father is."

"Like enough. Took her from some village, did they?"

"I don't know. You would have to ask her." Then again he asked me, "Will you operate?"

"Why would I? If none of the other surgeons were fool enough to agree to it, why should I be that fool?"

"None of the other priests agreed to give her the sacrament."

"Enough, priest," I said. "Don't tell me that."

"So, what will you do?"

I threw up my hands. "Very well. But let me talk to her first." I went back into the tent.

"Her name is Dorothea," he called after me.

I sat down beside Dorothea, lifting a cup of water to her cracked, parched lips. For all the claggy warmth of that space, she was shivering.

"The priest tells me you want the child taken out of you," I said.

Weak as she was, there was no mistaking her nod.

"You know it's no simple thing. I can't say that it's ever been done successfully where both mother and child live."

"I don't want to die. I don't want my baby to die."

"That's what I'm saying. I might well save your baby, but I can't say how you'll fare."

"I'm dying now anyway."

It didn't matter what I said. She looked back at me with clear gray eyes, and though her strength waned, her resolve did not waver. I felt her womb again, but the child had not budged. So, I went to collect my surgical tools, cursing and recriminating against myself the whole way, and instructed the priest to prepare a basin of water and some rags.

"I'll need an assistant," I told him when I returned. "Is there anyone who could lend a hand?"

"Let me," he said.

"Are you certain you're not the father?"

He pressed his lips together in a thin line. "I've kept my vows, Miss Dorn."

I readied my tools, and then I instructed the priest to sit the woman upright and to keep her from wrenching herself this way and that once I started cutting.

"And take care to empty your stomach out there and not in here," I added.

"Understood." He smiled, but already he had a pale and liverish look to him.

I lifted the knife, but he stayed my hand. "A prayer first," he said.

I closed my eyes while he called on Our Lady, the Mother of God, and on St. Luke, the patron of physicians, and last of all on St. Jude, the patron of lost causes. I confess, I heard little of his prayer. All the while he spoke, I was picturing Salomon's musty books, filled with woodcuts and sketches of the human anatomy—of muscle, organ, and bone. I tried to picture the part that we call womb, but which in Latin is called *uterus*.

For how many thousands of years have humans lived, eating and shitting, rutting and giving birth, going all the way to Adam and Eve in that first garden, yet we understand so little of our bodies, the very bodies with which we do all of that eating and rutting and birthing?

All my life, I've had a womb, and since I was twelve, it has been the torment of me, twisting me up in pain every month or so at inconsistent intervals and bleeding often for weeks at a time. It has plagued me with desires I could scarce understand, let alone master. Yet for all of that, what did I know of wombs? Only a handful of misshapen diagrams copied into a book. I'd never seen a womb nor touched one outside of my own birth.

I've always had a steady hand when it comes to surgery, but that day my hand shook as I lowered the knife. Even so, I endeavored to make quick, confident cuts. It would do no good to prolong the woman's suffering by cutting too timidly and being forced to cut and cut again to enlarge the wound.

I was well pleased with the first incision, which went deep enough to slice through skin and muscle. The girl gave a shrill cry, but the priest held her fast. I reached inside the incision, feeling for the womb, and when I was sure I'd located it, I used a dilator to hold the first wound open and went on to the second.

This cut I made more timidly than I would've liked and would've been best for the patient, and I had to cut a second time to extend the first. I was afraid of harming the infant, which I'd been instructed to save.

The weak girl slumped, passed out from the pain.

"Keep her upright," I reminded the priest.

He'd looked away while I worked, but now he was forced to turn, supporting the woman's weight on his shoulder. He made a gagging noise when he saw the bloody mess.

"I'm sorry," he said quickly.

"What do you have to be sorry for? It's men who take their pleasure and pay their fee and don't think about the consequences who should be sorry. Someone in the Tross should have helped her be rid of it."

He looked to be sick again. "Life is sacred."

"Look where you are, priest. How many years have you been at war? How blind do you have to be to still say life is sacred?"

After the second incision, I reached into the bloody opening and brought out the child. She let out a wail almost immediately. I handed her to Isidoro, who scrubbed her clean and swaddled her while I cleaned out the womb. Young Dorothea was yet breathing, so I took care to stitch her up and apply a cataplasm of eggs, rose oil, and breadcrumbs steeped in cow's milk to the wound, in case she might survive the ordeal.

The priest baptized the infant, and I, I stumbled out of the stifling tent and retched.

The priest handed the child to one of the camp women, who by that point had gathered in quite a crowd to see the outcome. The woman lowered her blouse and put the child to her own breast to suckle.

I remained on the ground. The fire that had coursed through my veins as I worked had all drained away, leaving my limbs jelly-like and unresponsive to my mind's commands.

Isidoro helped me to my feet. "It's a marvelous thing you've done. That God's done through you."

"She's not out of the woods yet."

He helped me pack my instruments, and we left Dorothea in the care of the camp women. I gave them instructions on how to tend to the wound and what she might need if she woke and promised to check on her daily.

Then the priest hobbled with me to my surgical tent. There, the runt bounded up to him with an eager wag of his tail, rolling onto his back while the priest stooped down to rub his belly.

I ordered the priest to take a seat and remove his left boot. The leather was wet and ragged and came away with difficulty. The cloth wrappings underneath were half-dissolved. Beneath them, the foot was hardened and discolored, giving off a stinking discharge.

"How long has it been like this?"

"Not so long."

"How long?"

"Three days?" he said, uncertain. "Four?"

"I should think you wanted to lose your foot."

He shrugged. "It seemed a minor complaint, and I was occupied."

"With what? Prayer? Your soul may be eternal, priest, but it needs your body to stay alive."

"Thank you for the reminder. I do seem to forget it." His smile made it hard to hold onto my irritation with him.

I handed him a bottle of brandy. "Here, drink."

"This is going to be painful, isn't it?" He took a deep draught.

"Be grateful if it is. It means the foot is not yet lost."

I sat myself down opposite him with a bowl in my lap and balanced his foot on the edge. "Hold still. If you kick me in the face, I'll charge you double."

With a nod, he gripped the edges of the chair. He twitched and grunted each time the razor bit flesh, and by the time I'd finished the scarification, his knuckles had gone white, and his face was coated with a sheen of sweat.

As I emptied the bowl of his blood and prepared the medicaments for his treatment, he spoke again, his voice still shaking from the pain. "I was surprised to see you here. I thought you were done with the army."

"I thought I was."

"What happened?" He flinched as I guided his foot into a bath of Egyptiac—vinegar and honey and sundry other ingredients, according to what's at hand.

"I don't know. Why are you still here?"

"The same reason as ever."

"Looking for goodness? I can't make up my mind whether you're naïve or just stubborn."

"Neither."

"Why do you do it then?"

"Faith."

I snorted. "Faith. Isn't that the cause of all of this? Catholics and Protestants at each other's throats over whose faith is the right one."

"Rather a lack of faith, I think. If more people believed in God as God believes in them, there'd be no need to take up arms."

"What sort of priestly babble is that? 'As God believes in them?'"

"You don't think God believes in humanity?"

"I can't begin to fathom what you mean by it."

"Why else would he give us the commandments? Why else would he come in the person of Christ, if he didn't believe we were yet capable of being better than this fallen world? We were made for goodness, and I don't think God has given up believing we're capable of it."

"And why would he believe that?"

"I know. It hardly seems possible sometimes. After my brother attacked me, I had an excess of time for thinking. For wondering what it was I'd done to deserve such suffering and why God had allowed me to endure it. But what I discovered was that even in misfortune, I was surrounded by goodness. The servant who took me for medical care, the surgeon who tended to the wound, the

Jesuit who helped me find my way. Whether they were good people or not, I don't know. But they did good to me at least. So, I look for goodness."

"And what about your brother? Is there good in him too?"

"We all have our stumbling blocks," he admitted. Then he looked down at the bowl. "How long must I keep my foot in this?"

"I'll tell you when you may remove it. No, I can't comprehend you. This war makes everyone worse and here you are, just the same."

"I don't think it's true that the war makes everyone worse. What about your surgeon friend? Or the woman, Katharina? What about your father? What about you?"

"The war made my father something else. He was not the man he started as. Salomon and Katharina were wise to leave it while they could. And as for me, I had my chance at peace, but here I am again. Why, you ask? Because I needed it. Because life didn't make sense without it. Because I don't know what to do with peace."

I lifted his foot from the bath and applied a poultice of more Egyptiac before wrapping it in a compress. "Come back in the morning and I will check on the progress. We may need to apply the treatment a few times."

"Very well." He pulled on his boot, wincing. As he rose to leave, he said, "The soul also gets wounded and needs tending, Miss Dorn. Take care you don't let it fester too long."

We do the work according to our skill and judgment, Salomon always taught. *But God alone decides who lives and who dies.*

Day after day, I came back to Dorothea, expecting to find her gone. She sank into a deep fever that lasted for weeks on end. I advised hearty and nutritive foods that would warm her and aid in healing, but it was a trial for any of the women in the Tross to get her to take food or drink.

After a few days, the wound started to suppurate, which I took as a hopeful sign that it was purging the infection, and I cleaned away the discharge and applied another cataplasm.

Then the army marched on, and the young woman remained behind with the other sick and injured. For two months, I had no inkling of how she fared.

When we returned at the end of those months, we found Dorothea hale, sitting up and chatting in her bed, holding her child in her arms.

Isidoro was quick to proclaim it a miracle, but I was slower to rejoice.

"She nearly died for some soldier's by-blow. Now she will be a mother with no husband, marching in the Tross. Where is the miracle in that?"

"Every life is sacred," he repeated.

"If you priests truly believed that, we wouldn't still be fighting this war."

But I confess I was quietly very proud of myself for having done what no other surgeon dared.

That year, 1628, was one of the quietest of the war. Our regiment hardly marched and did not fight, for the Danish king had only the scraps of an army left and had retreated to the island of Copenhagen while we occupied the peninsula.

In the east, General Wallenstein laid siege to the ship-building port of Stralsund in hopes of securing a fleet. He failed, but in August that year, he defeated the last of the Danish king's army, forcing him to terms.

That winter was as cold as any I could remember. The winds sped in from the North Sea, the sort that could knock a grown man flat on his backside. The camp was overrun with the sick and the frostbitten. I lost countless patients to illness and the cold.

And then one evening the priest too collapsed, his skin burning hot with fever.

I found myself praying for the first time in years. They were grudging, angry prayers, which is to say, they were sincere. I rolled my father's rosary beads between the tips of my fingers, muttering the *Ave*, and the *Salve Regina* in fitful, half-remembered bursts. "He believes in you," I prayed. "Damn it all, he believes in you."

One evening, I arrived to find another priest seated at his bedside. I put my hand to my mouth, imagining the worst. But when I drew closer, I saw Isidoro sitting upright, color in his cheeks, carrying on a conversation.

"Did I worry you?" he asked, with a charming, knowing grin.

"Only that you might have passed without paying what you owe me for treating your foot," I lied.

Almost a full year to the day after I'd rejoined the army, the Emperor, the Catholic League, the Danish king, and the pretender all put pen to a treaty. We'd been on the march most of that year, east through Mecklenburg and Brandenburg, then west and south into Hesse and the lands near Frankfurt, hardly passing more than a single night in one place. It was outside of Frankfurt that word of the peace reached us.

Those were heady days in the camp. The officers were eager to keep the discipline, but each day the air was punctuated by fresh outbursts of celebration. No amount of effort could temper the soldiers' excitement, their joyous relief at what seemed to be the end of a long and bloody campaign. The harder questions would come later—of what to do next, and who would pay them, and where would they go?

There wasn't enough wine, beer, or brandy to slake the thirst drummed up by a decade of war, though the Lord knows we all tried. At the end of the first week of celebrations, I woke well after noon with my head pulsing, only to find a line of men outside my surgery, nursing the wounds of their jubilations. I spent the day treating all manner of injury, and no sooner had I patched the men up than they went right back to their drinking.

The priest came to me early one evening as I was clearing my surgery of the day's work. I'd seen him only a few times since his illness. Now, he bared his teeth in a tipsy grin.

"Peace at last," he said, raising a jug of wine aloft. "And where are you? Working, of course."

"I might have more time to celebrate if these lackwits wouldn't let their drink get the better of them."

He laughed, and then he started to sing. The song was Spanish; I didn't know the words. But he took me by the arms and swung me around in a dance. What a fool he was, all long limbs and full-bellied warbling. Like a crane that has no idea it's not a robin.

We tripped and fell on our backsides, shaking with laughter, and he uncorked the jug. But as I reached to take it from him, he interposed his lips, kissing me deeply. His mouth tasted of wine, but his eyes were focused and clear.

My breath caught in my throat, and I scrambled to my feet. He stood too, wrapping his arm around my waist and kissing me again. I wheeled backward until I hit the edge of a table, but he stayed with me, step for step. A third time he kissed me.

"You're drunk," I said, pushing him away again.

"I'm not," he said.

"Then you're mad."

"What's wrong with that?"

How could I explain it? He was beautiful, and he was willing, and at one time that would've been all the encouragement I needed.

"We've been here before," I said. "The music, the bonfires, the drink. You told me then that I wasn't in my right mind. You were right. About me, especially, but also about us. If we do this, you'll surely regret it, and I will too. You'll say I seduced you into breaking your vows. You'll wake up in the morning feeling bitter and deceived. I couldn't bear it."

He shook his head emphatically. "No, no, no. Listen to me. I'm not drunk, and I'm not mad. You say this war hasn't changed me, but it has. It has taught me that when you find some scrap of goodness, you must do whatever you can to hold onto it. If you don't want me, say so. But don't tell me that I don't know what I want."

"And what about everything you said back then? About your vows? About what's best for you?"

"Don't you see I was trying to convince myself?" He inclined his lips toward mine once more.

I'd not had a lover in over a year, not since Eleonore.

"You started this," I said. "I didn't seduce you."

"You didn't seduce me," he repeated.

I led him into my tent. There we fell to kissing again. His face grew warm as I undid the strings of my bodice, tugged my blouse over my head, and wriggled free of my skirts. A moan rattled in my throat as he planted kisses all up and down my chest and stomach, as his lips grazed my hip bone.

I uncinched his cassock next, and soon he was as naked as I was. A jagged pink scar ran eight inches across his chest, starting at his collar bone and ending just beside his right nipple. I ran my fingertips along it, then let them wander below his waist.

As his hands found my hips, I felt my longing grow. I opened my legs for him.

"Are you sure?" he asked, as if my heart were not beating loud enough for both of us to hear.

"Aye, priest. What are you waiting on? Do I need to show you where to put it?"

He leaned into me, his mouth seeking mine, and then slid himself inside me with a grunt. We moved together, and for a too-brief spell, I managed to forget Eleonore, forget the broken drunks in my surgery, forget the war.

When our coupling was done, he dressed himself and went out.

It was just as well with me; I needed the space to catch my breath and order my thoughts. But he returned shortly after and eased in beside me on the narrow bed, draping his arm around my waist.

All night I waited for him to leave. What lover of mine had ever remained? But he didn't leave. The whole night he was there, breathing softly as he slept. And in the morning, when I woke having hardly rested at all, he was there too, awake, and searching my face with serious, thoughtful eyes.

"So." He brushed a strand of hair behind my ear. "Do you regret it?"

"Don't ask stupid questions," I muttered.

"Good. Neither do I." And then the fool said, "Let's marry."

16

Fool

1629

"Let's marry," he said, and if I'd been clothed at the time, I think I should have run right out of the tent.

As it was, I sat upright, tugging the blanket over my bare chest, and said, "Don't you do this to me, priest."

Isidoro's expression was guileless as a newborn pup. "I'm sure I don't know what it is you think I'm doing."

"I knew this would happen if I let you bed me."

"You knew that I'd ask for your hand in marriage?"

"I knew your conscience couldn't abide it. I thought you might resent me for it, but this is worse."

He propped himself up on his elbow. "How is it worse?"

"Because you're a priest, Isidoro. You're more a priest than any priest I've ever met. You can't give that up, not on my account. I'd not be worth it."

"I'd hardly be the first priest to marry."

I rose and pulled on my shift. "So, you want to keep me as a secret bride in a village somewhere. Or else, what? You'll join the Lutherans? You've not thought this through."

"Is that all?" he asked. "Or is there something besides?"

"I can't think what you mean."

"If I were not a priest—"

I sat on the edge of the bed with a sigh. "If you were not a priest, I shouldn't like you half so much. But I like you very much indeed, if that's what you're asking."

"Even after last night?"

"Especially after last night. That's just the trouble. If we married, I would ruin you."

A miserable little smile flickered on his face. "I should be going," he said. "There's a Mass to prepare in thanksgiving for the peace. Doubtless there are more drunks waiting for you that need stitching."

"Just a moment," I said. I went to the back of the tent and peered out. "Best go out the back to avoid questions."

"Good thinking." He paused a moment before he went, casting his eyes around as if searching for something he'd lost. We'd each run out of words, and all that remained was the stale air of the tent and a cumbersome mass of unspoken thoughts, heavy enough to crush us both.

What was wrong with me, that I couldn't give him what he wanted? What was wrong with him, that he came back to me anyway? That very evening he returned, strolling into my surgery and sitting down beside me as I ground up herbs with mortar and pestle.

"Perhaps you're right," he said, taking a sprig of parsley and stripping the leaves from the stems. "Perhaps my conscience was troubled this morning. I'm a priest; I took certain vows, and then I broke one of them. Perhaps there was some part of me that thought I could fix one broken vow by making another."

"So, you admit it was foolishness."

"No. That I'll not admit. You said I hadn't thought things through. Well, now I have. I've thought it over, and even if I allow that some part of me was feeling guilty, that can't possibly account for everything. I remember the moment I first thought of giving my life to God. It was in the hospital after my brother cut open my chest. All at once, the sensation came over me, like I was standing in the woods at night, when all is still and sleeping. Nothing but calm and quiet all around me."

"Then you haven't been in the woods at night," I interrupted him. "It's anything but quiet."

"Please, let me speak. Until that second, I'd been sick with anger. At my brother, at my father, at God."

"I can't imagine you angry."

"I was. I was bewildered, at sea. I couldn't understand what I'd done to earn my brother's wrath. I couldn't understand why my father went to such lengths to protect him and to send me away after. But when the old Jesuit asked me if I'd considered giving my life to God, that feeling of peace came over me, and it stretched in every direction, and each time I tried to find its limit, it grew wider and wider."

"You've lost me, priest. What does this have to do with this morning?"

"This morning, I felt the same thing when I woke and saw you lying next to me. Like I could spend my whole life searching out the edges of that feeling, that love, and never once find them."

Love, he said. What a troublesome word. I was sure I knew what love was. I felt its sharp pangs still, gnawing at my insides. I'd forgotten them only briefly when he was in my bed.

"There's your mistake." The herbs were long since reduced to paste, but I continued to mash them. "Love is anything but peaceful. And anyway, it doesn't change the fact that we can't marry."

"Be at ease. I didn't come here to ask for your hand again. I think, if you wanted it, we could find a way. But it's clear to me you don't, whatever the reason. Either you don't return my feelings, or..." His voice shook. "Well, I don't dare speculate."

"Isidoro, please, don't—"

"I only came to ask if it would be all right with you if I went on loving you anyway. If you will not have me as a husband, will you have me as a lover?"

He was a fool indeed. A magnificent, God-addled fool.

"Damn it, priest." I let the mortar and pestle fall.

"Is that a 'yes,' then?" he smiled, hopefully.

"You deserve better than me. One day you'll realize that."

"I don't think I will." Then he leaned over and kissed me.

What was wrong with him? What was wrong with me? Love, I thought, ought to burn. It ought to be relentless and irresistible, a conquering army, bombarding the heart's defenses until it cracks apart. How many hours had I spent waiting on Eleonore in the shelter of that old ruined church, hoping for a kiss, a touch, a single glimpse of her smile?

I wanted Isidoro. I enjoyed his company. But I didn't suffer for it. When his body trembled on mine, I felt pleasure, but my heart didn't flutter for fear I'd lose him. He was never gone long enough for that. How could I call it love, if it didn't feel like it would tear me apart at any moment?

How many hundreds of nights in the woods had I weathered while my father and I were on the road? Not a one of them had been quiet. There was always the rustle of the breeze in the leaves, the distant howls of the wolves, the screeching birds of prey, the insistent chirping of insects and frogs. No, I told myself, love is no quiet thing. The only thing that's quiet is death.

The peace held through the end of the year. Twenty weeks we waited in that land near Frankfurt before moving on to winter quarters in Westphalia. Our initial joy had long since faded, replaced by a restive mood. There was no war, but neither did we receive our discharges. We were an army without an enemy, restless, bored, and on edge.

That year, the Emperor moved to do in Germany what he'd done in Bohemia after the capture of Prague—that is, to claim Protestant lands and cities for the Catholics. He issued a new order, which he called the Edict of Restitution, declaring that all lands and cities that had gone to the Protestants after the settled peace of the previous century should revert to their former Catholic state.

He began with Augsburg, that holy city of the Lutherans. A part of the army was sent to *enforce Restitution* there, by which was meant to turn the city Catholic. When Augsburg was Restituted without bloodshed, he turned his eyes to Magdeburg, Speyer, and Nördlingen. The Protestant princes and their subjects objected, as did the defenders of German liberties, but neither party had the means to do anything about it. Which is to say, they didn't have an army.

It was hard to find any great enthusiasm for the Emperor's Restitution among the soldiery. Many were Catholic, true, but money knows no faith, and we counted a fair number of Protestants in our ranks.

But neither was there any great resistance. We were a miserable people, long ago resigned to march where our leaders pointed, to die at their command, to steal for survival, to kill for another man's policy. Eleven years of war, and we lacked even the strength to cry out, "Enough! Enough!" Perhaps it's true, what the English say, that Germans are good for only two things: drinking beer and stuffing our bellies with bread.

So, the year went on, and we went about our business. Isidoro was a regular presence in my surgery and in my bed. He made no more mention of marriage. Word spread that the Swedish king was planning to enter the war on the part of the Protestants, but what could any of us do about that?

On Christmas eve morning, I woke with an unease deep in my belly. My sleep had been troubled with nightmares, but that wasn't the whole of it. Isidoro had made a breakfast of bread and cheese and warm beer, but I took one look at the food, and my stomach lurched, bile bubbling up in my throat.

"Are you well, *Corazón*?" he asked, his brow lined with worry.

"Don't trouble yourself," I tried to reassure him.

"You talk in your sleep, you know."

My shoulders tensed, wondering what he might have heard. "Oh?"

"You sounded frightened. I didn't know if I should wake you. Is there something on your mind?"

He cocked his head. As ever, his expression was open, inviting. I leaned toward him and picked a crumb of bread from his beard. "It's nothing. Just a nightmare."

He planted a kiss on my forehead. "I expect to see you at Mass tonight."

"And if you don't?"

"I'll have to come to your tent and hear your confession."

"You're such a fool."

"I've never denied it." He lifted the canvas to slip away, turning back only to add: "Eat your breakfast."

Once he'd gone, I gave my food to the runt and curled up once more in my bed. The tears followed soon after. It'd been three months since my last monthly sickness, which was a long delay even given my courses' irregular comings and goings. I knew well enough the chance I'd been taking, but as summer faded into autumn and nothing came from it, I'd begun to think perhaps I was incapable of it—that is, of getting a child. It was plain enough now I'd been wrong.

Though I was one-and-twenty years old by then, I hadn't given more than a passing thought to being a mother. I neither longed for it, nor feared it. A woman's role is known, of course. One day, I would take a husband and have children. One day, when I was far from the army and had finally managed to purge that unquiet spirit in me, the one that would not let go of Eleonore, the one that would not let me be at peace.

Yet here I was, a year and a half later, still thinking of her. What was wrong with me? The same thing that had ever been wrong with me: a cord twisted 'round my gut, wanting someone I couldn't have, in a place I could never call home.

I spent the day in the company of that bitter epiphany as I plucked a small hen for the Christmas meal and roasted it on the spit. Come evening, I was no less troubled, but I pulled on my overcoat to join the congregation for the Mass anyway.

The Christmas eve Mass was a frigid, dark affair. We stood shoulder to shoulder in the chill of that winter's evening while priests by the dozen prayed and read from the Scriptures and preached.

Isidoro was cantor, and he sang out the liturgy in a smooth, honeyed tenor. Latin flowed from his tongue more naturally than German or even Spanish. I pushed my way to the front to hear, but even then I caught only every other syllable.

"*Magnificat anima mea Dominum,*" he sang. And: "*Deposuit potentes de sede, et exaltavit humiles. Esurientes implevit bonis, et divites dimisit inanes.*"

He has put down the mighty from their seat and has exalted the humble and the meek. He has filled the hungry with good things, and the rich he has sent away empty. Oh, if only!

We pulled our coats tight and stamped our feet for warmth while another priest spoke a homily. He praised the Emperor for taking up the defense of Catholicism and warned against the Swedish king who had designs on spoiling our hard-earned peace. After that, I stopped straining to hear.

When the preaching and praying was done, we all lined up to receive the host. Isidoro met each person with a welcoming smile and spoke each one's name as he placed the bread on their tongues. Hundreds of faces, and he didn't once falter or misremember even a single name.

"*Corpus Domini Nostri Iesu Christi custodiat animam tuam,* Josefine, *in vitam aeternam. Amen.*" He laid his hand on my shoulder after he'd fed me the host. I nearly broke down crying right there.

I left after that, retreating to my tent as the first chords of joyful singing sounded from the crowd, filling the air with bright music. It was too much: the child, if he acknowledged it, would ruin him. If he didn't acknowledge it, it would ruin me. Wish though we might for the world to be different, it was not. The mighty still sat on high, the lowly still perished at the hands of soldiers, and the days when virgins gave birth to holy infants were long since past.

He found his way back to my tent in the early hours of Christmas day. We sat side by side, warming ourselves by the fire. The meat from supper had gone cold, but he shoved it into his mouth hungrily. I'd resolved not to tell him, to wait another month and be sure. Perhaps I could even find a way to rid myself of the problem quietly, without his ever suspecting.

But as I watched him eat, that uneasy feeling in my stomach returned, and my resolve broke. Tears, unbidden and unwelcome, ran down my cheeks.

He set his bowl aside and held me in his arms without asking what was wrong. My tears came faster then, soaking into his cassock. The scents of incense and roast hen mingled on him.

I told him, then.

"You're certain?" he asked when I'd finished. His expression, normally so revealing, was illegible in the dim light.

I nodded. "There can be no other explanation. It is what happens, after all, when a man and a woman carry on as you and I have."

He covered his mouth with his hand and made a strangled, sobbing sound.

"I'm sorry—" I'd begun to stammer out an apology when I realized he wasn't sobbing at all. No, he was laughing.

"But this is wonderful news," he said. "Why are you crying? You had me scared witless. I thought you must be ill or dying."

"Wonderful news? You got a bastard on me, and that's wonderful news?"

"A new life, Josefine. Our new life."

"You're mad, priest."

"That may be so," he laughed. "But only a little. There are worse things to be than a bastard. She'll have no jealous older brothers, at least."

"You've decided on a girl already?"

"Yes, one who knows her mind like her mother and with a heart just as big."

"Listen to yourself," I said. "What sort of unruly child are you condemning me to raise?"

He grinned. "I never once knew your father to complain."

"He was as big a fool as you are."

He kissed me, then, tumbling me onto the cold ground. I half thought he meant to take me right there, in the plain view of a dozen other tents. Instead, he broke off his kissing and pulled off my boots, tickling the stockinged soles of my feet.

"Oh, but you're an ass, priest," I sputtered between fits of ticklish laughter. I wriggled free of him and retreated into privacy of the tent, and he followed.

In the closeness of that place, his playfulness gave way to passion. His kisses turned long and lingering, and his hands massaged their way up my legs and under my skirts, sliding my stockings away from my thighs.

His name came, cracking, from my lips: "Isidoro."

"Yes, *Corazón*, what is it?"

"This is exactly how you got me into this trouble."

His hand drew nearer to the pulsing warmth between my legs. "Do you want me to stop?"

"You always ask such stupid questions."

"I'll take care of you both," he whispered, pausing to stroke my cheek with his fingertips. "I promise."

And how will you do that, I wanted to ask. But his eyes shone bright as starlight, and I couldn't bear the thought of darkening them with my worries.

17

The God Who Gives and Takes

1630

The fool asked me to marry him again. It was Silvester, the eve of 1630, and there was light snow on the air. He said I didn't need to answer him, not right away. If I agreed, he'd write the head of his order, asking to be released from his vows. But in the meantime, there was a town thirty miles away where we could pay our gulden and have the marriage entered in the register, and the old bishop there would agree to overlook the fact he was a priest.

"Consider it only before you say no," he said. "I know I have little means in this world, but once I'm released from my vows, I can get work as a clerk or traveling scholar. Not lucrative professions to be sure, but better than a vow of poverty for caring for a family."

"I have my surgery," I reminded him.

"Yes, you do. But you'll need another pair of arms to hold the child at very least—unless you intend to operate with her strapped to your back."

"You're still sure of a daughter." All week long, he'd been proposing girls' names.

"Yes," he grinned wide. "A little... Carlotta. No, Isabella."

I shook my head.

"Magdalena? Yes, I like Magdalena. It's a hopeful name. Witness to our Lord's resurrection. Our little Magda."

"I'll think about it," I said.

"The name or marriage?"

"Both."

I've had better nights' sleep with my blankets laid out on a bed of roots than I did in the days that followed. I was damned if I let him give up his priestly vows for my sake—better to compel a nightingale to give up its song than to drag so pure a fool into Hell with me. But I was damned just as well if I tried to mother the child on my own, unwed and in the Tross. Over how many such mothers and children had he prayed the funeral rites in the last year alone, taken by illness, hardship, and hunger? It was no life I'd chosen for myself, but at least I'd chosen it with my eyes open. How could I choose it for a child, who knows nothing of the world, who doesn't even choose to be born?

All my aches and pains and restless nights were wasted, of course, for it was not my choice to make, not truly. I might refuse him marriage, but he would never deny the child, even if I begged him to. He would go on trying to take care of the both of us, even if it ruined him. The truth of the matter was, he'd given up his vows the moment I allowed him into my bed, sinning.

So, at the end of the week, I gave him my answer.

"I'll do it," I said. "I'll marry you."

He smiled wide, and his plain delight only served to deepen the aching in my conscience. Why should this fool be so happy to be damned? I lowered my head so that he wouldn't see my misgivings, but not soon enough.

He took me by the hands. "Listen. I'll give you no cause to regret it. I'll still be me, priest or no. I'll still drive you utterly and completely mad."

"You'd damn well better," I said.

But my insides were a snarled mess, which all his reassurances could hardly untangle. Even then, I still knew nothing of loving. I was still searching for that feeling, hot and loud and irresistible, that I'd felt in the shadows of the ruined church, waiting for Eleonore to appear, consumed with anger and longing and jealousy when she didn't.

I never had to wait for Isidoro to appear. He was a rooted tree, and if I let him, he would grow knotted and ancient, waiting out the seasons for me to love him.

It took us a few weeks to prepare for the wedding: first, to write to the bishop, and then to plan the journey. Heavy snows delayed us further, but as January ended, everything was in order, and we laid plans for the second week of February.

Isidoro's easy joy set my own ambivalence in relief. I loathed myself for it. Each night, he caressed my belly and asked me questions without end—how was I feeling, had I felt the child quicken yet, was I happy?

I smiled and smiled and strove to keep my dark thoughts from staining his joy. But each day, I thought on the child growing inside of me, expecting to feel some measure of excitement or anticipation, and each day, I felt only the creeping fear that my lack of eagerness signaled some larger defect in my soul—that I was unfit, perhaps, for mothering.

It was a naïve fear, in the end.

The pangs started in mid-January. I labored through them, hoping they would pass. Patients came to me, and I bled or stitched or bandaged all those others, while setting my jaw against the flashes of pain in my own belly.

One afternoon, a farmer was seated in my chair. He'd been found beaten along the roadside, though no one would admit to the crime. It took some time to stitch up the gash in his head, and by the time I was done, my arms and stomach were so wet with his blood, I hardly noticed the liquid sensation on my own legs. But the world rocked, and when I looked down, blood ran down my stockings in a slow stream.

I was alone, apart from my patient, and he was barely conscious. I stumbled toward the tent of the nearest midwife, but I didn't make it very far. A sharp, lasting pain wrenched my belly, and I doubled over. The runt danced around me anxiously, whimpering and pawing.

"Help. I need help," I muttered to the first person who approached me.

What can I say about the rest? Time and memory compress it to the flash of a knife, but I know better. Somehow, I dragged myself back to my tent. The midwife arrived soon after. Certain details haven't left me—the dark red blood, almost black; the midwife's cold hands on my fever-licked skin; the sharp air of that chill, dry January day. I closed my eyes, and my pain appeared to me as a bright burst of yellow, like a marigold in bloom.

I remember voices, too: my own, screaming and disembodied; the runt's insistent yowling until the midwife drove him off; the midwife's frail encouragements, urging me along. Such nonsensical words: *Come along, you're a strong girl, not much longer now, you're doing a fine job.* A fine job of what? I could not think it.

At one point, I was certain I heard Isidoro's voice outside the tent: *I need to see her. You can't keep me from her.* But the old midwife answered him: *You've caused the poor girl enough trouble, don't you think? And you, a priest. You should be ashamed.*

It took a day of the midwife coming and going, of the camp whores checking in on me and standing watch over my tent. Too quick and too slow, all at once.

When it was done, the old woman wrapped the birth in a cloth so I could not see it. I don't know if it would have been a girl or a boy, or if it had died before anyone could tell. The bundle was impossibly small; unbelievable that so tiny a thing could have caused so much pain. The midwife left me soon after: she had another birth to see to—a living child.

I slept for the rest of the day, and even when I was awake, I didn't want to move. I stared at the canopy of my tent, running my hands over my stomach, but feeling no difference. You'd hardly have known that a thing had gone out of me, but gone it was, and I was only starting to account for all the things it had taken with it.

What was it, then, that I'd lost? It seems wrong to call it a child; there'd been no quickening, no flutter of life, of soul. There was no funeral. They didn't even show me the body. Neither was there a baptism. The sacraments, after all, are for the living. If the midwife suspected I'd forced the matter, she mercifully did not report it to anyone. Likely she thought it for the best—one less bastard mouth to feed.

No, it wasn't a child I grieved, yet I grieved all the same.

The day after, the cold winter sun shone bright on the camp. I gathered up the linens and my ruined clothes and burned them. Then I went to buy cloth to make new ones. The merchant overcharged me by half, but I'd no strength left for haggling.

Back at my tent, I remade my bed, and laid everything back in its place and took to sewing. The steady in-and-out of the needle proved a much-needed diversion. The runt wandered in confused circles, sniffing the new bedding and burrowing beneath it with his nose.

That afternoon, I thought to go to find Isidoro among the priests' tents, but the midwife's words rattled in my head: *And you, a priest. You should be ashamed.*

How easy it is for a careless word to plant a suggestion in a gloomy mind! Why shouldn't he be ashamed, I thought to myself. Who could blame him? Perhaps he'd finally come to his senses and remembered that he was a priest. In the end, it had been such a small thing that bound him to me, and now it was with the refuse.

So, I stayed put. I rose in the morning, filling my kettle and boiling my water and picking over my breakfast, sitting alone grieving a thing that never was.

I opened my surgery, but had to break off working at midday, when the front of my blouse grew strangely damp and uncomfortable. It wasn't until I'd retreated into my tent and unfastened my bodice that I understood that the dampness I'd felt was mother's milk, leaking from my swollen breasts. I broke down and wept until my throat was ragged.

Isidoro came back that night. I was seated by the fire at my sewing when he announced himself with a cough. I looked up at him, huddled in his overcoat, the breath puffing white from his pink lips.

"She's...?" he began, letting the rest of the sentence drift unspoken.

"Gone," I said.

"And you're...?"

"Here."

"I meant, are you..." He pursed his lips as he sought out the words once more. Small wonder he couldn't find them. I don't believe they exist.

"I know well what you meant," I said. "And 'here' is my answer. It's the best I can do."

"It's enough." He slumped his shoulders, exhaling another cloud of mist.

"Will you sit?" I gestured to the place beside me.

He nodded and sat. I went back to my sewing. He said nothing. For a while it seemed as if we were both content to let the spit and crackle of the flames speak for us.

"I'm sorry," I whispered.

"You're not to blame," he said. His jaw tensed, as if biting back tears. "It's a common enough thing. God alone knows why, and I'll not pretend I understand it. I don't. He gives and he takes, and no one knows the why of it. We can only hope that in the end we will see things as he sees them, and it will all make sense."

He gives and he takes. *Shall the faultfinder contend with the Almighty?*

The lines of his face cast heavy shadows in the firelight. I'd not noticed them until then—the little cracks and crevices where the last seven years of war had made their mark, however slight, however imperceptible. For the first time, he was a shape I recognized.

He raised a fist to his mouth and stifled a sob. I set my sewing aside and held him. He shuddered against me, and I brushed the tear-matted locks of hair away from his face.

"I'm sorry," he said. "I wanted to be there, but they wouldn't let me near you."

"There's nothing you could have done."

"Still," he said.

I nodded. My own eyes burned with tears, but I rubbed them dry.

He placed his palm on my cheek as if he might kiss me, but he only looked at me. In the firelight, his suddenly old, suddenly sorrow-limned eyes seemed to blaze. No, he was not a conquering army or an endless wood. He was a spring, burbling up from groundwater deep beneath the earth. I let my forehead come to rest against his, drawing comfort from its warmth.

And then the fool sniffed and cleared his throat and said, "I suppose we've no need to marry now."

My own throat felt as if it had been stopped up. I couldn't breathe. Take everything away—the child, my lingering love for Eleonore, his being a priest—take away that whole heap of excuses and what was left? Love, cool and refreshing and nothing like a fire or a battlefield, but no less deep, no less consuming.

"No," I said once I'd regained my voice. "Don't do this to me, priest. I'll not allow it. I'll not allow you to spend months telling me how much you love me, prattling on about endless forests and other nonsense, getting me pregnant and promising, insisting on marrying me, and then... and then walk it all back. I told you I was sorry. I swear to you by all the saints, I didn't mean for it to happen. What more could you want from me?"

I'd been waving and gesturing wildly all the while I'd talked, and now he took my hands and held them fast, held me fast.

"No," he said. "No, you have it all wrong. I thought you only you agreed to marry me on account of the child."

"And what if I did? I agreed to it, didn't I? I said I'd marry you. But if you're telling me you've changed your mind—"

"—I haven't changed my mind."

"Then don't say such stupid things. Not today of all days."

He smiled then. "Josefine?"

"What?" I snapped.

"I swear to you, you'll not regret it."

It was early March when we at last set out to be married, almost two months after our loss and a delay of more than two weeks from our original plans. The fool was sensitive both to my health and my state of mind, which wavered from day to day. But as the winter frost gave way to milder spring, we knew we would have to break winter quarters soon, and if we marched, we might lose the opportunity entirely.

I left the Tross a few hours ahead of Isidoro and waited down the road. He followed after on horseback, so that no one, especially the other priests of his order, would see us leave together and try to stop us. He left his cassock behind and dressed in plain jerkin and breeches.

He looked unaccountably strange in ordinary clothes, but not so upsetting as I'd feared. His hair still hung loose around his shoulders; he still grinned easily. We had two accomplices with us, a pair of Spanish mercenaries who were trusted friends of Isidoro's. The roads were too fraught with dangers to go without an escort.

It took us two days to reach the town where the bishop had agreed to carry out the secret wedding. The runt trotted alongside us at a slow but steady pace. I rode with Isidoro's arms around me, his head peering over my shoulder. We made camp at night on the way but slept in separate tents.

The bishop was exactly Isidoro's sort of fool. He'd been a Franciscan priest before he became a bishop, and he still wore the brown habit of his order. He'd long ago donated the traditional bishop's palace to the townspeople as a hospital, while he was content to live in the gardener's hut with an ornery pair of black-and-white cats he'd named Clara and Franz, after the saints.

The country around his bishopric had long ago turned Lutheran, but the people there tolerated his presence, as he lived a humble life, tending to the poor and refusing to stir trouble.

He met us on the front step of his little house, his two cats hissing at the runt from the windowsill. He was a short, round man, with shriveled, spotted skin, and all his hair and most of his teeth missing.

When I asked him, he said he'd stopped counting his years at eighty, as it seemed like arrogance to go any higher.

He invited us in and offered us bread and beer, apologizing that he didn't have more to give. Soldiers had been through, trying to enforce the Emperor's Restitution, reclaiming all the Protestant lands for the Catholics.

"I told them they're welcome to try," he said. "The land around the town is controlled by close to twenty different families, divided into some forty different estates, and they'll be lucky to find even three Catholics in the whole region with wealth enough to manage it all. It's simply not practical."

We sat in his main room on plain wooden chairs, eating bread and drinking watered-down wine, while he asked Isidoro questions about our plans: where we would go (back to the Tross, until my contract as field surgeon was done); how he planned to provide (as a clerk); was there any other reason for our wanting to be married?

At the last question, Isidoro's gaze fell to the floorboards. I took his hand and answered for him, "No, excellency."

The bishop nodded. "It used to be priests married all the time. It was something of a gray area. Neither permitted nor forbidden."

He took a sip of wine. "Different times, I suppose. The pastor of the Lutheran church here has a very pretty little family. I used to dine with him on Saturdays. That was before the war started and it became unseemly for Lutherans and Catholics to eat together. I hope he and his wife are well.

"I never minded celibacy personally; my vices lie elsewhere. My garden, my books. I'd have wasted away in selfish idleness if I'd not joined the Franciscans. They sent me out into the world to care for other people. To some it comes naturally, but to me, it was difficult. I always preferred my solitude, my peace."

He addressed Isidoro directly, then: "Young man, I understand that celibacy is difficult for some, but so is marriage. It's not a thing to be entered into lightly. If you're restless, might I suggest you find yourself a whore and leave this poor girl alone."

Isidoro blushed and started to stammer a response, but I interrupted. "Trust me, excellency, there's no budging him. I've tried it and look where it landed me. Instead of talking him out of it, I got talked into it."

The bishop chuckled and scratched his chest. "Well, in that case, let's not delay any longer, shall we?"

He led us to a small, drafty church. The building was in a state of heavy disrepair. No Catholics meant no funds. No matter, he said. He was likely to be the last bishop in this place anyhow.

"It doesn't trouble you, seeing the Catholic faith vanish?" Isidoro asked, ever the Jesuit.

The bishop shook his head. "If goodness and generosity were to vanish, that would trouble me. Besides, if the faith is to thrive, it won't be the way the Emperor goes about it, at spearpoint."

Then he cleared his throat and turned to the marriage ceremony. It was begun and ended far quicker than I'd expected. The bishop knew the words by heart and raced through them without lingering. We each made our vows, and Isidoro slipped a simple ring on my finger, and thus the contract was bound. The runt and the two Spanish mercenaries were our only witnesses.

After, we walked across the town to the inn on the square. The mercenaries slept in the common area downstairs, but Isidoro had rented us a room.

It was a plain room, warmed by a metal stove, with a bed large enough for the two of us to share.

At the bedside, Isidoro knelt and motioned for me to do the same.

"Pray with me?" he asked.

The last I'd prayed was during his illness, two winters before. But I knelt beside him and threaded my fingers through his. He laid out all his hopes in that prayer. He prayed for a child; he prayed that he would always do right by me; he prayed that we would have a household full of peace.

We'd been chaste as blushing virgins since our loss. Now, we were timid, fearful even. What if we no longer fit together as we had before?

By way of reassurance, I kissed him, then I opened his shirt and let my fingers trail down his chest, along the jagged line of his scar...

"If you're not ready, I can wait," he said, between kisses.

... down his stomach, along the strip of dark curls that disappeared beneath his belt...

"It's enough that you gave me your vow."

... and finally, below his waistband.

His next words were swallowed up in a grunt. He leaned back against the edge of the bed. I stayed with him, stroking his cock. He fumbled with his belt. I waited for him to finish undressing, then pushed him down onto the bed. He drew me toward him, tugging at the strings of my bodice.

Then he lowered my blouse over my shoulders. He hesitated.

"No," I said. "Don't stop."

He laid slow full kisses first on my breastbone, and then on my belly, and finally he took my breast in his mouth and gave the nipple a gentle suck. I lowered myself onto him, and we were joined.

18

Ordinary Time

1630-1631

In the quiet hours, after the sun has set, when lovers and children are in bed, I still catch myself wandering time-worn roads back to that year. I wish I'd written it all down back then, every smile and every God-addled word of nonsense that tumbled out of his beautiful mouth. It would be my private missal—a year of marriage recorded in feasts, in fasts, in the reliable march of ordinary time. Instead, I must rely on memory.

We married in secrecy in the middle of the somber, meatless Lenten season. Fitting, I think—we'd never done things the right way around. A few days after our wedding, we rejoined the Tross. Isidoro wrote to his order, asking to be released from his vows, but their reply was slow in reaching us, so he carried on, fulfilling his duties as a priest by day and his duties as a husband by night, with only the two of us and a pair of Spanish mercenaries knowing the whole truth of it.

Can a person be a home? No more, I think, than he can be a tree or a spring. No more than love can be a forest. What's the use of all these metaphors, except to try to build a bridge across the chasm of the inexpressible? These two things are nothing alike, and yet in one way, held up in a certain light, it is possible to see the one reflected in the other. In the end, a man is not a tree, and he is not a spring, and love is only ever love and nothing else. To say otherwise is to lop off parts of it, as in some gory fairy tale, to make it fit a certain shape.

We made a home together, in the quiet of my tent, calling each other "husband" and "wife" when no one else could hear.

Easter 1630 fell at the end of March, and still there was no war in Germany. Yet anyone could see that the peace of the previous year was fraying. The Emperor's Restitution outraged the Protestant princes, and even his general, Wallenstein, enforced it only grudgingly. The noises of war from the Swedish king were growing louder. In darkness we waited, like the dead lying in their tombs—but what sort of world would we be resurrected in? One of peace or one of war?

That was a season of confessions and baptisms, of marriages and confirmations, and I hardly saw Isidoro during that time.

"I'm afraid I've been a neglectful husband," he said one night as he laid his head next to mine for the first time in two weeks.

I touched my thumb to his mouth. "Serves me right for marrying a priest."

His lips parted in a smile, but his eyelids were already drooping, and soon he was sound asleep.

A month later, he surprised me in my surgery at midday, wearing a lusty smile. He pulled me toward the tent. I laughed, feigning protest. Yet no sooner had I stripped the cassock from his body than I saw his chest was pocked with red bites.

I pushed him off me, inspecting the garment in the harsh sunlight. The offending creatures were near invisible against the black cloth, except when they leapt into the air: fleas.

I ordered him to strip and piled all his clothes into the kettle for boiling. Then I had him stand in my wash basin, where I scrubbed his skin till it was pink all over. Once he was clean, I took my scissors and razor to the top of his head.

Tears marbled my vision as his black locks fell and collected at his feet like crow's feathers, but an army cannot abide fleas. They spread disease as fast as anything.

After, he ran his hand over his head with a sheepish grin. "I'll not hear the end of this as long as I live, will I?"

"At least not until your hair grows back," I said.

Come the end of the Easter season, we had cause to hope on a child, but by Pentecost my monthly sickness returned, as fickle as the spring weather.

"It will happen when it happens," he said.

"Or not at all," I said.

"Whichever it is, all will be well." How strange to find that I believed him.

I'd understood him better, since our loss. For years, I'd thought him like any other priest, willfully turning his face from the world's brokenness in stalwart defense of his God and his faith. I thought that because it hadn't made him angry or bitter, the war had not touched him. It had, only he'd chosen another path.

"This is where goodness dies," I'd told him, countless times.

"Only if we stop doing good," he'd said, resolute.

He collected goodness the way I collected herbs for my potions. He gathered up joys like poppies, and he held onto them, keeping their petals pressed in the pages of his soul. That was where he went when the enormities of the war bore down on him. He retreated into prayer, giving thanks for births and baptisms, for sweet plums and well-seasoned beef, for fair sun on a day that had threatened rain, for the laughter of children, for the wagon that did not break, for the patient that did not die, for the battle that did not come.

In May, he prayed a double funeral for the prostitute Dorothea and the child I'd cut out of her almost two years before. They'd both succumbed to smallpox. He spent the weeks after buried in his prayer book and muttering his *Aves* as he walked through the camp.

"Do you know what I think must be true?" he said to me while we were in bed one night, not long after.

"I never know what you think," I teased.

"I think that God must be everywhere and at all times."

"Aye, that is a very priestly thing to say."

"What I mean is, I think he must not see things as we do, one after the other. I think he sees it all, as if it's all happening at once. I think when he looks on all the suffering we have made in this world, he must see all the joys as well. I think the joys must be so bright that they blot out the pain and blot out the grief, so that God sees only the beauty."

"It's a pretty little thought," I said.

He chuckled. "That's what you say when you think I'm talking nonsense. But I think it must be this way, otherwise, how could God look on any of this and still believe it's good?"

He went on: "What if we suffer so deeply now because we cannot see how the flowers will bloom on our graves? We cannot see what the next moment will bring, let alone the world to come. We cannot see how our own kindnesses burn like the sun in God's eyes, rendering him blind."

"What does it mean," I asked, "to say that God is blind to suffering? What justice is there in God looking the other way?"

"Not blind then. But he sees what we can't. He sees how it ends. He sees how it's all made right. It must be made right."

I rested my head in the curve where his neck met his shoulder and breathed him in.

"You think it's nonsense," he said when I didn't speak. There was a disappointment in his voice, as if he'd been seeking my affirmation all along, though I couldn't fathom why.

"I want to believe it's not," I said, clutching his arm.

His smiles were harder to come by in those days. I fought for each one, coaxing them out of him with kisses and teasing and bawdy talk that made him blush.

It was around that time that General Wallenstein visited our camp. I glimpsed the general as he rode through the Tross toward the officers' tents. He rode stiffly on horseback, clad in forbidding black garments, his eyes like black beads set under a monstrous forehead: vision and contempt all mingling in one man.

He was in a particular rage then, shouting short, clipped commands at his officers and spitting invective about his rivals in the Imperial court loud enough for any to hear. "I wage more war with a few ministers than with all the enemy," he declared.

The cause of the general's anger was soon made plain. The Emperor had ordered him to send thirty thousand soldiers south, and the general had refused. Wallenstein was convinced that the Swedish king intended to invade and that the best means to stop him was to keep a strong force on the northern coast.

But the Emperor overrode him, and at the end of May, the greater part of the army marched south under the command of the Italian General Collalto. Our regiment was one of the few that remained in Germany.

June marked a year since the treaty had been signed and two since I'd rejoined the Tross. I'd thought to be done with the war by then, but Isidoro had yet to receive a response from his order about his vows. So, I signed on for another year, and he wrote another letter.

The next month Isidoro helped kill a boar. A pack of wild pigs stampeded through the Tross, tearing up the tents and making off with rations. A whole army of soldiers was standing by, but my gangly, narrow fool of a priest took it on himself to run one of the creatures down, cornering it from the rest and driving it toward the spearpoint of a readied pike.

"And if it had turned around instead and charged at you?" I asked him. "And if you'd been gored?"

"You'd have cursed me out and stitched me back together," he laughed. "In that order."

"Not likely. Rather let the devil take you for being so stupid."

Oh, but what a fuss was made over that hog! No doubt the princes of Germany, well-fatted on fresh meat and exotic fruits, would have laughed in bewilderment to see it. Isidoro got a portion of the belly and the haunch for his contribution to the hunt, and we shared it with all the widows, beggars, and whores of the camp. That night, we laughed and danced and sang rowdy songs until the sun came up, imagining the meal was dates from the East, oranges from Spain, and venison from the Emperor's own woods, and our watery beer was fortified wine.

While we celebrated, the Swedish king and his army made landfall, and whatever hope we had of peace died at his landing.

And where was the Emperor in 1630? Where were the German princes? Secure in Regensburg, drinking and fighting amongst themselves. Naturally, they were in no danger of freezing to death of a winter, of starving in early spring, of contracting typhus or smallpox. They'd not die beaten to death by soldiers or burned in their own homes.

The priests in the army led us in praying for peace, remembering each of those lofty princes by name. The more fools us. While they bickered over religion and titles and their precious German liberties, peace, it's clear to me, was nowhere in their minds. Nor, I'm sure, did any of them pause to remember us in their prayers.

The country they fought over was not a people, but an idea: a collection of cities, religions, and liberties, that which could be drawn on a map or written into law, no more or less. Where in their meager imaginations was there space for flesh and bone, for love and pain and joy, for death and birth, for all the human needs and longings that play out on the face of the earth, even in times of war?

Of course, I wasn't in Regensburg. I can no more say what they discussed than I can peer into God's mind and know his thoughts. I only know the outcome. Wallenstein's rivals won the day, and he was removed from command. In his place they appointed General Tilly of the Catholic League—a pious old soldier well into his eighth decade. The princes rejected the Emperor's Edict of Restitution, but it was too late to keep the Swedes off our shores.

In August, a miller in the Tross had his arm crushed when the axle of a wagon that was hauling one of the millstones broke, and the ropes snapped, loosing the heavy wheel and sending it rolling. The damned soul had rushed in to try to steady it.

"I suppose we'll go to meet the Swede next," Isidoro remarked as I handed him a rag to squeeze onto the man's tongue.

I shrugged. "I heard we're to march east, not north." Broken bone poked through the tradesman's skin at two places, and I could tell from feeling along the upper and lower arm that there were still more breaks beneath the surface. "You'll want to look away, priest."

He shook his head. "How many years since you've been back, and you still think I'm the weak-stomached boy you met in '22?"

"Very well. Keep your pride; just keep your stomach." I leaned all my weight on the poor man's bone, forcing it back beneath the skin. He hollered and convulsed, and the priest had to pin his shoulders to the chair to keep him from toppling forward. There was a sick sucking sound as the shard popped back into place.

Isidoro blanched, but he didn't turn away.

I moved to the next bone. "Rumor is Duke Maximilian has struck a deal with the French, and the French are on the side of the Swede."

"So where does that leave us?"

"In the strappado," I said. What a mess it was. The Emperor would have Tilly strike at the Swedish invaders at once, but Tilly took his pay and his orders from Maximilian, and Maximilian's agreement with the French prevented exactly that.

The miller sputtered and coughed. "Watch out," I warned Isidoro.

The priest stepped back from the chair just as the patient heaved up his insides. The poor man was a deathly pale color, and his skin had gone cold and damp.

"Damn it," I hissed.

Isidoro helped me prop him up, so I could continue my work, but it was plain the pain was getting the better of him, and I'd as good as lost him already. Sure enough, he started to shake uncontrollably soon after, and his skin took on a greenish hue. He was gone within the hour.

My mood turned bilious, and I stormed about the surgery, cleaning and packing my instruments, while Isidoro searched out the man's family and readied the funeral.

"You gave it your best," he reassured me by the fire later that evening as he stuffed a wooden pipe with tobacco leaf. It was a habit he'd picked up from the soldiers, who'd learned it from the English mercenaries.

"Of course I did," I said. "If anyone could have saved him, it was me. Only, they always send me the hopeless cases, and I'm sick of it."

"They send them to you because they know your skill."

He passed me the pipe, and I sucked in the smoke and breathed it out. I handed it back to him, and he reclined on his elbows, blowing smoke rings with his tongue.

"They send them to me because I'm a woman, and they want to see me fail."

Even my fool of a husband knew better than to deny it. He sat up and planted a gentle kiss on my shoulder.

As predicted, when next we broke camp, we marched not north, in the direction of the Swedish forces, but east toward Saxony, where the prince there had yet to choose between the Swedish king and the Emperor. We attempted to cross into Brandenburg, but were driven back on our heels by the Swedes.

Marching, when the weather is good, is not such a bad time. Retreating, on the other hand, is laborious. The pace is quick, the marches are long, and you sleep in your wagon or under the open sky; there's rarely time to set up a proper camp. I took care to inspect Isidoro's feet each night and to wrap them fresh in dry wool each morning.

I'd never known him to be anxious, but a melancholic mood settled over him during those marches. At first, I waited for it to pass, like one of those dark clouds full of false threat that casts its shadow without bringing any rain. But it didn't pass. His sighs grew deeper; his sentences broke off at the midpoint.

Now I sat on the edge of my bedroll with his foot propped in my lap in the dark pre-dawn hours and said, "Will you tell me what's weighing on you, or must I pry it out of you?"

"I can't hide a thing from you, can I?"

"Tell me the truth. Is it about children? Am I a disappointment to you?" Six months we'd been married, and my monthly sickness continued in its irregular way. The other women in the camp assured me that six months was not so long a time to wait on a child, but we'd both been eager to put our loss behind us, and we'd certainly been making the effort.

"What? No, and I don't know how you could think it."

"You're certain? If you're having regrets—"

"It's my order," he said. "No word from them in months, and now we have the Swedish army on our tails. I don't know when I'll be released."

I set his foot aside and crawled closer to him. "It will happen when it happens."

"And if it doesn't?"

"All will be well." I kissed him.

"I'm not sure I like you levying my words against me."

"Now you know how the rest of us feel, priest."

Advent brought hunger as our food supplies dwindled. The cause of our trouble was the former General Wallenstein. He may have been dismissed from command, but by virtue of his land holdings, he controlled our food supply. To spite Tilly and his enemies, to make clear just how deep the Emperor stood in his debt, he cut us off, and we starved.

I'd been hungry before, as a child on the road with my father, but never like this, a hunger so deep it ceased to gnaw; it simply became part of us, like any other ache. On Christmas eve, Isidoro scavenged a stub of a candle and stuck it in a chunk of acorn bread. We split the loaf between us and nibbled at it, imagining the dense, bitter taste was that of dried fruit.

In the middle of that unabated fast, we celebrated one year of marriage. He roused me before dawn, and we left the camp for a spot by the banks of the Oder. The weather had been mild, and we took advantage of the pleasant morning air to sprawl in the grass and bury our recent hardships in the pleasure of each other's company until a spring rain drove us back, laughing, soaked, and muddy.

Almost nothing that year had gone to plan. He was still a priest, there was still a war, and we had no child to look forward to. Yet when I think back on it, I'm unwilling to let go of a single moment. I keep them pressed between the pages of my memory, like the dried petals of a poppy flower, a reminder that happiness is not the opposite of pain. It's not the opposite of want or cold. Happiness exists in and through and despite all these things.

That spring, the Swedish advance drove our half-starved, sickly army to the gates of Magdeburg, the maiden city of the Elbe. What happened there, I could spend the rest of my life trying to forget.

19

Magdeburg Mercy

1631

Two months into the siege of Magdeburg, I woke with hunger gnawing at my belly. I left Isidoro asleep in my tent and went to find food. The runt, now thirteen years old and a gray old dog, looked up at me wearily with his one good eye as I left, then rested his head once more at the priest's feet. Outside the light was low and the wind whipped the banners around the camp.

I returned some time later with a half loaf of acorn bread, some discarded chicken bones, and a handful of broad beans. While the broth bubbled on the flame, I scavenged my dwindling medicines for dried herbs. Isidoro crawled out and sat on his haunches in front of the fire. He prayed over the bread and then broke it, handing me the larger half. I tore off a piece and fed it to the runt, who struggled to chew it.

We ate in near silence, soaking our bread in the watery broth and watching each other through a hunger fog. He planted a kiss on my forehead before going off to his daily ministry, praying for the souls of the soldiers who bombarded the walls of the city daily.

There was food in Magdeburg. All we'd heard for months was that there was food in Magdeburg. Great grain houses piled high with wheat and barley and rye. Breweries overflowing with fermenting beer. Fisheries and butchers and storehouses bursting with cheese and butter and lard and oil and more exotic things besides—spices and fruits shipped on the Elbe from the northern ports. Plums, grapes, peaches. The mouth watered to think of it. The stomach ached.

Months we'd been outside the city, which had openly allied itself with the Swedish king. Months in which the city had refused to surrender, despite having only a small garrison and no hope of holding out. But on this day, the order had finally been given to storm the walls.

The thunder of cannon began at the usual hour, and the wind carried the sour odor of gunpowder over the camp. As I doused the fire from breakfast, shouts of fighting came from the city's southern bulwark.

I didn't make anything of them at first. I checked the dressings on the injured and readied my surgery for what bloodshed the new day would bring.

By mid-morning, I knew that the walls had been breached. The first injured came in from the New Gate, and I busied myself pulling out bullets and stitching up saber wounds. But as the morning wore on, ragged battle cries gave way to shrill screams.

The first of the soldiers returned, dragging behind them the women they'd taken from their homes near the walls. They took them to their tents or, in some cases, they didn't wait, but fell on them in the open. Their commanders shouted orders to restore the discipline, but the soldiers were a-froth with battle fever.

I went toward the screams, looking to treat the abused women, and found Isidoro in the midst of the disorder, enjoining the soldiers to remember their Godly morals and to leave aside wickedness. A pikeman struck him over the brow with the pommel of his sword. The priest fell like a dummy made of straw.

I pressed my hand against his forehead to stanch the flow of blood. We stumbled toward my surgery just as the sky began to darken with smoke and the thunder of collapsing timber shook the city walls.

By midday, the city was a luminous halo on the river. Pitch-colored clouds loomed over her, blotting out the sun. The wind whipped up both flame and fume, and soon the whole camp was choked with soot and ash.

Isidoro and I huddled beneath the surgery canopy while I stitched up the wound on his forehead. My eyes filled with smoke, and I struggled to see clearly.

Isidoro prayed. He prayed over the injured, he prayed for the city, he prayed until he was hoarse. Was God not listening, I wonder, or was it simply that he could not hear over the heat and noise of the inferno, the shuddering of timber as the city and all her grain houses and breweries and storehouses collapsed, one by one?

Some insist it was an accident: the gunpowder from our cannon sent up sparks and ignited the southern gate, and the wind that day did the rest.

Our soldiers offered their own explanation. They said that the treacherous citizens of Magdeburg had started the fires out of petty spite, to deny plunder and much-needed food to the sacking army.

There is a third possibility—that the city burned in an act of self-defeating vengeance for its long resistance, for allying itself with a foreign king, for refusing to bow to the Emperor's Restitution. That our soldiers set it ablaze deliberately in a blind and ravenous fury.

I don't know which explanation is the true one, but for my part, I cannot blot out the memory of those rage-blind pikemen, working out their frustrations on the city's women.

As the day went on, a number of those women found their way to my surgery, where I put salves on their wounds until I ran out of herbs and Isidoro held their hands and prayed over them. Most of them were too dumbstruck to speak. Some grew fearful when the priest approached them. But I told them he was my husband, and they were reassured.

"Thank God. I thought he was a Catholic," said one.

Isidoro, I noted, didn't correct her.

"There should be more wounded," I said, once the last of the women was resting under the canopy. There were thirty thousand in the city, and the fires had been burning and our soldiers pillaging throughout the day. The smoke still billowed profusely overhead, obliterating the sun and the sky. Yet it must have been hours since the defenses fell.

"They will come." Isidoro squeezed my hand, and I knew that he didn't quite believe his own words. "Perhaps the other surgeons…" he began, but I shook my head.

We both knew the other surgeons' tents were as empty as mine.

The next morning brought uneasy quiet. The fire in the city had died down, and the sky was a clear, gentle blue, with just a hint of smoke floating on the air. I gathered my surgical tools at first light and made my way toward the gates. Isidoro accompanied me.

The main wall stood fast, but the scorched framework of the secondary fortifications groaned and cracked as we passed them. Banners emblazoned with the black and gold Imperial eagle had been hung from the stone ramparts overnight. The city's old emblem, the maid of Magdeburg, had been torn from the gate, but the motto could still be made out under the soot: "Who shall take her?"

The answer to the question lay all around us.

As we entered the city, we were forced to cover our faces to keep from choking on the stink. Isidoro gagged, and my own stomach lurched. The scent was like to that of a hog fired on a spit, but denser, heavier.

All along the main thoroughfare, we stepped over bodies. A few of them, the members of the garrison, died clinging to weapons or clad in breastplates. But the greater number bore no weapons other than their own fists, and no armor other than the homespun wool they wore on their backs. They'd been cut down fleeing or pleading for mercy.

We stumbled over the corpses of sheep, pigs, horses, and dogs as well. Isidoro came to a halt and stared stupefied at the body of a black-and-brown dappled mutt. "What quarrel did we have with the dogs?"

"They were Protestant dogs," I remarked. He didn't laugh.

Onward we went, searching for some sign of the living. Our own soldiers were still moving about the city, entering crumbling buildings and rifling through the furniture.

We stopped outside the charred skeleton of a baker's shop. We knew it by the iron sign that had fallen onto the front step, blocking a blackened lintel where hung a set of empty hinges with no door. Warped and discolored pieces of glass littered the ground in front of the windows. Only the brick oven remained, the chimney crumbling.

Amid the rubble lay several lumpen figures. I studied them for a minute or more before I made sense of their shape—an arm here, shielding the face, a leg extended there. *People.* Isidoro made the sign of the cross in front of the doorway.

"We oughtn't be here," I said to him, turning away from that hellish scene. "We have nothing to offer them."

"We may still pray for their souls," he whispered. His face was white as pearl.

One of the rafters broke free of the beam that was supporting it and crashed on the figures below. The noise rattled our souls in our bodies, and we hurried away.

I cannot describe the incongruity of that place: an entire city reduced to a vast, ash-covered plain. The only sounds the intermittent pop of the last flames, burning themselves out, the creak of charred timbers, the breeze whistling through them.

The only visible structure for a mile was the cathedral. We went toward it. Across the square from the church, we stumbled over a line of children, no more than nine or ten years old, their bodies rent apart by the sharp edge of a sword. A wild dog gnawed on the shoulder of one of them. My own solid stomach failed me then, and I heaved up bile.

Our generals had managed to post a defensive line in front of the cathedral, preventing the pillaging soldiers of their own army from entering, and there at last, we found the living. A few thousand, no more. They'd sheltered through the night under the church's eaves. We were allowed to enter to pray and treat the injured, but it was two more days before the pillaging ended and those poor folk were allowed to step outside and see what had become of their city.

In the following days, the survivors were permitted to ransom back their women. If there was no one to pay the ransom, the priests encouraged the soldiers to marry them.

In thirteen years of war, I'd not seen the like of it. In all, twenty-five thousand bright souls were extinguished that day. Enough to field an army. Enough to fill every bed in Nördlingen three times over.

For days after, we dragged up the bodies, which the flames had transfigured into shapes scarcely recognizable, and cast them into the Elbe like refuse. There wasn't time enough to dig so many graves, not before the flesh began to rot and spread disease.

Just when we thought we'd finished the gruesome work, we discovered another body, hiding in a well, or buried beneath crumbled rafters. Even the great river struggled to swallow them all, and for weeks after, bloated bodies washed up on the banks to become food for buzzards and wild dogs.

Since then, the destruction of that city has taken on many pretty names— *The Magdeburg Wedding*, *The Magdeburg Sacrifice*, *The Magdeburg Offering*—poetic sorts of names for the pamphleteer to deploy, invoking a city of martyrs to lend nobility to the Protestant cause.

I can't stomach any of them. What happened in Magdeburg was as ignoble a thing as has ever been done by human hands, and what did all those hapless martyrs get for their sacrifice? Sixteen years it's been, and their blood has been repaid ten- and twenty-fold—an endless procession of martyrs covering the whole of Germany—and still this war has not reached an end.

No, I prefer to call it, simply, *das Magdeburgisieren*. New horrors must birth new words to describe them. How else can one hope to give utterance to the unutterable?

Five days after the city burned, Tilly ordered the cathedral and the city to be re-dedicated to Our Lady. When Isidoro heard this, he quaked with rage. Never in all the time I'd known him had I seen him lose his good nature so entirely. He refused to attend the re-dedication Mass.

I was all at a loss, a very poor wife indeed, for I didn't know the first way to comfort him.

"God did not will this," he said, clenching his fist.

Aye, I wanted to say, but he allowed it. He allowed men to do it in his name. And we'd been there too; I, healing and he, praying.

We hadn't struck the match, but we'd accepted our part without protest, mindless as the flames leaping on the wind.

So, I said nothing. I stayed awake by his side, night after night, while he rocked back and forth with his arms on his knees and his forehead pressed against his prayer book. "Minister to a massacre," I heard him say when he thought me dozing.

Finally, after a dozen such restless nights, I spoke to him plain. "Tell me what's on your mind. I'm your wife. Don't keep it all for God. He doesn't deserve it."

"We must go," he said then.

"Aye," I agreed. That much was obvious.

But where would we go? In Brandenburg to the north, the Swedish army gathered, and rumor was that the people there suffered even more dolorously under the invader than we did in our ration-starved army. In Berlin, it was said, they'd taken to eating their own dead, while the Elector of Brandenburg feasted on roasted duck with the King of Sweden.

To the south and west lay the rich and relatively untouched lands of Saxony. The prince there was a Protestant, but he wavered yet between his loyalty to the Emperor and to his faith. There, at least, we might find food if not welcome. From there it was not far to Bohemia, Catholic lands.

Once he'd spoken the words, he relaxed. We were both happier for having chosen a course of action, and we put our minds to planning our escape.

As it happened, we weren't the only ones in the army who'd had their fill of war after Magdeburg. It was no great number, but between the starvation and the raw horrors of that day, we managed to find about a dozen others who were ready to go with us.

We left before dawn one morning. I packed my tools and my medicines onto my horse, but left my cart behind, so that when they first noticed me missing, they'd think I'd only gone to one of the nearby towns for supplies and delay their search. Apart from that, we took only what we could carry on our backs. The soldiers snuck out with their wives and met Isidoro and me in the hills. From there, we cut across fields and woodlands before reaching the road leading south and east toward Bohemia.

We were an odd little band, made up mostly of former foot-soldiers and their wives and children. We parted ways with half of them a few days later. They were mercenaries by profession and had decided to journey north and seek employment with the Swede. The rest of us made our way to Saxony.

Along the way, I plied my trade as a surgeon, and Isidoro went to the towns with the rest of the men to find work, just as my father had once done. He had no trade, but he was educated, and when there weren't contracts to be transcribed and letters to be copied, he made a few gulden reading the war pamphlets in the town's square. Only on Sundays did he reveal himself a priest, when he consecrated our bread and broke it.

He remained troubled, walking through those days unsmiling, and at night he tossed in his sleep, muttering and groaning.

"What is this dream that turns you about every night?" I asked him.

He shook his head. "I don't know how to tell it. When it begins, I'm back in Magdeburg. But there are no men there, only beasts, the devil's own legion. The flames are unquenchable. I think it must be a vision of Hell, or else the end of the world."

"The end of the world would be a mercy," I said. "The trouble with the world is, it goes right on."

"No," he said. "I don't believe it. If this is the end of the world, then where is the hope in that? There must be something left that's worth saving."

"Aye," I said, pulling him into my arms. "It's you."

By pieces, his smile returned. He slept more soundly. We put Magdeburg behind us in miles and in days, until I had the feeling it had been just one of his nightmares, nothing more.

In early July, we found ourselves in a little town just north of the Bohemian border. The whole day long the sky had been that kind of unnatural hue that portended storms, and so we'd decided, with the others, to take our chances spending the night in a local tavern.

At suppertime, Isidoro and I sat by ourselves in the corner, sopping up our stew with chunks of fresh bread, while the others of our band took to drinking with the townsfolk. The runt, who was walking more stiffly those days, settled beneath the table, nibbling half-heartedly at the scraps we tossed him.

By and by, the conversation in the room turned to the war. The townsfolk were Protestant, and one of them raised a toast to the Swedish king: "To Gustav Adolph, may God be with him."

One of our own, deep in his cups, spat on the floor by his feet.

"And what do you mean by that?" The man who had raised the glass was stout and round-bellied, his face twisted in a perpetually sour expression.

"No self-respecting German should raise a drink to a Swedish invader," came the drunken reply.

"Who should I toast instead? The Emperor in Austria? Or perhaps the King of Spain, his cousin? At least the Swede fights for the German, for the true German religion. With God's help, he'll drive the Catholic butchers of Magdeburg back to their countries."

"Say that again." Our man was on his feet now.

"Or what, Pope-lover?" the other hissed.

"At least I'm not lining up for the chance to suck Swedish cock."

The inn's proprietor intervened. An angular, sharp-eyed woman of about sixty, she ordered both men to sit down on their benches and be quiet. "There'll be no more talk of the war, or I'll toss the whole lot of you out into the storm and keep your gulden."

The rest of the night was quiet, apart from the rumble of thunder and the pelting of raindrops on the tavern roof. By morning, the storm had cleared, and we'd as good as forgotten the incident from the previous evening. We set out for the next town.

But on the road from town, men were waiting for us. I recognized the round-bellied man and his drinking companions, but there were several other men besides. They held makeshift weapons—tools and wooden switches. One carried a sword.

The closest house was half a mile behind us. On either side of the road grew dense, coarse thicket. Our men corralled the women and children behind them and moved toward the waiting townsfolk, hands at their swords, ready to draw.

"Listen." Isidoro stepped forward, palms raised. "I am a man of God, and I see no reason why we should be at each other's throats."

"A man of God? You mean, a priest?" It was the round-bellied ringleader.

"Yes, of the Society of Jesus."

"A Jesuit! But you have a wife."

"I do. We have more in common than you might think, Protestants and Catholics. This band of travelers left the army, seeking peace. We don't want any more violence. We just want to pass on our way to Bohemia. So, please, I don't know what you're intending, but if there is any mercy in your—"

"Mercy! The priest talks of mercy," the man scoffed.

There was a flash as the man stepped toward Isidoro, morning sun glinting on metal. He thrust his fist toward Isidoro's stomach in too little time for even a warning. My priest let out a strangled breath, and crumpled forward, clutching the knife still stuck in his ribs.

"There's your mercy, priest," the man spat. "Magdeburg mercy."

Shouts and violence followed. Our band charged at the townsfolk, who lost their nerve and scattered, leaving two dead behind them, including the man who'd stabbed Isidoro. I dropped to my knees beside the priest, pouring all my strength into turning him on his back. His hand was stiff on the knife. His blood bubbled up, hot, beneath it.

"Water!" I heard myself scream. "Bring me water! Bring me my instruments!"

All the color had gone from his lips, and his body was racked with shivers. One of the other deserters tried to unclench the priest's hand from around the weapon, but there was no use in it. Isidoro looked up at me, eyelids fluttering, and his mouth parted in a trembling smile. "*Corazón*," he said. "Pray for me."

Oh, but my fool of a priest, I did. You had to have known when you asked it of me that I would. Even now, I pray for you, every night and morning. Though God knows, I'm the one who needs praying for.

It's sixteen years now you've been gone. Sixteen years since we buried you, on a little grassy hillside half a mile from that spot. Who knew that it was possible for a person to lose one's heart and yet live so long?

20

Gottschalk

1631

My dear priest, you said I would find peace in the writing of this account. But tell me, what peace is there in digging up old bones? My mother, my father, you. What peace is there after Magdeburg? Is there a soul left alive in all of Germany who knows the word? God help us, if peace should come, we'll cast it into the street as a stranger.

It's been months now since I last picked up my pen. What a state I was in after I last wrote! I couldn't have anticipated the power that terrible day still holds on me, even after sixteen years. It was as if I'd killed you afresh with paper and ink.

I had a mind to abandon the whole endeavor as hopeless after that, but here I am. What a fool you've made of me—there is still more to tell.

The world goes on, you see, and that's precisely the trouble. Magdeburg blazed with apocalyptic flame, and the next morning the smoke dissipated, and the sun rose and set with familiar indifference. What could we do but rise with it, take our breakfast, and go about our work? Isidoro died, and the world went on, and I went on, too. I tucked his pipe and his prayer book into the same pouch where I carried my father's rosary. I placed a lock of his hair between the pages.

The wives in our band of deserters all scurried about me, doing my washing and urging me to eat, though I had no appetite. They filled the silence of my tent with their patter, as if to ward off grief with noise. I drove them away, preferring solitude, and they clucked their tongues behind my back and called me a strange one. "Thinks she's better than us," one said, thinking me out of earshot. "Working a man's profession."

At night, the runt sniffed Isidoro's scent on the bedroll and let out a disconsolate whine.

"I know," I said, scratching behind his ear. "I know."

The dog shuffled, listless, before finally curling up beside me.

Not two days after, one of the other deserters, a musketeer named Schultheiss, approached me as I was binding herbs into bundles. Illness and injury don't wait for grief, and in any case, I was glad to have the activity. The musketeer stopped a few feet away from me and lowered his hat, patting down the tufts of his beech-colored hair.

"The men have been talking," he began. His voice was thin and uncertain.

"About me?" I prompted him.

"Aye," he said, but did not continue.

"What is it, then? Spit it out. I can earn my keep if that's the concern. Though I'd have hoped you'd consider waiting more than two days afore you cast a man's widow to the dogs."

"No, we'd not considered it... that is, we've no intention of... We respected Father Isidoro very much. He baptized Krohn and Enderle's children. He was at my confirmation when the bishop of Mainz visited the army."

I studied the man in front of me. His appearance havered uncertainly between youth and maturity. Lines of hardship and hunger cast world-weary shadows around his mouth and eyes, but look at him in the right sort of light, and he still looked every bit a boy.

"How old are you?" I asked.

"Sixteen. My father was a musketeer before me, killed at Dessau Bridge."

I shook my head. He'd still been suckling at his mother's teat, no doubt, when the war started. "My father was a pikeman, killed at Stadtlohn," I said.

He crossed himself. "May God grant them a joyful resurrection."

"If the others haven't sent you to kick me out, then what?"

"Well, we started talking. And we all agreed that it wouldn't be right to leave the good Father's widow without anyone to care for her. And since the others are all married—"

I began laughing before the words had left his mouth. "You poor boy."

He furrowed his brow in confusion.

"Tell the men I appreciate the offer." I stood, slinging my basket of herbs over my arm. "But I'll not be marrying you or any of them. And wipe that crestfallen look from your face. If the good Father were here, he'd tell you that I'm stubborn and Godless and a whole host of other unfavorable qualities besides. I'm sure you'll make a good husband one day, just as I'm sure I'd make a very poor wife for you."

I patted the boy on the shoulder and returned to my tent, to my solitude. I thought I saw my priest enter behind me, robed in black, but when I turned to observe him directly, it was only the shadows of the trees, playing on the canvas.

I went on—whether I wanted to or not. I parted ways with the deserters. I was sick to death of war, of flitting from town to town, and further, it was plain by then that the runt didn't have so many years left in him.

He deserved better than to be left in a ditch on some God-forsaken stretch of road. He deserved to lie down in the loam of Rachel's garden one last time, running down rabbits in his dreams, until death should see fit to take him. After all we'd been through together, I thought I might at least give him that. I resolved to live by my profession and make my way back to Öttingen.

Before I left, the boy Schultheiss asked me once more if I would reconsider the offer of marriage. I assured him that if we each survived, if he did not hang for deserting or skirmishing with the villagers, I would most certainly come to his wedding—just not as his bride.

I hoped to reach Öttingen by the fall, but God or the devil—who can say which—had other plans. For two months I wandered as all manner of misfortune conspired to keep me from my destination. Near Dresden a company of soldiers waylaid me and demanded the use of my horse. They paid me half what it was worth, though they at least let me unpack my supplies before taking the beast. From then on, I traveled by foot.

Work proved hard to come by, not because there was no need for surgeons, but because most people looked askance at a woman practicing the trade. When I'd been with the soldiers, I'd at least had them to recommend my skills. My money dwindled, and I took to mixing potions for sale.

Even so, I should have made it to Öttingen easily enough, but at the end of August I fell so ill I couldn't breathe without pain. For three weeks I lay on the floor of a sick house in Bayreuth, and when I'd recovered, I found I was several *kreuzer* shy of covering my stay. They were gracious and let me go on without paying the balance, but I had nothing left.

So it was that I arrived in Nuremberg, penniless and in poor constitution, with only the runt for company.

"Well," I said to him as we entered the city, "our wandering is over. Either I will find work, or we will both die here." He stuck out his tongue, panting, and his tail gave an uncertain wag.

All the Empire knows Nuremberg. It's the hub of a wheel of roads connecting Vienna, Leipzig, Frankfurt-am-Main, and Prague. Then as now, all the wealth of the Empire flowed, at some station or other on its journey, through that city.

The city I entered in July 1631 had declared its neutrality in the war and then buried itself like a tortoise behind its high walls. Crowds of people pressed into the markets and scurried up and down the streets, chasing down the day's business. I was struck dumb at the sight of it, the apparent thriving regularity of the place, in contrast to the dwindling and deserted towns I'd passed through on my travels.

But the more I wandered its streets, the more I recognized the signs of war. People moved past them and talked around them, but they were there all the same: lanes of abandoned houses and boarded-up shops, posted with months-old yellowed notices: "No stock today." Masterless dogs digging in the gutters for scraps of food. Refugees turned beggar in the streets.

High walls might keep an army at bay, but they cannot keep hunger out when the roads are no longer safe, when the fields are stripped of their harvest before it reaches market, when the people who would pay for sugar and silks and leather and wine have all been driven from their homes. The war was slow in coming to Nuremberg, but it was coming.

I sought out the lane where the barber-surgeons had their shops and went from door to door, knocking and inquiring if any of them needed an assistant. I knew I'd get nowhere trying to convince them I knew their art, so I didn't even try.

Most of the men I spoke to that day shook their heads and mumbled vague excuses. A couple of them simply laughed. Another helpfully suggested I might try the local whorehouse, as my services might be better suited to that setting. The last one told me I might ask at Mr. Gottschalk's, on the next lane over. He smiled slyly as he said it. I couldn't fathom the meaning behind such a smile, but I wasn't in a position to question it, either.

I found Gottschalk's with some difficulty. It was not well marked—the name was painted in worn black lettering on a dark blue door. The curtains on the windows were drawn, and there appeared to be no light inside. But when I knocked, I heard the thump of heavy footsteps from within.

When no answer came, I struck the door with my open palm more forcefully. "I can hear you lumbering about, so you might just as well answer."

I was about to knock a third time when the door opened.

"Damn your racket. If it's money you want, go away." First came the voice, then the smell, in short succession. He was a gaunt, red-faced man of indeterminate age. I'd have guessed sixty, but he might have only appeared old. His hair was matted and gray, and every inch of him reeked of sweat and brandy.

"Mr. Gottschalk?" I asked.

"I'm the one." He crossed his arms over his chest, looking me up and down. "You're a woman."

"Aye, I'm aware."

"Not a debt collector then. What's wrong with you? Got yourself in the family way? Well, this isn't the place for that. Mrs. Hoffmann, across the square. That's who you're looking for."

"I'm looking for work."

He sniffed. "Work, you say? What sort of work?"

"Whatever work you have to offer."

"I suppose you know how to scrub the blood out of linens? Boil water? Mix herbs?"

I nodded to each of his questions.

"You don't have a weak stomach, do you?"

"I was with the army."

"That doesn't mean a thing."

"I helped dig out the bodies from the rubble of Magdeburg."

He fell quiet. "Very well, then," he relented. "Come in."

I followed him into his workroom, a cramped space not much bigger than a soldier's barrack, made all the smaller by the disorderly way in which he kept it.

His chair was in the middle next to the small table where he kept his instruments. Much of the space on the table was currently taken up with a small copper bowl, in which four blackened molars rested. A set of bloodied pliers was balanced across the rim. Shelves lined the other walls, crammed to bursting with books and medicines. In the corner, peeking out from the mess, was a brick fireplace with a rusted kettle dangling over the hearth. Glass bottles, some still half-full, were scattered around its base.

A noisome, boggish odor lingered in the air. I twisted up my face.

"I thought you said you were at Magdeburg," Gottschalk remarked.

"Magdeburg was sacked. You don't have any such excuse." I went to the window and tried to push open the shutter. It stuck fast.

"Been like that since I first rented the place," the barber-surgeon shrugged.

I struck the wood with my elbow, and it swung open. The scent of wet straw wafted up from the street to the room. Nevertheless, it was an improvement.

Gottschalk had no need of another surgeon to assist him, let alone a female one. What he needed was a maid. But I wagered that as long as I was working for him, the chance to prove my skills would come in due time.

Each day, I rose at sunrise to scrub down the room and organize his instruments and mix his medicines. I fixed him his meals as well—that is, when I could coax him to take anything but brandy. In exchange, he let me have a room in the upstairs apartment and promised me a small weekly salary. But as I soon came to find out, his bills were almost always in arrears. All told, I managed to collect less than half of what he owed me.

The surgeon's reputation is often a questionable one. It's not taught in the high seats of learning, but passed down from practitioner to practitioner, just as I'd learned it from Salomon. It is often bloody work, and the patients who come to us often suffer as greatly under our cures as they do from whatever it is that afflicts them.

Gottschalk, for his part, combined a casual indifference to the suffering of others with a brutish directness in the application of his work. If he had any philosophy of medicine, it was this: cut away the rot, and the body will heal. He took a perverse pride in the amount of blood that accumulated on his apron over the course of a day.

Each morning he took a swallow of brandy for breakfast, and on days when he operated, he might finish half a bottle before he even touched an instrument. I asked him why he drank, and he reflected a moment, squinting, then said, "Can't remember anymore. I suppose I started once and decided I didn't want to stop."

I gathered that he'd been with some army or other at one time, but as with so many people I've met, I could not say if war had made him what he was, or if this was who he'd always been. He squandered most of his earnings on games of chance and was forced to borrow money often.

I could do little about his gambling, but for his patients' sake, I tried to clear the house of drink. In sobriety, however, he developed such a tremor in his hand, I feared he would slip and slit the throat of the man whose beard he was trimming. So, I returned the bottles, but rationed their contents.

I went on, and Nuremberg went on.

Oh, Nuremberg: what a magnificent, wretched city! Its people moved through each day in a performance of happier times. The burghers carried on, griping about the cost of fruit and fortified wine and other fine things. In the market they haggled in raised voices, a gulden for this and ten for that and this much for silks to swaddle themselves in. Bargaining for comfort as if it were a substitute for peace.

And I was no better. Stuck in the crevices of grief, I played pretend. My monthly sickness had stopped once more, and I nurtured the secret hope that some part of Isidoro still remained with me.

But when my stomach neither swelled nor gave any other sign of being with child, I was left to accept that he was gone entirely. Hunger and illness alone were to blame for my missing courses.

In autumn, the runt developed a racking cough. For nights on end, he kept me awake with his retching noises. He stopped taking solid food, and I had to coax him to lap milk from a bowl for nourishment.

"If you need a hand putting him out of his misery, just say the word," Gottschalk offered one morning after a particularly hard night.

"It's just a little sickness. It will work itself out." I wasn't ready to contemplate another loss.

It was during that period of sleepless nights that the chance I'd been waiting for arrived at last. Some hours past midnight, there came a pounding at the surgery door. I was awake already, holding the runt to soothe him, so I pulled on my clothes and took a candle downstairs to see what was the matter. I found Gottschalk passed out on the floor of his room, sleeping heavily. When I tried to rouse him, he slurred his curses and turned over to resume his drunken slumber.

The hammering at the door grew louder and more insistent. "Come on, now. Don't be a heartless bastard," a man's voice called. "Let us in. It's a matter of life and death."

Gottschalk had the habit of keeping the door barred, even in the daytime, for fear of the debt collectors that were always at his throat, but at this hour, I judged it unlikely to be creditors. I lit the lamps and let the men in.

Two men, their faces and hands bloodied and swollen with fresh bruises, carried a third between them, his head lolling on his chest. I cleared the chair and the men lumped their companion into it.

"Where's Gottschalk?" one of them asked.

Without thinking, I said, "I'm Gottschalk."

The men glanced at each other sideways. "You?"

"You said it was a matter of life and death. Do you want to waste time questioning me, or will you tell me what sort of trouble I'm looking at?"

"He—he fell," one began.

"I'll need a mite more to go on. Where? How far? Did he land on his head or some other part of him?"

"Down a flight of stairs," the other clarified. "Struck his head several times on the way down." He clutched the bloody knuckles of his left hand close to his chest.

"Tripped, did he? Or did one of you help him along?"

"Not us, no," came the hasty denial.

"But you were drinking. And brawling."

They each gave a shameful nod.

I set to work, quick as I could. The man flitted in and out of wakefulness, and his left eye was bloodshot. His companions looked on dumbly, uncertain whether to protest when I began to shave away the hair from his head.

"Is there anything we might do?" the one asked as I readied the drill.

"Hold him down," I said—though he was hardly stirring. "And pray." I paused then, too, modulating my breath. It was the first time in years that I didn't have Isidoro beside me, mumbling his Aves. I muttered the words myself and made my cut, peeling away the scalp so that I could drill into his skull and relieve the pressure, as I'd done countless times before.

After I'd stitched the man up, I examined the wounds of the other two. Most of them were superficial, but the one with the bloodied knuckles had broken two of his fingers. I set them and bound them up.

When all was done, I took the men's money and sent them on their way. "Get your rest. Your friend will still be here come morning."

I went back to my room to check on the runt and found him curled up on the bed, slumbering soundly. I lay down beside him for a spell, and the exhaustion of the previous sleepless nights took me.

Some hours later, Gottschalk throttled me awake. He yanked me from the bed by my blouse, and before I could raise my arms in defense, he rained blows on my face and shoulders.

Curses tumbled out of his mouth. "What the devil were you thinking?"

I wriggled free of him and ran to the other side of the room, placing the bed between us. The runt growled, then broke off in a fit of coughing.

"I'll warn you not to strike me again." My jaw pulsed with a bright ache as I spoke.

"You'll warn me?" He was shouting. "Have you forgotten your place here, woman? You have no business warning me of anything. I took you and your mongrel in."

"I've more than earned my keep, and I'd be gone by now if you paid me what you owed me."

"And you think that gives you the right to call yourself by my name and operate in my stead?"

"You were passed out drunk. I might have saved your reputation."

"By killing a man?"

I felt my heart pulse in my throat. The morning sun glowed warmly through the curtains. The man had been sleeping when I left him, but I'd not intended to fall asleep myself. "*Did* I kill him?" I asked, not wanting to hear the answer.

"No," Gottschalk admitted. "But you might have."

"Not likely," I said, hoping he hadn't noticed my moment of doubt. "I didn't spend three years as an army surgeon to be lectured by a drunken barber who couldn't pull a musket ball from a bullet wound without making a bigger hole than the one it went in by."

"An army surgeon? You?" he scoffed.

"They don't teach trepanning to seamstresses."

"I should come over there and clobber you, just to teach that tongue of yours manners," he said, but his temper had already cooled, and the threat was half-hearted. "You might have said you were a surgeon sooner."

"You wouldn't have believed it."

He scowled, but he nodded. "No, I wouldn't have. I'm sure I don't believe it now, except there's a man downstairs on my table with a beautiful row of stitches in his scalp, and it wasn't me that did it."

"Will you allow me to check on him, or will you try to strike me again?"

He huffed, then took a step back and gestured toward the open door. The runt jumped to the floor with an awkward thump and followed behind me, a low growl rumbling in his chest as we passed.

The injured man was sitting up talking when I entered the room. His eye had begun to clear up and his memory was sharp. By and by, his companions returned to collect him. They paid me the fee directly.

When they'd gone, I counted out half and gave it to Gottschalk for the use of his name. The rest I kept for myself. Then I returned to my room and went back to sleep. When a man came in later that afternoon in need of bleeding, Gottschalk knocked on my door and woke me.

After that, we reached a sort of understanding. I'd handle the simpler cases that crossed his threshold, and he'd allow me to keep an even split of the payment. Besides which, I made certain he understood that if he so much as raised a hand against me again, I'd leave and set myself up with a rival.

The war, as well, went on. Whether I was in the Tross or far away, it went on. The Emperor's starved and beleaguered army marched into Saxony. In September, reinforced with fresh recruits, they captured Leipzig, but proved unable to hold it. The Swedish king was relentless, and when the two armies finally clashed outside that city, Swedish artillery splintered the Imperial defenses like so much rotted wood. For the first time since the start of the war, the strength of the Catholic League army broke.

In Nuremberg, news of the battle of Breitenfeld was greeted with celebration up and down the streets. The bells of St. Lorenz rang all hours of the day. Thirteen long years, the Emperor and the Catholic League had held the Protestant by the throat. Though the city maintained an official policy of neutrality, in the hearts of its citizens, neutrality had perished with the dead of Magdeburg.

The sermons preached that Sunday cast the Catholic League's defeat as a holy reckoning, with King Gustav Adolph of Sweden as the avenging angel of the Protestant cause, exacting with interest the price for every one of the souls claimed at Magdeburg: twenty-seven thousand Imperial soldiers, their bodies even now sinking into the earth.

Even Gottschalk seemed to cast aside his sour disposition for a spell.

"Good morning," he greeted me when I came downstairs to the surgery, the day after the news reached us. He took a pair of glasses down from a high shelf and tipped the contents of his latest bottle into them. A bit of the liquid dribbled down the neck of the bottle, and he caught it with his finger and slurped it up.

"Expecting company?" I asked, though I knew well enough he had few friends and none that came around.

"I thought we might drink a toast," he said.

"What for?" I asked.

"Ah, yes," he nodded. "You marched with the Catholic devils. I forgot." His grin was all smugness, and I was sure he hadn't forgotten at all.

"That's got nothing to do with it," I said. "A slaughter's a slaughter." No number of Catholic League dead would cause the souls of Magdeburg to rise from their river-grave. "I've seen too much of death to drink to it, regardless whose it is."

"Not to death, then," Gottschalk amended. "To rest. For the souls of Magdeburg." He raised his glass and downed the drink.

"Aye," I said. "To rest."

The brandy hit the back of my throat and filled my nostrils with fire. My eyes watered and my head gave an involuntary shake. Gottschalk let out a bellowing laugh, then poured us both another.

I can't say when the torpor set in. But by November, I'd all but forgotten that I ever intended to leave. Nuremberg had swallowed me up in its false reality.

Öttingen, meanwhile, seemed impossibly far, both in distance and in spirit. It was a place that had been home to another person, and the plans to go there had been made by someone else—another Josefine. The runt's cough finally cleared up, and I'd managed to set aside enough gulden to be on the road again. Yet I delayed.

Who knows how long I might have gone on like that? That's what grief does—it sticks you in place; the only way to survive it is to go forward, but somehow going forward seems a betrayal to the ones you've lost.

A year later, and the city would welcome the Swedish king. General Wallenstein, newly restored to command of the Emperor's forces, would lay siege to it. Ten thousand of Nuremberg's citizens would perish within her walls, washing away the illusion of peace like sand on the shore. Perhaps I would've been one of them, stuck in that place until starvation or plague took me.

But one evening, as I was cleaning out the surgery, there came a quiet knocking. Gottschalk had gone out to indulge his vices and had left the door unbolted behind him.

Before I could ask who it was, the door opened, and a woman walked through. No, not *a* woman. Eleonore.

She hovered in the open doorway without speaking, and two things were at once very plain to me: her face had somehow grown more beautiful in the intervening years, with soft lines framing her mouth that hadn't been there before. And the second thing: her belly was large with child.

21

Eleonore's War

1631

The corner of Eleonore's lip twitched, but she did not smile. "It's true then," she said only.

"What's true?"

"I heard talk of a woman surgeon, and I felt compelled to investigate. I did not think there could be two in the whole of Germany. It seems I was right."

"Come in," I said, my hand shaking as I set out a chair for her to sit on. "How long has it been? Three years?"

"Nearly four." She stepped inside but did not sit.

"You look well," I said.

She shook her head. "You look…" She couldn't quite manage the lie. "Your color is good."

"There were lean times in the army, but I'm eating better of late."

She exhaled a deep sigh. "The devil with this farce! The two of us, pretending to be old acquaintances and nothing more. You left, Josefine. How could you leave?"

"You were getting married," I said.

"You didn't tell me you were leaving. You didn't write," she continued. "I waited for you at the ruined church. And when you didn't come, I went all the way to Pflaumloch, thinking to drag you from the house and tell you off for being stubborn. But the Jewess there—"

"Rachel," I provided.

"Rachel told me you'd gone back to the war." Eleonore's jaw flared. "I've had years to think on why you did it, but I still don't understand. Were you trying to punish me? Was it that unforgivable that I was getting married? You knew what little choice I had in the matter."

"I didn't do it to punish you."

"Then why didn't you tell me you were going? Why did you let me hear it from a stranger's mouth, standing in the living room of a stranger's house, trying not to fall to pieces?"

"Because I couldn't bear it," I said quietly. "I couldn't say goodbye to you."

"Why not?"

"I might not have been able to go, for one."

"And would that have been such an unbearable thing?"

It was hard for me to remember just then. Somehow, all the immediacy of those intense feelings had faded. Somehow, three years, almost four, had passed, and there had been so many other things—Isidoro and our child and Magdeburg and his death.

"You were getting married," I said again. "You would have been a burgher's wife, and there was no place for me in that. I'd have married some village boy, and we would have been as strangers. I didn't think I could survive it."

"I thought I would never see you again. I didn't think I could survive that."

"I should have at least written to you. I'm sorry."

She looked as if she wanted to say something else, but she didn't speak.

How can I describe the weighty sadness she carried? She wore it like a veil. In Nördlingen, there had long been a quiet melancholy hiding beneath her playfulness. But this was something more. When she smiled, the muscles in her face strained, and she looked like she might break.

"No one's to blame," I said. "For us. I loved you, and I think you loved me, but we both knew it couldn't last. Nördlingen is your home. It was never mine. It would have been foolish for me to stay. Better to let you get on with your life and find mine elsewhere rather than tormenting myself with what I couldn't have."

"Do you really believe that?"

I was no longer sure. "You look well," I said again, and then, gesturing toward her pregnant belly, I added, "Felicitations."

She broke then; she collapsed into the chair sobbing.

I was ill-prepared for her tears. Another time, another place, and it would have been the most natural thing in the world to pull her to me and hold her, to make myself a bulwark against whatever pain it was that now assailed her. But there, in Nuremberg, after so many years apart, I no longer knew what was fitting between us. Instead, I warmed the stove and prepared her an infusion of herbs spiked with warm brandy. Her sobs had already begun to settle by the time I put the drink in her hand.

"Thank you," she said and held it close to her face, letting the steam warm her cheeks. "I'm sorry."

I sat down opposite her. "Will you tell me what happened? Why are you here?"

By and by, she told me everything about how it had gone for her in Nördlingen in the years since I'd left.

In the first place, she'd married the cabinetmaker, Konrad Lehmann. He received his citizenship in the town around that same time, and they moved into a house a few doors from her father's, where Konrad set up his woodworking shop.

There were small difficulties from the off. She admitted to being so anxious on their wedding night that she made herself sick. She wouldn't let her new husband touch her. He was patient, but it was a month before they managed to consummate the marriage. "And then when it happened, it was fine," she confided. "Nothing so dreadful as I'd feared, yet somewhat less than what I'd hoped. Bearable."

For a while, they were more or less contented. Konrad was skilled at his work, and his business quickly grew, even during the war. Love was slow in coming, but they adapted by pieces to each other's ways and habits.

He could be difficult, but not in a cruel way. He spent long hours in his workshop, and often when he was home, his mind was in the shop still, thinking on some unfinished piece that held all of his attention.

Meanwhile, she enjoyed having the run of the house and the ledgers. She found a particular satisfaction in the precise and irrefutable logic of numbers, in seeing the house and the business prosper. "Everything in the right place," she said. "Just so."

Konrad traveled often. Back and forth to Augsburg, to Frankfurt, sometimes as far as Hamburg or Leipzig. His work was in high demand. Sometimes she traveled with him, sometimes not.

"I missed him when he was gone," she admitted. "The house felt large and lonely, and he was good company when you managed to coax him out of his own head." *Was*, she said, taking a sip of her drink. I noted her dip into the past tense but let her continue.

The next year, 1629, was a trying one. Imperial soldiers arrived in Augsburg to enforce the Emperor's Restitution. Before long the soldiers were rowdy and restless, harassing the city's Protestant citizens in the streets. In autumn, Konrad's father was attacked and beaten while he was walking home from the market. Konrad went to Augsburg to look after him. He wanted Eleonore to join him, but her stepmother Margarethe was ill, so she stayed behind.

Konrad was gone three months, returning to Nördlingen only for a brief spell at Christmas.

In February, his father died. Eleonore went down to Augsburg to join her husband. He took the death hard.

"I'd never seen him in so dark a mood. Everything was wrong. His food, the fit of his shirts, the way I looked at him. It wasn't just me. He picked and snapped at his mother too. Neither of us could make him happy."

In April, she discovered she was pregnant. "It felt like a calamity," she confessed. "All I could think of was my mother, how weak and pale she was after she birthed my brother, just before she died."

Still, she did her best to put on a smiling face for Konrad as she told him. She hoped the news would provide some lightness after his father's death. But instead of being joyful, he was full of suspicions; he questioned her about what she'd been up to while he'd been away—who she'd seen, how long she'd known she was pregnant, and why she hadn't told him sooner. All as if trying to catch her in a lie.

"There was no question whose child it was. I've never known another man. I couldn't imagine wanting to," she added.

"I should have gone with him to Augsburg in the first place. That was my mistake. Something changed in him after his father's death. After that, it was him against the rest, and I'd made myself part of 'the rest' when I remained behind."

When they returned to Nördlingen, he took the shop's ledgers away from her. He said she'd made errors, and he would handle them himself.

("I hadn't. They were perfect.")

He demanded that she work on the shop floor where he could keep an eye on her. She had no finesse for the work and cut and burned herself often. Each time, he scolded her for her clumsiness.

"Every day was a fresh battlefield. He thought I was trying to ruin him."

Their son was born in November 1630. They named him Georg Peter after both their fathers. "I was glad for a boy," she said. "I thought a boy would put all his suspicions to rest. I thought he would be content. For a while, he was. He was beside himself with pride."

But the peace didn't last. She soon caught him staring at the child, studying his every feature.

"He'd remark that his nose was rather large, or his eyes—no one in his family had that color eyes. I told him that a baby's eye color can change, and his nose was a normal size. Everyone said how much he resembled his father, but Konrad wouldn't have it. One day it was the shape of his mouth, the next his hair color. There was always some fault. He said he should divorce me for being unfaithful. The thought terrified me. I begged him not to."

She lurched forward with a strangled cry, hugging her middle. I laid my hand on her knee, and she clutched it tight. She settled herself a moment later. "I'm sorry," she said. "I'm sorry."

The infant Georg was sweet-tempered by day, but his nights were long episodes of wailing interrupted by short bouts of sleep. Konrad earned good money, but even so they couldn't afford a nurse to sit up with the child, so it fell on Eleonore to rise with him.

"I was bone tired, Fi. I felt my soul draining out of me, like a leaky pitcher. One night, I ..." The words caught in her throat. "I didn't wake up. I didn't hear him."

The next morning, she found her son lifeless in his bed.

"Oh, Eleonore..."

She paused, and I was left groping for words to fill the silence. In the end, I settled for holding her hand. When she resumed, her gaze was fixed not on me, but on the stove on the far wall.

"It was *his* doing." Her voice was a whisper, but she spoke with conviction. "I saw how he looked at him, at our son. The terrible thing is, he was right. Oh, Georg was his son, there could be no doubt of that, but about me? He was right. I didn't love him. I hadn't betrayed him, but I was not a good wife. In my heart, I was not faithful."

"That's no justification."

She turned to me, and the hurt in her eyes reached out and pierced me in the heart. "Isn't it?"

Piece by halting piece, she went on to tell how she found the boy, pausing to linger on the sorts of trifling details only a mother might remember. The way his small hand rested on his chest, how perfectly the blanket was tucked beneath it, unnatural for a child who slept as fitfully as her son. She screamed, and Konrad rushed in. Immediately he started berating her for not waking up in the night to check on the boy.

"How would he know?" she asked. "How could he know I didn't wake up?"

She asked Konrad if he'd done it, if he'd killed the boy. He warned her to shut up, but she was out of her mind by then. He struck her, again and again, until she tasted her own blood. Her stepmother Margarethe found her and the boy later that day and fetched the surgeon. Eleonore couldn't prove Georg's death had been anything other than an accident. But Margarethe insisted on taking her out of the city. They left for Nuremberg the next day.

Eleonore broke off her account, and her hand wandered to her belly. "That was five months ago. I didn't know..." Her voice cracked.

"What will you do?"

There was no hesitation in her answer. "I'm divorcing him. After the baby's born. That much is settled. The city council will not refuse me. The surgeon will testify to how badly bruised I was, and so will Margarethe. The time I spend here in Nuremberg will count toward the separation period."

"Konrad won't let you go lightly if you have his child."

Her lip trembled. "Yes, I know. That's why no one will know of it. I'm giving it to the church."

"The church? Are you sure?"

Eleonore tugged her hand free of mine and stood. "Spare me your judgments. I needed you. I don't care what else we were to each other, you were my truest friend, and I needed you."

"I'm sorry," I whispered.

"It's the only way, Fi. I can't risk Konrad knowing. I can't risk what he might do."

"It's no easy thing to be an orphan in this world."

"I know. But what other choice is there? Margarethe's too old for childbearing, and if she returns with a baby, everyone will suspect, including Konrad. My aunt and uncle are older still, and she's half-blind. They raised eight children of their own. Neither of them is in fit shape to raise another. The church is the only option."

Listening to her, she seemed sure enough of her chosen course. But when she looked at me, her gaze was searching, pleading.

Eleonore lingered till her nerves settled, and then I offered to walk with her back to her aunt and uncle's house. She looped her arm through mine as we walked, holding me close.

Since Isidoro's death, I'd been cocooned in a kind of numbness, but her touch stirred feeling in those deadened parts of me once more. The ache that I'd once been so sure was love welled deep in my gut and spread through my limbs—not a shout, as it once was, but more than a whisper.

The runt, too, seemed to come alive in her presence. He loped alongside us, looking more spirited than he had in months. Her mood brightened as he turned his good eye on her, tail wagging.

By and by, the corner of her lip turned upward in a smile, the old glint returned to her eyes, and she chuckled to herself.

I gave her an inquiring look.

"Nuremberg, remember?" she said.

I'd not forgotten. How many times had we played that game in the aftermath of our passion in the ruin of the old church? Running away together, settling down somewhere new.

"It's a little different than we imagined, isn't it?"

She gave my arm a squeeze. "I don't know. I rather imagined us walking arm in arm, just like this. I like it here. It's not so small as Nördlingen, where everybody knows your business. We can be whoever we want."

"And who do you want to be?"

"I think I'd like to run my own shop."

"What sort of shop?"

"Cloth, I suppose. Margarthe's taught me everything she knows. But it hardly matters. I could just as well see myself managing your surgery. Keeping your books in order; keeping it well-stocked and at a good price. I've become quite good at haggling. The sellers at the Pentecost Fair are all intimidated by me." She caught herself then. "Not that I'm saying—it's just a fantasy. I know we're... you're married now, and—"

I laughed. "Where did you hear I was married?"

"Everyone calls you Mrs. Gottschalk."

"Ah. That's a business arrangement, nothing more. I pay Gottschalk for the use of his name, but he sleeps in the backroom downstairs. I *was* married, but that good man's four months dead in the ground now, God rest him."

"I'm sorry to hear it. But he *was* good, this husband of yours? Truly?"

"I sometimes fear he was all the goodness that was left."

It was my turn to relate all that had happened since I'd left Nördlingen. When I told her about mine and Isidoro's wedding, she broke into my story with a giggle. "I'm sorry," she said. "It's just—of course you would end up marrying a priest."

"Of course? What do you mean by that?"

"Fi, you are the most contrary, willful person I know. I don't think you'd ever be happy with someone you were allowed to be with. I mean it admiringly, truly. I'm wildly jealous of you for it. I always have been. That's the trouble between us, isn't it? Each of us wanting what the other has, resenting each other for it as much as we love each other for it, maybe even a little bit more."

"I don't resent you."

"You don't? I was so angry when you left without telling me; partly because I wished it had been me. I've always envied your freedom, but I'm too much a coward. I could never have left, no matter how much I wanted to."

"You're here now," I said.

"Yes," she said with a slow nod. "I suppose I am. But I interrupted you. Please, tell me about this priest of yours."

"He was a strange sort of priest. He came to the war looking for goodness, of all things. He would've been better served staying in a monastery somewhere, contemplating God, but he loved the world too much for that. For some reason, he loved me too."

I felt the pressure of fresh tears building behind my eyes. My voice faltered.

There were times in the army when our marches took us through a wild, storm-swept country, where the roads were worn away and our feet stuck in the mud up to the ankle. The land itself fought us, dragging us half as far back with each step, and when we finally crested one hill, another, yet larger hill lay just ahead.

It was four months since Isidoro's death. Four months I'd been trudging up that hill with no sign of reaching the top. As I told Eleonore about him, I felt myself slip. Down and down I slid, unable to find solid footing on the treacherous earth.

She wrapped her arm around my waist and caught me.

Outside her aunt and uncle's house, we embraced. The runt, too, pawed at us until she knelt to scratch behind his ears. When she stood again, she reached out, unthinkingly, to lay a hand on my cheek.

"I'm sorry for leaving," I said. "I was jealous back then, it's true. I was angry. But not at you, I don't think. You were right enough; one of us would have had to get married eventually."

"Tell me I'll see you again and all will be forgiven," she said.

"You know where to find me."

"Promise?"

"Aye. Promise."

Then she disappeared into the house, and I went back to Gottschalk's.

When I returned to the surgery, Gottschalk was there. He couldn't have been back long, for the door was still swinging slightly on its hinge when I arrived, and he was stumbling around the room, rifling through cabinets, all the while clutching his nose with his left hand. Blood seeped between the fingers.

"What have you done this time?" I asked him.

"What business is it of yours? And where the devil were you? Don't I pay you to run the surgery while I'm out?"

"It was closing time. No one else was coming. And you don't pay me for anything. I take my pay from the patients I operate on and give you your share. Now, will you let me look at your nose, or are you going to go on bleeding everywhere and making a mess?"

He grunted and lowered his hand. As I'd suspected, his nose was broken. I instructed him to sit down while I prepared a poultice and soaked a bandage in vinegar water. He was a surly patient, and when I put pressure on the injury, he made as if to bite me.

"Very well. Do it yourself." I threw the bandage down in exasperation.

"No, no, I'm sorry. It was reflex. I'll do better. I just need a drink."

"You've had several drinks, from the smell of you."

He reached for a bottle anyway. He took a long draught, then tilted his head back and stared at the ceiling, exhaling. If I hadn't known him to be a Godless heathen, I might have thought he was praying.

"All right then," he said.

I applied the poultice and wrapped the bandage.

"Listen," he said when I'd finished. "I need to borrow—"

"No."

"—a few gulden," he pressed on. "I'll repay you. The next patient that comes in here, whatever their complaint, you can keep the whole fee."

"No, you'll get your half, just as we've agreed. I know better than to have you in debt to me."

"Come now." He stood up and held his arms out. "What's a little pocket money between friends?"

I cleared away the scraps of my work and wiped his bloody fingerprints from the cabinet doors. "It's not pocket money, and we're not friends."

"Just a few gulden, to tide me over till the end of the week." He tried to smile, but the action caused him pain, and he winced.

"My money's too precious to be lending to the likes of you."

"Do you want to see me in ruins? Is that it? Haven't I been kind to you?"

"You've been a grudging host and an unreliable business partner." I moved to the other side of the room, putting the chair between us.

"I took you and your mongrel dog in when no one else would!" His voice was raised.

"You hired me for a maid, and now I do half your surgeries."

"Ungrateful bitch!" He stalked toward me. The chair scraped against the floor as he brushed past it.

My back was against the wall. I raised a hand. "You remember our arrangement. If you touch me, I'll take my skills elsewhere. Don't think I won't. Without me here, you won't make even half the gulden you gamble away."

He stopped then, close enough for me to smell the brandy on his breath. "Damn you, woman," he hissed. "Damn you." Then he stormed off to the backroom and slammed the door behind him. The jars on the shelves rung for seconds after.

My nerves still rattling, I climbed the stairs to my room. The runt labored up after me, whining. I checked the bedpost, where I kept my money hidden away. It was all still there. Then I jammed a chair in front of my door for security.

I fell asleep that night clutching the lock of Isidoro's hair I kept pressed between the pages of his prayerbook. I thought it might still hold his scent, but it smelled only of paper.

It's unfair, I maintain. God has all the saints that ever lived in Heaven to attend on him, but I had only Isidoro. How was it that God took my fool of a priest to himself but left the likes of Gottschalk and Konrad Lehmann to live and torment us?

22

Death and Birth

1631-1632

Gottschalk disappeared a few days later. I'd been making my rounds through the market to restock our shelves, and when I came back, I found the surgery unlocked and the door to my room wide open.

Stalks of straw were strewn all over the floor, spilling from a foot-long tear in the mattress. The bed itself was overturned, and several of the floorboards had been pulled up in haste. The lockbox where I kept the keepsakes from my father and Isidoro had been pried open and lay empty in the middle of the floor.

My first confused thought on seeing the mess was that I didn't remember leaving the room in such disorder when I left it. Only with grudging slowness did I understand what had happened, that I'd been robbed.

A queasy feeling came over me. I stumbled back, catching myself on the stair rail. I descended the stairs, rather than look on that mess any longer. Rather than stare at the empty box and think on what was no longer in it: my father's rosary, Isidoro's pipe, his prayerbook, the locks of his hair.

Downstairs, I banged on the door to Gottschalk's room, but there came no answer. I opened it, but the room was empty. He was gone.

In the main room, I searched through the glass bottles piled beside the stove until I found one with liquid still in it. I uncorked it and drank until I no longer felt the burning in my throat. Only then did I muster the courage to ascend the stairs again.

The room wasn't in so bad a shape as it first appeared. On lifting the discarded mattress casing, I found Isidoro's prayerbook with the lock of his hair still tucked safely inside. I was able to recover most of the straw from the mattress and sew the tear closed with about an hour's work. The bedframe was broken beyond hope, but in his clumsy search, Gottschalk had somehow missed the hollow post where I'd hidden my gulden. All that trouble, and all he'd managed to take were my spare dresses, Isidoro's tobacco pipe, and my father's rosary.

I removed my money from the broken bedframe and dragged it to the top of the stairs. With a shove, I sent it careening down. It thudded between the railing and the wall before landing in a splintered heap at the bottom. I left it there, with a mind to have Gottschalk clean it up when he returned.

But Gottschalk did not return. As the sun came up the next morning, I cleared away the broken bedframe myself, taking a bone saw to the rails and posts and stacking them by the fireplace for fuel. In the afternoon, I opened the surgery and waited. A few of Gottschalk's regulars came for their shave, but I was no barber, so I turned them away.

That day passed and another and still another, until it'd been a whole week, and Gottschalk still hadn't returned. I took to lying on his behalf, saying he'd just gone out to purchase this or that sundry thing.

The woman who did his washing came to call, and I paid her. The distiller who brewed his brandy came to call, and I paid him, though he was none too happy when I told him there was not an order that week. The landlord came to call, and I noticed that he winced and rubbed his jaw as he spoke. I asked him what the trouble was, and he said he had a rotten tooth. I removed it for him, and in exchange he agreed to take just one month's rent and wait for Gottschalk's return to claim the rest.

Bit by bit, the money I'd saved went to paying Gottschalk's debts. He'd managed to rob me after all.

When the second week turned over, and the man was still absent, I picked up his scissors and his razor and tried my hand at barbering. I thought it must be simple enough, if the likes of Gottschalk could manage it, but I soon learned I had no taste for it.

In surgery no one tries to strike up a conversation while you work, nor do they make suggestions, telling you to cut a little deeper there, or make the stitches closer together here. But a man hangs a great deal upon the appearance of his beard, and in the meantime, he expects to be able to ramble on about everything that troubles him, while you listen and agree.

They complained of their wives most of all. One spent all her husband's money. Another was an unrepentant gossip. Another harangued her man continuously, such that he had no peace at home. Money troubles had forced them to move to their third set of apartments that year and each one, she complained, was smaller and draftier than the last.

"She was beautiful once. Now she's an ever-present thorn in my side. Does nothing but moan about her gout and accuse me of gambling away all our money. I only gamble to get away from her screeching."

"Colder temperatures can cause gout to flare," I said, drawing the razor up his neck with a steady hand.

By and by, I put Gottschalk behind me. He was gone, God alone knew where, and good riddance to him. I continued to run his surgery, and I made good money keeping all my earnings, though his creditors turned up as regular as the snows and had to be bought off, a little at a time.

One Sunday in early January, I answered the door expecting to encounter the landlord or the miller or the apothecary. It was none of those three, but a member of the city watch.

Eleonore was with me, as had become her habit. She came direct after the Sunday service, bearing a basket stuffed full with sausages and pork belly and brown bread, and spent the afternoon making sense of Gottschalk's books while I took stock of the surgery.

The watchman was so tall he had to duck to enter. Once inside, he doffed his hat and smoothed his mustache.

"Mrs. Gottschalk?" he addressed me.

"According to whom?" I asked in reply.

"You are the woman who has been living with Melchior Gottschalk, the barber-surgeon who rents these premises, are you not?"

"Aye," I said. "As his assistant and housekeeper. Not his wife."

The watchman coughed into his fist. "My apologies for the error. Have you seen him of late?"

"Why do you ask? Does he owe you money?"

"I'll ask again, have you seen him of late?"

"Again, I'll ask, what business is it of yours?" By then I was growing ill-tempered with the watchman's vague questioning.

"There's been a body discovered in the river. Washed up by the rising waters from the snow and rain."

Eleonore inhaled sharply.

My chest grew tight. Gottschalk was a surly drunk, a wastrel, and a thief. Yet I wondered if I oughtn't to have made more of an effort to find him when he disappeared.

"You're telling me this body you found is Gottschalk's?"

"It's only a suspicion," the watchman was saying. "The state of the body... we've not been able to confirm it."

"Very well. Take me to him." I pulled on my boots. Eleonore brought me my shawl.

The watchman shook his head. "It's not a sight for a fair woman such as yourself. Better if you can tell me when last it was you saw him and anything that might identify him. How he was dressed, what he might have been carrying."

"I've seen dead aplenty. Take me to him."

Seeing that I wouldn't be budged, the watchman donned his hat and relented. Behind me, Eleonore pulled on her own boots and cloak. The watchman looked her over, at the fine stitching of her cloak and the round belly peeking out from under it, and sighed.

It was a difficult trudge downhill toward the river. Where there were paving stones, the way was slick. Where there was only wood, the boards were covered over with mud and threatened to break apart beneath us. The watchman offered Eleonore his hand, but she refused it.

He led us to a spot near the Hangman's Bridge, where the rainwater and melting snow had churned up the body and trapped it against the bridge's supports. A boatman rowing by had spied the body and brought it ashore, where it yet lay as we approached, giving off a boggy odor.

"Try not to breathe it in," the watchman warned, a little too late.

I covered my mouth and nose with my shawl. Eleonore made a gagging sound.

Best not to describe the state of the poor man's body. Let's say that it's the fate that awaits all of us, one way or the other, and leave it at that. Best, in fact, not to think of it as being Gottschalk at all.

Oh, but that's a rank lie! The priests would have it that our souls are the only part that matters, but without a body, what's a soul? If it were anything at all, then Isidoro would still be here with me, chiding me, no doubt, for all the ways I've done ill in my descriptions of Gottschalk.

He was a drunk and a gambler, it's true. But he also healed the sick and brought comfort to the dying on more than one occasion. He was a listening ear to each of the men who came to him for their shaves. He took me in, though he couldn't afford the help. He wasn't a good man, yet there was goodness in him. For that alone, he deserved a better death.

I stooped beside the remains to get a closer look. His face could hardly be recognized, but for the unhealed break in his nose. His overcoat was in tatters and stained with river mud, but I flipped the breast open and found a leather purse still tied to his belt. I reached in and drew out a rosary of amber beads and a clay tobacco pipe.

"Aye, it's him," I said, stepping back with a cough. "It's Gottschalk."

"You're sure of it?" the watchman asked.

I showed him the rosary and the pipe. "He stole these from me before he ran off. No doubt he was hoping he could sell them."

"When was that?"

"November."

"You didn't think to report him missing?"

"He was deep in debt. I thought he didn't want to be found."

The watchman nodded. "He was in debt? Did he ever talk about giving back God's most precious gift?"

"You mean killing himself?" I was incredulous. "No, Gottschalk was many things, but he wasn't the despairing kind."

"My apologies. I had to ask."

"So," I asked him. "Do you have any notion how he ended up in the river?"

"I suppose he slipped. Everyone who knew him has said he had a fondness for the bottle." He shrugged. "Without any witnesses, who can say?"

"Might he have been killed?"

"He might have, but if it happened in November, like you say, there's little chance of finding out who did the cruel deed. Anyway, it's not worth the trouble."

I walked back toward Eleonore. She held a gloved hand over her mouth and nose, but she'd not taken her eyes off the body.

"What will happen to him?" she asked.

I shrugged. "He had no money. It'll be a pauper's burial, most likely."

She nodded somberly.

The air was filled with light mist as we trudged back up the hill to the surgery.

"And how are you bearing up?" she asked once we were back inside the cold, dark room.

I busied myself with starting a fire. "Fine, only—"

My mind rocked. Gottschalk was dead. No longer "missing," no longer "stepped out for a drink and yet to return." The bastard had gone off into the night and fallen into the river and drowned.

"What is it?" Eleonore interjected into my thoughts.

"Everything's in his name. His surgery, his tools, his medicine. I wasn't his partner. I wasn't his wife. His creditors will take everything." I laughed bitterly. "When his landlord finds out, I'll be homeless."

Eleonore draped her cloak in front of the fire and stared thoughtfully into the flame, chewing on her bottom lip. When she spoke again, her eyes shone with familiar mischief. "Not until tomorrow. That's plenty of time." She cast her gaze about the shelves. "Which of these things has any value?"

"You're a criminal," I laughed.

"He owed you money, didn't he?"

For the next hours, until the sun set, we tore through Gottschalk's shelves, sifting through pots of medicine, mildewed books, and jars stoppered with decaying corks, searching anything of worth. Gottschalk had doubtless sold off his most valuable items long ago to keep his creditors at bay, but there were still some treasures to be found.

Secreted behind a jar of leeches, I found a pot of fragrant saffron. In another box, we found assorted gems for sundry medicinal purposes. On the highest shelf, which I had to climb to reach, was a leatherbound book. The pages were thick and smooth, and the ink smelled faintly sweet, but the printing was in an unfamiliar, flowing script.

"Hebrew?" Eleonore guessed.

I shook my head. Salomon and Rachel had a Bible printed in Hebrew, and the characters bore little resemblance. "Arabic, I think."

"Did Gottschalk know Arabic?"

Cobwebs clung to the pages. "Not likely."

"Perhaps it was a gift."

It was hard to imagine Gottschalk receiving a gift, especially one so dear. But then, I didn't know the man really, only his habits. And of those, only the ones he'd had since I met him, which didn't amount to much when weighed against a whole lifetime.

By the time we'd finished plundering Gottschalk's stores, we'd assembled a small trove of items. Eleonore piled them into her basket. We agreed it was for the best if she used her uncle's connections to sell them and gave me the money afterward. The book I kept, thinking it might be of interest to Salomon if ever I made it back to Pflaumloch.

We quickly set the shelves back in order, so that no one would have cause to suspect anything missing, and then we both dressed to leave.

"Where will you go?" she asked.

"The inn, I suppose."

"No, not the inn. Come with me."

"To your aunt and uncle's house?"

"Please. Just till you find your feet again. I don't care for the thought of you sleeping on the floor of some dingy inn. My aunt and uncle are good Christians. They won't turn you away."

"Very well," I relented, "But only if you're certain it will be no trouble."

Eleonore's aunt and uncle lived in a stately stone house on the Burgstrasse, three floors high with glass windows and a gabled roof.

Her uncle was a quiet man with trembling, spotted hands and a hitch in his gait. He walked with his arm looped through his wife's for support. That woman was a thinner, frailer version of Eleonore's stepmother. Her eyes were glazed over and she relied on her husband to lead her from room to room.

They were warm hosts, and Eleonore's stepmother was especially doting. Eleonore explained my circumstances, although she gave the truth her own embellishment. In her version of the story, it was Gottschalk who'd taken advantage of me, stealing a poor widow's small inheritance and trapping her in his debt.

They had a servant bring me wine while another drew me a bath. Margarethe laid out a fresh shift on the guest bed. "You poor brave woman," she clucked. "You're well rid of that awful man. Don't you worry about a thing. We'll see you on your feet."

A servant scooped embers from the stove and filled a round metal pan, which she slid beneath the bedcovers. "What the devil is that for?" I asked.

"For warming the bed, Mrs.," she said.

The runt sought out a warm spot near the stove and curled up there with a contented snort.

Eleonore came into the room as I was dressing. Her shift flowed around her curved form, and the candles painted her face with golden light.

"Thank you," I said. "This is far better than the inn."

"See," she said. "I told you it would be no trouble."

She drew down the blankets and slipped into the bed. "Come," she said, patting at the space beside her.

I hesitated. "We're not the same people we once were."

"No, we're not. But we're still friends, aren't we? Please," she said. "Just to sleep."

"Just to sleep," I repeated.

My weary body sank into the down-stuffed mattress. Eleonore rested her head next to mine, filling my nostrils with the scent of lavender, vinegar, and gall. There was another scent besides, one I smelled mainly when I closed my eyes: wildflowers and honey in a candlemaker's shop.

She guided my hand to her belly, where the baby stirred restlessly.

"It'll be ready soon," I said.

"Yes, soon," she agreed.

Her eyes were full of pleading. "You'll help me, won't you?"

"Yes, of course."

"Thank you," she murmured as her eyelids drooped shut.

It was the twenty-seventh of January by the Protestant calendar, the sixth of February by the Pope's, when Eleonore's pangs began. We'd been ready for it, but even then we were surprised by the strength and intensity of her labors. Her waters broke almost immediately. She'd only just dressed for the day, but already I was helping her back into bed and undoing her bodice so that she might breathe and push when the time came.

Her stepmother sent for the midwife, but I'd been present for many such births in the Tross, and I knew this child would not wait. I set to work heating water and preparing warm rags and a poultice of herbs. I also readied my needle and thread, should there be the need.

For the first hour, Eleonore gritted her teeth and grunted through the pain, but as she entered the second, her cries loosed from her with increasing ferocity, and she gripped the sleeve of my blouse until her knuckles turned white.

"Please," she said between cries. "Please, Fi, I don't want to die. Don't let me die."

"Hush now. You're not going to die. Breathe slowly." I brought Eleonore's head to rest against my breast and ran my fingers through her hair, whispering encouragements all the while. But the fear that gripped her was terrible, and even though she made good progress, she continued to cling to me, pleading for her life.

Shortly into the third hour, the baby began to crown.

By then, I'd seen so many babies birthed that I'd ceased to see anything remarkable in it. Being born was no guarantee of survival, in any case. But when Eleonore gave the final push, and the child, a girl, slid into my hands, just as natural as if that was what they'd been built for all along, when I wiped her clean and she screwed up her face and let out that first fragile wail, when she opened her eyes to take in the world, and they were just like Eleonore's—brown and pierced with flecks of golden light—I'd have sworn I heard Isidoro's voice in my ear: *A new life, Josefine. Isn't it a miracle?*

Eleonore lay on the bed when her exertions were finished, breathing heavily, her skin pale and beaded with sweat. Blood blossomed across the bedsheets between her legs, and she moaned.

"There now," I said to her. "It's done. You've done it. She's a healthy one."

I swaddled the girl and laid her in a basket by the bedside prepared specially for the purpose. Then I went to work stopping the flow of blood.

To my great relief, the bleeding proved superficial, and with the poultice and the warm rags I was able to stanch its flow. Eleonore gave another cry, and with the pangs that followed, she passed the afterbirth.

I cleared everything away and propped her up with cushions behind her back. She looked uncertain as I placed the child in her arms.

The baby's mouth made searching sucking movements, so Eleonore took out her breast and began to nurse. It was then she started weeping.

I set the basin of water and dirty rags aside and climbed into the bed beside her. She rested her head on my shoulder while shuddering sobs rippled through her body. Now and again, she tried to speak, but I shushed her and held her. If anyone ought to be able to weep without explanation, it's a woman who's just given birth.

The infant began to cry too, so I took her and rocked her gently. In time, she settled and searched for the breast once more. Eleonore had just calmed beside me, and not wishing to start her weeping again, I undid the laces of my bodice and let the child suckle at my own teat. I had no milk to give her, but for the moment, the girl was content.

"Let me take her," I said then. The words tumbled out of me, taking me by surprise. But as soon as I uttered them, I knew I meant them.

"What?" Eleonore asked.

"Don't give her to the church, to be raised as an orphan. Let me take her."

"Fi, please, don't," she pleaded. "Only say such a thing if you mean it."

"I do mean it."

"How will you raise her on your own?"

"I won't be on my own. I'll take her back to Pflaumloch. I'll beg Rachel and Salomon's forgiveness if I have to. They won't turn their backs on a child." I added: "You could visit, too, from time to time. You could see for yourself how she's growing up and chide me for all the ways I'll ruin her."

"But Konrad…"

"I'm a stranger to him. What reason would he have to notice or care?"

She fell quiet, and I worried she'd refuse. At last, she said, "Very well. But only if you're sure."

"Aye," I said, stroking a tuft of the girl's wispy brown hair, soft as a flower's petal. "Let me take her."

Part 3

Mother

23

Wonderful, Difficult Things

1632

Some parents go mad by pieces, but I went mad all at once, the moment I laid eyes on her, on my daughter. I didn't know the first thing about rearing a child. I knew even less of how it would consume me. That's what love does: it digs a little hollow for itself in your soul, and from then on, you're not you anymore—at least, not only.

I understand my own parents better now. My father's stubborn determination to be everything for me, even after it was clear that he could never be enough. My mother's need to keep me working at her side, so she could teach me all she knew in the short time she had left. I even begin to understand why they broke.

How ill-equipped for mothering I was! In the first place, the child was ever hungry for milk, but I had none to give. I spent the days chewing on fennel and lucerne and choking down potions brewed with each. Whenever the child cried out, I put her to my breast, until my teats were sore and cracked.

Eleonore helped with feeding while we waited for my milk to come in. The child thrived with her, and a flickering, jealous fear kindled within me each time I saw them together.

"Well, now, hasn't she been at it long enough?" I'd snap.

"She's still suckling," Eleonore said, ever patient.

"Aye, and then she'll fill herself up, and she won't try with me. No wonder my milk won't come in."

"Your milk won't come in because you storm about all day and tie yourself up in knots with worry. You need to be at ease."

"How can I be at ease when I can't feed her?"

"And what will happen if you can't feed her?" she asked.

"She'll starve."

"You won't allow that to happen. You'll feed her pap, and she'll grow strong just the same."

"Your stepmother and aunt will force you to give her to the church."

Both her aunt and her stepmother had been taken aback when Eleonore told them I would raise the child. They were still less pleased when they learned that I had no intention of having her baptized.

It seemed to me then as now that we'd all suffered enough grief on account of our baptisms. So long as the child was healthy, I hoped to spare her the trouble of being called Protestant or Catholic, Christian or Jew. Eleonore's aunt and stepmother didn't see the matter my way.

"It's not their choice who I give her to," Eleonore said. "It's mine."

I knelt beside her as she nursed, laying my head on her knee. "I just wanted to be her mother."

Eleonore stroked my hair. "You are. You clean her and bathe her, and she goes to sleep in your arms quicker than for anyone else. Just the other day, Margarethe remarked how she searches for the sound of your voice when you enter a room. Think on how many children take their feedings from women who aren't their mothers, and don't let it weigh so heavily on you."

I looked up at her. "An easy thing, coming from you. You have no such troubles. You're her true mother."

"No. I'm her wet-nurse. Now, stand up."

I did as she asked, and she rose from the chair, withdrawing her breast from the child's mouth. The infant fussed.

"Take the chair," Eleonore commanded. "And don't hunch yourself so. Be at ease."

She handed me the child, and I put her to my breast.

"Georg didn't take to the breast at first. And when he did, he seemed to hardly get anything from it. He was always hungry, always dissatisfied. Margarethe hired a nurse, and she showed me the ways to cajole him to feed properly. It's just one thing, Fi."

"A rather large thing, if you ask me," I said.

"But not the whole of it."

A few days later, my milk came in. Just a few drops at first, and then a trickle. But the more the child fed, the more I was able to give her.

What did I know of being a mother? My own mother hadn't lived long enough to instruct me, and the only advice I had from Eleonore's family came from her aunt, who'd raised eight children, but with the help of half as many servants.

Most of what I knew I'd learned from the women in the Tross. If a child cried too much or too little, either could be a sign of an ill temperament. If they were left too long swaddled, they might grow up lame. Keep the child close at all times and you'd spoil it, but leaving it too long in its basket could be a sign of neglect. The younger children in the Tross were not raised singly, but in groups, passed from woman to woman as needed. The older ones fended for themselves and helped look after the young ones.

But I was alone when I set out with my daughter for Öttingen at the end of February. I had no husband, no servants, no army of women to help me. Eleonore and I agreed that I should go ahead of her, so as not to arouse Konrad's suspicions. She would remain in Nuremberg until she'd healed from the birth and her milk had dried up.

As we made our farewells, she said, "Remember, Fi. The child's moods follow the mother. Don't fret, and you'll get on fine." Sensible advice, even if I had a poor time following it.

The child and I rode in the back of a poulterer's wagon, squeezed between crates of chickens, with the runt at our feet. I'd brought a basket with me for laying the girl in, but each time I set her down, she gave a heartrending wail. For fear of seeming over-indulgent, I tried to let her cry until she settled herself, but I couldn't bear the sound, and neither could the chickens. So, in the end I kept her resting almost the whole way on my chest.

At a waystation, the driver stopped to water his animals, and I took the girl down to the stream to clean her. As I unwound her blanket, I saw that her skin had turned rose-red and mottled. My imagination raced ahead of my sense, and I cried out in panic.

The driver rushed over to me.

"Something's wrong with her," I cried.

"Show me," he said. I held her out so he could see, and he broke into laughter.

"I don't see what's so funny."

"Nothing's wrong with her. She's been in her blankets too long. That's all."

I looked again and saw he was right. The child was sweating, but not feverish, and the rosy splotches on her skin bore none of the markers of any disease. She was, simply, hot. Though it was yet winter, I'd been holding her swaddled beneath my cloak for hours under the warm sun. I left her unwrapped a while and dabbed a few drops of cool water on her face to lower her temperature.

The driver was still chuckling to himself when I climbed back into the wagon.

The days it would take us to reach Öttingen stretched out before me. The nights, even more so. All in all, she was a sweet-tempered baby, but she woke often for feeding, somehow timing her cries to the very moment sleep took hold of me.

During those restless hours, I went over all the things I planned to say to Rachel and Salomon when I saw them again. I would tell them how wrong I'd been, and how impossible it was for me to repay them all I owed them, but I would promise to try anyway. Then I'd take out the book I'd found among Gottschalk's things and offer it to Salomon. He'd sworn not to speak to me again if I left, and I wouldn't ask him to take back his oath, just to give me the chance to prove my sincerity.

More than anyone, I longed to see Rachel again. She could set me on the right way; she would know how to guide me through this mad thing I'd decided to do.

I parted with the driver at Nördlingen. From there, I went by foot to Pflaumloch.

It was just after midday when I arrived in the village, climbing the low hill to the place where Jewish houses stood in a neat little round. It was a Sunday, and everything was still.

But it was the wrong sort of stillness. All was dark. No sounds of work or play echoed in the yard. No smoke curled from the chimney. The garden Rachel had kept with such care, expanding it row by row each year, was overgrown. Even the winter herbs were dead.

I knocked on their door, and it drifted open. The latch had broken away from the jamb. Inside, the cupboards were ajar, the tables and chairs overturned, and the brick stove was thick with dust and ash. It looked as if it hadn't held a fire in a season. Two meager logs rested beside it. There was a hook in the ceiling where the Sabbath lamp once hung, but the lamp was gone.

I struggled to make sense of the sight. Everything was in disarray, but nothing was broken. There was no blood, no sign of violence. I rushed upstairs to the bedrooms, calling their names, but found the rooms cold and empty. In one, a cat hissed, startling me, before leaping out of an open window onto a neighboring tree branch.

With the rest of the houses, it was the same. All abandoned, all stripped bare of anything of value.

The child grew restless and hungry. I set a chair upright in Rachel and Salomon's kitchen and began to nurse. The baby's eyelids drooped with contentment as she suckled, ignorant of all troubles. How I envied her!

When she was finished eating, I went back down the hill to the Christian part of the village. There, too, much had changed. For every house where a candle burned, two more sat dark, including the one belonging to the Bauers, the old Catholic couple who'd taken me in years before.

My heart cracked on seeing it. I crumpled into the dirt beside the village well. All those miles, only to arrive at nowhere. I couldn't hold back tears any longer. The child fussed in my arms.

What could I do? Go back up the hill, start a fire in Salomon and Rachel's stove and live there until someone drove me out? Or go to Nördlingen and pray that someone in that indifferent city would take me in? I thought I might rather go all the way back to Nuremberg.

A family passed by on their way home from church. I scrambled to my feet, brushing the tears from my cheeks, and asked them what had become of the Jews.

"All left," the husband answered. "A year or two ago, not longer. Looking to escape the war."

"Where did they go?"

"Sundry places. Are you seeking someone in particular?"

"Aye. The physician, Salomon Frankfurt. Do you know him?"

"He and his family went to the city," the man said.

"The city? You mean Frankfurt?"

He shook his head. "Nördlingen."

"Jews aren't permitted in Nördlingen," I said, perplexed.

The man shrugged and sniffed the air. "Well, there are Jews in Nördlingen now."

The city moved lazily around me as I entered. It was Sunday, and the church service had ended, and though there was much to do, no one was in any hurry to do it. The soldiers were Protestant now, thanks to the Swedish king, but apart from that it was the same place I remembered it being, close and busy and to a stranger, indifferent as the stream is to the person drowning in it.

The child slumbered in my arms, which by then were sore from carrying her, but I breathed deeply and assured myself it would not be much farther now. I didn't know whether I could trust the villager's word, but I couldn't then contemplate the alternative. I asked directions of the first people I met, and they directed me toward a cluster of buildings near the western wall.

The windows in that quarter were open, releasing the scent of warm pastry into the lane. I was reminded that I'd not eaten that day.

The directions I'd received led to a small door in narrow alley behind a butcher's shop. The door stuck in the jamb and shuddered when I finally managed to wrench it open. Inside, the staircase was cool and dark. I climbed to the third floor, pausing at each landing for the runt to lumber up behind me, and knocked.

Rachel answered. What a sight she was—plump and ruddy with health, not so different from when I'd left her. Just a little more gray in her hair. What a sight I must've been—caked with the dust of the road, face red and stained with tears, and all while holding a baby not much more than a month old.

She reached for my arm, groping at it as if to convince herself that her eyes were not liars.

"Praise God," she said at last. Then she pulled me in tight, until the baby squirmed. "Praise God for bringing you back to us."

She ushered me into the little set of apartments and ordered me to sit down and take food. As she made up my plate, she went right on asking where I'd been, and how I was doing, and did I have any trouble finding them?

Finally, she looked at the baby, stirring in the crook of my arm. "And who is this then?"

"Magdalena." There'd been no question of the name. He'd chosen it that hopeful winter, two years before. "My daughter."

"A beautiful name," she said. "And a beautiful little girl. You've done well." Rachel moved around the small kitchen, taking down a bowl and mixing together flour and butter. I laid Magdalena in her basket on the floor and rose to help her.

"That's not necessary," she said.

"Please," I said. "I've come back to you empty-handed. The least I can do is help."

She stepped aside and picked up the baby. "Hardly empty-handed, I'd say. But if you insist. It's lucky I was home when you arrived. We went to the synagogue this morning. Salomon and the children are still out walking."

As it happened, I'd arrived on a feast day, which the Jews call Purim. The story is written in our own Bible as well: how the Jewess Esther stood up to the cruel Persian king, her husband, and in so doing spared the lives of all the Jews.

I sprinkled the table with flour and started rolling out the dough. "I went to the village first. The house was empty. I feared the worst."

"Aye, well, that's a story, isn't it?" she laughed.

Two years before, the city council had invited Salomon to settle in the city and practice as a physician. There was an ever-growing need on account of the war, and he already had many patients within the walls, including a few of the councilmen themselves.

"If it'd been up to Salomon, he would've refused," Rachel explained. "He didn't even want to consider it. He remembered what you'd told him about your experiences as a Catholic in the city. 'If they'll turn on a Gentile child, you shouldn't doubt what they'll do to Jews,' he said."

In the end, it was the other families that convinced him. Since the start of the war, they'd debated amongst themselves what was best for the community, whether they should seek refuge somewhere better protected from the passing armies.

"The men sat him down one evening," Rachel said. "It was Purim then, too. I remember because they said to him, 'Perhaps God has chosen you to go to Nördlingen for just such a time as this.'"

"I can imagine how Salomon responded to that."

"He didn't like it one bit, not least of all because he couldn't think of a way to say no."

"And what was your opinion on the matter?"

She lowered the baby into the basket and started to rock her. "I didn't see why it should be so complicated. Better to have a home here than to run to the walls as a refugee every time an army marches through. But then, I didn't grow up as he did. I didn't truly know what it was like to be a Jew in this country until I became one."

"And if you'd known, would you still have done it?"

Rachel did not answer as she took down a pan and started stirring together a poppy seed custard. By and by, she said, "It's the wrong question, I think. Life is full of wonderful, difficult things. Things we might never attempt if we knew how trying they would be at the outset. I couldn't know how hard it would be, but I couldn't know how happy I would be, either. The better question is, would I give it up? The answer to that is easy. No, not for anything."

Salomon entered the house then, carrying a girl of about two, followed closely by their boy Daniel and his older sister Hannah. He stood stiff when he saw me. My heart threatened to stampede out of my chest. I stopped my work.

"Don't just loom, Salomon ben Judah." It was Rachel. "If you have something to say, say it."

He set the youngest child down. "How long has she been here?"

"You might ask her that yourself," came his wife's short reply. "I've enough to do this afternoon without relaying messages between the two of you when you're standing right here in the same room. If you had any sense, you'd be grateful for it. God has delivered her out of the wilderness. He's brought her back to us, safe and well."

Salomon cleared his throat. "Will you give us a moment?"

Rachel sighed and took the custard off the stove. "Fine. The filling needs to cool anyhow. But I'd better not come back to find you've eaten it all. You know how costly sugar is." Then she rounded up the children and led them into the next room, leaving me and Salomon alone.

He sat down at the table, and I took out the book with the fine leather binding I'd found among Gottschalk's things.

Then I made my speech as I'd rehearsed it, the one Rachel hadn't given me a chance to deliver. I told him I was sorry for being an ungrateful child, and that I didn't expect him to take back his oath, but I hoped he'd at least give me the chance to earn his forgiveness.

He thumbed the pages of the book. "Avicenna," he muttered. "In Arabic." Then he snapped the book shut and let it fall on the table with a heavy thud.

My flesh went cold. "Please," I said. "If you could give me some sign, some reason to hope that you might one day forgive me…"

Salomon took the custard and set it in the center of the table. "Do you know—" He stuck a finger in and licked it clean. "Do you know what's more foolish than making a hasty oath?"

He held the bowl out to me. I hesitated, but he nodded, urging me on. I dipped my fingers in. The taste prickled my tongue.

"The only thing more foolish than making a hasty oath is keeping one."

The sound that came out of me was half-formed, some middle thing between a laugh and a sob. I covered my face with my hands. Next I knew, he was standing beside me with his hand on my shoulder.

"Can you forgive me?" he asked.

"What do I have to forgive you for, old man? You've only ever done right by me, even from our very first meeting, when you fixed my hand and didn't take the fee."

"Now, who said—"

"Rachel told me the truth."

"Yes," he said with a knowing nod. "She can always be relied on for that. But it's not true. I haven't always done right by you. I didn't do right by you the night you left. I'd helped you and trained you in your profession, and because of that, I made the mistake of thinking that I was your father. That I had a claim on you. I didn't. I had no right to try to keep you or to force you into a marriage you weren't ready for. As usual, Rachel saw it clearly well before I did."

"You *were* a father to me," I whispered.

"Not by blood."

"But in every way that mattered."

He gave my shoulder a gentle squeeze. "Then give me a chance to say what I should have said when you left. You are always welcome here, do you understand? Whatever happens, you are welcome."

"Thank you. I promise I'll repay the dowry just as soon as I can."

"Forget about the dowry!" he laughed. "I don't want to hear mention of it again."

The baby stirred and gave a small cry. I picked her up from the basket and rocked her.

"Well!" Salomon exclaimed. "When were you planning to tell me about this little one? She's yours, is she?"

"Aye."

And then he asked the question I'd long been girding myself for. "And the child's father? Where is he?"

"He's... he died," I answered him.

Then I told him all about my marriage to Isidoro, the whole honest tale of how it came about, except that when I reached the end, I made one small alteration. I told him that after Isidoro's death, I discovered I was with child. I meant to come to Öttingen straight away, but was waylaid in Nuremberg, where I gave birth.

My dear priest, I pray you'll pardon me the lie. I only hoped to give you the child you so dearly wanted. I told myself you wouldn't mind.

24

For Everything a Season

1632

Life is made up of seasons. Seasons of quiet and seasons of noise; seasons of activity and seasons of rest; seasons of satiety and seasons of want. My return to Nördlingen marked the beginning of one of the more restful periods of my life. That was well with me: I'd my fill of worries, raising up Magda. But I've often found that such restful periods are rarely so restful as they seem, for it's in those periods that the troubles of the future breed.

Looking back, certain events appear to prefigure the things to come. In hindsight, a too-small apartment resembles a siege, while ordinary cruelty and every day rancor sicken like plague. The peace we purchase for ourselves is dear. We tighten our grip when we feel it being ripped away, and in the process it tears, and we're left to try to stitch it back together.

I'd arrived at home, or at least, to the closest place I'd known to a home since my mother's death, fourteen years before. I was resolved this time to keep it—for Magda, if for no other reason. But how? It seemed to me that each time I'd found a place for myself I lost it again, whether because of the will of strangers or the war or my own muddled discontent.

I wanted Magda to grow up in the peace and security I'd so often longed for. I wanted her to grow up among people who cared for her and knew her name, to never have her know the hardships of the road or the bitter, isolating experience of being a townless stranger beneath the world's notice. I didn't know the first thing about how to give her any of that. I thought if only we had a roof over our heads and a hearth to return to each night, it would be enough. I thought we would be safe within that city's strong walls. I prayed for it dearly.

On my first arrival, Nördlingen seemed little changed. The Spital, the square, the tanneries, the grocers—they were all just as I'd left them. Baker Ruppel was older now, his hair almost gone entirely, but his booming laugh still echoed down the lane.

Even so, the changes were there. The walls, though sturdy as ever, couldn't hold back the tide of strangers who came seeking shelter behind them, nor could they keep folk in who thought they might leave and escape the war entirely. Magda and I were far from the only new faces to join the masses of humanity seeking refuge in that city.

The burghers and the council approached the situation with a steady pragmatism, levying taxes each year to pay off the armies that marched through and to secure the grain harvest safe inside the city's storehouses, while the Spital and the church carried on in their sober work of sheltering refugees. The council's justification for admitting the Jews had been likewise calculated: admitting the Jews meant admitting their purses as well.

The people prayed. They prayed that the war might end, that they might be spared the Emperor's Restitution, that there might be bread on their tables and peace in the streets. Above all, they prayed for the Swedish king, Gustav Adolph, to deliver them. They prayed for him so faithfully that it seemed to me he'd displaced God himself, or at very least, had joined the ranks of the saints while he was yet living.

Make no mistake, none of them wanted war. Only, after fourteen years of it, they knew no other way to pray for peace. It was one conqueror or the other, and they preferred the Swede's mercy to the Emperor's, if only just.

We stayed with Salomon and Rachel after our arrival, squeezing ourselves into their too-small quarters, which were less than half the size of their former house in Pflaumloch. A half-dozen swine rooted around the yard below them, and the smell was such that the family was compelled to keep the windows shut during the day, even during the heat of summer.

They had just three rooms: their bedroom, the kitchen, and the living room which doubled as the children's bedroom. It was not nearly enough space for the five of them, even without adding Magdalena, the runt, and me. But for Rachel it was out of the question that we would stay anywhere else, so on our first evening they moved the children's bed to their bedroom and laid out blankets in the living room for me to sleep on.

"We'll get you a proper bed tomorrow," Rachel said. "Salomon has been talking to one of the city councilmen about finding more rooms. But there are none in this part of town, and folk are yet wary of living next to Jews."

"They're never so hesitant when they need someone to smell their piss for disease," Salomon muttered.

"Aye, love, I know." It was a weary sort of answer, as if they'd had this conversation a dozen times before.

"Do they think Jewishness is catching?" he grumbled.

Rachel planted a playful a kiss on his lips. "I caught it from you."

Salomon grunted something unintelligible, then trudged to the bedroom.

She sighed. "He's not wrong. Only what good does it do to point out the obvious? It just puts him in a bad mood. I wouldn't refuse bigger apartments, though."

I was grateful for the hospitality. I'd been right about Rachel setting me straight. It was a mercy just to have a second pair of arms when Magda was restless and refused to settle, but Rachel was full of motherly wisdom besides.

She had a trick for everything—a way to coax a willful child to nap, a way to soothe rashes, a way to tend to nipples cracked from too much suckling. She was a continual source of encouragement—that was, perhaps, her greatest trick. She had a way of making me feel as if I was doing everything just as I was supposed to, even when I was making a mess of things.

But it wasn't long before the living situation brought us to strife. The three adults were ever bumping shoulders or tripping over one of the children or the runt, who rarely budged from his spot on the floor. We snipped and snapped at one another with such regularity that the two older children, Hannah and Daniel, echoed our saltier language back at us, both to our amusement and our shame.

It all came to a point one afternoon, when, in the midst of explaining some new medical procedure, Salomon leapt up from the kitchen table in a fit of excitement, took a stumbling half-step to avoid stepping on the runt's tail, and elbowed Rachel's bubbling soup pot off the stove in the process. Rachel only just managed to jump clear of the steaming liquid as it splattered onto the floor.

Salomon poured out apologies for his carelessness, but Rachel's patience was spent. She stormed into the bedroom and informed Salomon through the door that he could clean up the mess, see to dinner, and then sleep in his surgery until he'd persuaded the city council to find them better rooms.

But she couldn't go an evening without sighing as she passed Salomon's empty place at the table or as she readied the children for bed.

I was the guest, the one who didn't belong, so after two such nights, I said to her, "I'll sleep in the surgery tomorrow. I'll take Magda and the runt with me after the midday meal. You'll have space enough to walk again, the children can have their bed, and you can have your husband back."

"Nonsense. That surgery's no place for a baby."

"Be sensible," I said. "Your husband's not dead. He's living and breathing, and you should have him at your side. Besides which, I can't abide another evening of your mournful sighs. I'll sleep in the surgery."

"Oh, very well," she relented.

So, a little more than a month after I'd arrived, I was on my own again.

Salomon's surgery was just a few streets down from the Spital. It was a comfortable enough space, even if it was no home. There was a recessed area in the back of the room with space for a small bed, and there was a pump in the yard just outside for drawing water. Over time, I made it nicer, adding a crib for Magda and a tub for bathing in. The runt was certainly happier; in the days after we moved in, he regained some of his old energy, jumping up and wagging his tail each morning at Salomon's arrival.

But I was less than a year out from Isidoro's death, and every waking was a fresh reminder of how different loving a dead man is from loving a living one. The quiet and loneliness of the surgery bore down on me each evening after Salomon left for the day. If I hadn't needed to rise on the regular to cuddle and feed Magda, little could have roused me from my bed.

Salomon spent the whole of the Christian Holy Week in a temper. He ordered Rachel and the children to stay indoors, but it was an impossible command. They needed food and cloth for mending garments and candles for him to read by at night, and none of these things would spirit themselves into the apartments on their own. So, Rachel and I went to the market one morning with the children, letting them dart in and out of the stalls in the cool spring air.

"Willful, arrogant woman," Salomon barked when we returned. "Won't you for once do what you're told?"

"Don't speak to me in that fashion, Salomon ben Judah," she snapped back, as she unpacked her basket. "I've always honored and obeyed you, but I'll not do it when you've so clearly lost your senses."

"Lost my senses?" he shouted, incredulous. "You know what the season is. You've seen their passion plays. Who kills Christ in them? The Jews, that's who. And who are we? The Jews. One of just four families in the entire city, and we don't need to draw attention to it."

"Draw attention to it? How is buying food for our family drawing attention? Do you think I don't know what's at stake? If they ever found that I turned my back on their Christ, they'd burn me alive for it."

On they went, arguing in a mix of Yiddish and German. I held my tongue.

"I am your husband, and when I ask you to keep your head down and out of sight, for your own safety, I expect you to do it. If you care so little for your own life, at least you can think about the children."

Rachel slammed a cabinet shut. The pans on the wall rattled with the force.

"Get out," she said, firm and quiet.

Salomon's expression went slack with shock. "Käthe, I'm sorry."

He tried to put his arms around her, but she stepped away.

"My name is Rachel."

"Rachel. It's this damned city—" he protested, but she cut him off.

"No, Salomon. It's you." She continued to move about the room as she talked, clearing away children's toys, folding the tablecloth. "We made the choice to move to this city *together*. We knew it would be hard. We knew it would be different than being in the village. I was ready to do it, though, because I knew *you*, the man I married, the strongest, wisest, kindest soul I know. I knew whatever happened, I'd be facing it with you."

She leaned against the kitchen table with a sigh. "But now I don't know who you are anymore. I don't know who this bitter, fearful man is, who comes into this house stamping his feet and lecturing me like I'm a child."

Salomon was silent. Rachel pressed her palms into her eyes and then stood up again. "I need to get the children their supper."

She picked up the kettle and made for the door, but Salomon blocked her path. He leaned to kiss her, but she turned her mouth aside, and his lips grazed her jawline instead.

"Please, forgive me," he pleaded.

"I will," she said, running her fingers along his chest. "You know I will. Just not yet. You must be better. I can't... I don't think I can go on living with you, behaving like this."

She went out, and he slumped into a chair and dug his fingers into his graying hair. I'd been standing in the corner cradling Magda, unable to leave without walking into the middle of their argument.

"I've made a mess of things, haven't I, Josefine?" he said.

I sat next to him. "It's nothing you can't mend."

"I'm glad one of us is confident." He exhaled. "I grew up in Frankfurt. Took my first wife there. Had my first children. Lost them all to smallpox. Still, I couldn't imagine leaving. There were close to two thousand Jews in that city. Enough that it was like having our own town. Enough that you might occasionally run into another Jew and only know half of everything about their life, their family, where they came from, and so on." He smiled at the memory.

"Some five years before you and I met," he continued, "a group of Christians came to the *Judengasse* to start trouble. They plundered our houses, and several Jews were killed. But to keep the peace, the city expelled the Jews. *We* were attacked, but we were the ones who had to leave. As if our very presence was disturbing the peace.

"Two years later, they captured and hanged the men who started it, and the Emperor ordered the city to let the Jews back in. But by then, I'd gone. I couldn't stay there any longer. The notion of home I'd had there, it was spoiled for me."

He tapped his fingers on the table in a nervous movement. "Ever since we moved into Nördlingen, I think I'm back in Frankfurt. I feel trapped, waiting for someone to attack us, or accuse us of something, or banish us again."

"Did you tell Rachel that?"

He shook his head. "What difference would it make? They're foolish thoughts, and I know it. Not because those things won't happen, but because fearing them won't prevent them."

Magda fussed, and Salomon reached out for her. I handed her to him, and he set her on his knee and bounced her up and down.

"I don't know anything about being a Jew," I said, "but I know just a little bit more about being a wife. After Magdeburg, Isidoro had terrible nightmares. The fear of them kept him awake all hours of the night. I'd never seen him so troubled; he was not himself. All I wanted was to be a comfort to him. I think I was. I hope I was. I'd wager that's what Rachel wants, too. She doesn't mind that you're afraid. She minds if you act as if you're alone in it, as if she's not there or can't help. She loves you."

"Does she?"

"Aye," I said with a chuckle. "That I'm certain of. It'll take more than this bit of trouble to dissuade her of that."

"I pray you're right," he said.

I wished there was something I could do for my friends' happiness, but much as I wanted to, I couldn't remake the world. Instead, I offered to run Rachel's errands for that week, if she would look after Magda. She was ill-pleased to trade away her freedom, but she agreed to it for the sake of peace in her household.

Eleonore returned to Nördlingen a few months later. She didn't delay even an hour in pursuing her divorce. The news spread from the mouths of every gossip in the city. The old women shook their heads and clucked their tongues: *The deacon's daughter and the cabinetmaker, such a young and promising couple. What went wrong?*

I'd left a message at Eleonore's stepmother's shop, letting her know where I was staying, and soon after her return I had a letter from her. It was by parts brash and playful. Over the following weeks, she wrote a dozen such letters. I've kept every one. I won't bother copying them all here. One example should suffice to reveal their nature:

Dear Not-a-boy,

I never did ask if you minded my calling you that. If so, I'm afraid it's too late to correct the error. I couldn't possibly break the habit if I tried.

I confess I'm glad you're not a boy, because if you were, I could not write half the things I know to be true. I could not confess to you how good it felt just to be in your presence in Nuremberg, or how miserable I was after you left. Until that time, I felt as if my heart had been turned to ice, and I did not know if I would ever feel again.

Am I confessing too much if I say that Nuremberg was the second time you saved me from drowning?

You surely think this letter is nonsense. It would not surprise me at all if you remembered that time in Nuremberg differently. Swear that if you do, you won't tell me. Promise to leave me to my happy memory.

I hope you and your little one are doing well. I promise to pay you both a visit when this awful business is finished. I wish I could do it sooner—oh, how I want to!—but I must deny myself, for now. Even one rumor could bring everything to ruin.

Until then, I am ever,
the girl who is glad you are not-a-boy,

Eleonore

As for my response, I no longer have it, but I'm certain I told her that I too cherished our time in Nuremberg.

It was midsummer, and Salomon had gone to prepare for the Sabbath while Magda had just gone down for a nap when I heard a knock at the surgery door. I muttered a curse, fearing the noise would wake the child.

But I forgot my irritation when I saw Eleonore in the doorway.

"Magda's just gone to sleep," I said.

"It's just as well. She's not the reason I'm here."

She drew toward me, till her breath warmed my skin, till she was close enough for me to count the flecks of gold in her eyes. "It's done," she said. "I'm free."

"You're free," I repeated.

She threaded her fingers through my hair. They danced along my ear, tracing the curve of my neck to my collarbone. I sucked in a jagged breath.

"We're not the people we once were," I croaked.

"No, we're not," she agreed, but her fingers had found their way to my blouse, and they slipped beneath the collar, caressing my bare my shoulder. "You're a widow now, and I'm divorced. We're free."

It was all I needed to hear. I made to kiss her, but she interposed a thumb. "I love you, Fi," she said. "I've loved you since were were children. But if you don't love me—"

I kissed her wrist, her forearm, the crook of her elbow. She shuddered as I gathered her in my arms.

We covered each other in eager kisses as we stumbled to the bed, leaving our bodices and blouses discarded on the surgery floor. I lay back, and she climbed on top of me. We paused only once, when we heard Magda start to fuss in the cradle nearby, and we lay there, waiting, half-frozen, for the child to wake. That silence lasted an age, until Eleonore broke it with a stifled giggle, and we fell upon each other once more.

Afterward, I held her against me, my nerves still thrumming.

"And to think," she said, "I was terrified you wouldn't want me."

"I don't think that's possible," I said. "Even if I wished it. I think perhaps we're bound to each other in some way. Bound to always find each other again."

"Well, that's a gloomy thought," she said.

"Is it? I didn't mean it that way."

"I'd rather think we chose each other. Outside of the church, I picked you out—the odd little baker's boy, too small for his coat, feeding scraps of bread to his dog. Do you remember?"

"Of course I remember."

"But when did you pick me, I wonder? Was it then, or later? In the tower, maybe, when you kissed me."

"No. Earlier."

"When?"

"When I jumped into the river after you."

She smiled then and reached across my naked stomach to weave her fingers into mine. "I thought so."

When it was time for her to go, my heart ached, but we both knew she couldn't stay. Her father and stepmother would both wonder where she'd gone off to. She was free of her marriage, but a young woman in this country is still not at liberty to choose where she lays her head.

The rest of that year rolled on, and for the first time since Isidoro's death I sensed some purpose left in my being alive, beyond the steady mindless march from one day to the next.

Salomon and Rachel were finding their way, at least if the swelling in Rachel's belly come August was anything to judge by. He didn't cease being anxious, but he learned not to bark and snap at her for it, which is all she'd wanted.

In September, the council finally agreed to let them resettle in larger quarters. Their new apartments were above a glazier's shop north of the church. We spent two days loading and pulling carts through the city, and when we were done, Rachel and I both agreed that Salomon had too many books.

I took over their old apartment above the butcher's. I'd been working in Salomon's surgery as much as Magda would allow it, and I'd saved enough to pay half a year's rent in advance. Even so, the landlord required a guarantee from Salomon before he agreed to let me the rooms.

The space that had been utterly insufficient with seven people in it was cavernous with just two. I'd no furniture of my own apart from my bed and Magda's crib. Over the following months, I kept my eyes open as I walked the streets, looking for castoffs and broken items. I found a solid tabletop and paid a carpenter to attach new legs. I salvaged broken boards for bookshelves. I purchased a tripod cauldron and an iron pan at a widow's auction. Eleonore brought cloth for blankets and curtains from her stepmother's shop, and Rachel helped me with the sewing.

Magda was a happy child, and each turning of the season brought new delights. She learned to smile and giggle, and she took to dragging herself across the floor. She found new ways to tire me out then, wedging herself behind the bookcase in Salomon's surgery while I worked and grabbing anything within reach.

But for everything there is a season, except for war, which knows no season, which goes on forever. All that year, the Swedish king's advance was relentless. The Protestant cities, Nördlingen included, oscillated between rejoicing and trembling.

For Nördlingen, the dilemma was the same as it had always been. Where did their loyalties lie? As a Free Imperial City, they were bound to the Emperor. As Protestants, they knew well that the Emperor was no friend. In the early days of the war, that had been an easy choice—the Protestant cause, however righteous, had also been a hopeless one. The weather changed with each of the Swedish king's victories, and Nördlingen went with it. The Golden King, they called him, their liberator.

Yet war is ever the same, regardless of who holds the upper hand. The war touched the city in all the usual ways. The price of bread rose, and sick and starving refugees arrived from Nuremberg. There were soldiers to quarter, Swedish instead of Imperial, but it made little difference to the city's peace.

A popular children's song echoed in the streets, warning of the arrival of the Swedish king and his chancellor, Oxenstierna:

Pray, children, pray
Tomorrow comes the Swede
Tomorrow comes Oxenstiern'
To teach the children to pray
Pray, children, pray

Protestant or Catholic, an army needs wealth for pay and equipment and food to fill its soldiers' bellies. The council did their best to pay off the armies and protect the city, but those outside it were less fortunate. We heard stories of Swedish soldiers pouring mud down farmers' throats and leaving them to die. Life under the liberator turned out to be much like life under the Emperor. Only the banners were a different color.

In the last days of October, the runt fell ill. For two weeks he lingered, scarcely eating, scarcely drinking, scarcely moving. As his condition worsened, Rachel agreed to look after Magda so that I could be with him.

It feels foolish to say how much I fretted over that dog. I know that to any onlooker he was just a dumb animal—a mangy, gangly, one-eyed beast that I'd pulled from a pile of moldy straw. There are thousands of such creatures born and dying each day in Germany.

What can I say by way of explanation except, when he looked up at me on a march with his tongue out, panting, he looked for all the world like he was grinning?

I wrote to Eleonore, and she came to the surgery to sit with the both of us, telling her father and stepmother not to expect her back at any usual hour. I don't know what I would've done without her there.

He passed at mid-morning on a cloudy day in mid-November, stretched out on the floor with his head on my lap. He'd not opened his eye the whole night, but at some point his ragged breathing slowed and then stopped. Eleonore sat beside me, one hand stroking his side and the other wrapped around my middle.

Shortly after, the bells of St. George's rang out a death toll and then fell silent. They remained silent, all day long, not even chiming out the hour. They were followed by cries and wailing, and most of the town poured into the church in a great procession to pray.

Call it one of fortune's little mockeries, but that morning, just as the runt breathed his last, word reached Nördlingen that the Golden King, the Protestant champion, Gustav Adolph, had fallen in battle never to rise again and save them.

While the city's residents gathered in the church to mourn their would-be liberator, Eleonore and I loaded the runt onto a cart and carried him through deserted streets, out of the city gates. He was so wasted away by then, he weighed almost nothing at all. Salomon and Rachel joined us with the children.

"He was a glutton, and he wasn't very clever," I said, shoveling the first bit of dirt over him. "But he never held a grudge. He lived long enough to become old, which is as good as any of us can hope for. I think he was happy. I'm glad he's at peace."

I buried him along the road between Ellwangen and Nördlingen. Between the long marches and the time my father and I had spent wandering from town to town, I figured the road was the closest thing the runt had to a home, and I had the funny notion he might like watching the people pass, wherever he was.

25

Siege

1634

If only the Swedish king's death had meant the end of the war. Magda and I might have settled into our new home untroubled. I might have brought her up with no notion of armies. I might have taught her the wayward joy of escaping the city walls on a Sunday afternoon and gamboling down to the babbling riverbed, of traipsing through the woods, ankle deep in a bed of dead leaves, for no other reason than the pleasure of hearing them crunch beneath her feet.

But the princes had not yet surfeited themselves with war. They each believed that what they had to gain by fighting or what they stood to lose from peace was greater than the cost of going on. Easy for them to say; it wasn't their cost to pay.

As the armies marched back and forth across the center of Germany, the flow of strangers in and out of Nördlingen was constant. They overflowed the Spital into the streets. They slept on the floor of the church.

In those days, Salomon and I went back and forth between the two places, treating the sick and injured. There were always sick and injured. Typhus and typhoid were most common, followed by smallpox. We'd heard there was plague during the siege of

Nuremberg in 1631, and we thanked God daily it had avoided us in Nördlingen.

I saw more of Eleonore's father the deacon during that time than I'd seen in the previous years combined. He was much as I remembered him—tall and spare with nothing excessive about him, either in his figure or his mannerisms. His normal expression was a mask of featureless piety, except when I brought Magda with me. He smiled warmly when he saw her and offered her little treats if he had them—a bit of dried fruit, a piece of communion bread. He didn't remember me at all.

That summer, the church teemed with sick. We moved as many as we could into the sacristy, trying to separate the afflicted from the well, but they crowded the space. The council paid to have a building near the church turned into a sick house, and the deacon, Salomon, and I spent the better part of a day moving those too weak to move themselves.

As we worked, the deacon asked me why he hadn't ever seen me at church services.

"I don't put much stock by church services," I told him honestly.

He arched his eyebrows. "You are a Christian, aren't you?"

"I was baptized one."

"Baptism is one thing; faith is another. Do you believe in God?"

"Do you?"

He hesitated before answering, "Well, of course. I'm a deacon in His church."

"A lot of churchmen say they believe in God, but I'm not so sure. If they did, surely they wouldn't need to drive so many people to their graves just to prove it, don't you think?"

We covered our noses as we entered the sick house. Three dozen people, maybe more, lay on the floor while the flies buzzed above their heads. The room was filled with the stench of soiled blankets. A young man lay pale and motionless; death had claimed him.

"I can't say what I believe, deacon." We wrapped the dead man and carried him out to the street. "I don't know whether God is living or dead, Protestant or Catholic. Maybe he's been a Jew all along. But I'm sure he's not the one the Emperor worships, nor the kings of Sweden or France."

He stared at me, mouth agape, just as if I were a brazen woman, a brothel harlot with her breasts hanging out of her bodice. "But what will you teach your young daughter? Will you raise her to be faithless?"

"I hope to raise her to live at peace," I said.

"I will pray for you both," he said.

During that time, Eleonore's ex-husband, Konrad, remarried. Eleonore told me the news on one of her clandestine visits to my apartments.

"She's a pretty little thing," she said as she pulled the pins from her hair. "I knew her in the Lutheran school, though I would hardly have remembered her otherwise. She was quiet, skittish, like a church mouse. I pray he doesn't destroy her."

I laid my hands on Eleonore's hips. "I saw Konrad the other day at the church. He wanted to help with the sick. Your father sent him right off, and he spared no fire on Konrad's account. If I didn't know what he was like, I'd have felt sorry for him. He left like a dog with his tail between his legs."

Eleonore frowned. "I don't know how I feel about you spending so much time with my father. You're supposed to hate him. I think I'd lose my mind if you started liking him."

I lowered the sleeve of her blouse over her shoulder and planted kisses all along it. She shivered.

"I don't hate him," I murmured into her bare skin. "I pity him. He has his God, but I have his daughter."

That year Nördlingen found itself caught between three armies. The Emperor's son, Ferdinand of Hungary, commanded one, marching west. His Spanish cousin, also called Ferdinand, commanded the second, marching up through the Black Forest to meet him. Between them was the Swedish Protestant force.

As summer wore on, we read the reports of the armies' movements with desperate interest. We hung on each report the way one looks at gathering storm clouds, with a mixture of awe and fear.

In August, Mr. Frickhinger, one of the city council members, paid Salomon an unexpected visit at the surgery.

"What's the trouble?" I asked him. "The gout again?"

"No, not the gout," he said, limping toward Salomon. "Or rather, that's not why I'm here. Doctor, may we have a word?"

"What is it you need? If you would eat the diet I prescribed, you'd feel much better."

Frickhinger laughed. "I know. My wife says the same. But I'm set in my ways. These times are hard enough without foregoing little pleasures, I find. No, the matter is money, doctor."

"My price is more than fair. Need I remind you, I'm not some quack peddling half-baked cures. I'm university educated."

"It's not about the price. It's about the city. You've been following the news of the army, I don't doubt."

"Perhaps you should have a seat," Salomon offered. I fetched a chair each for the councilman and Salomon.

The man smiled at me gratefully and sat down. "Ferdinand of Hungary will be in Donauwörth soon. The Spanish Ferdinand will be looking to meet him and join their forces before they confront the Swedish army. The likely place..." he trailed off.

Salomon nodded. "The likely place is here, you mean."

"Yes. If the Swedish army intervenes in time, they might drive them off. That would be for the best. But if they don't... well, no one wants another Magdeburg."

"So, levy a war tax. You surely didn't come all this way on a bad leg to tell me that."

"We're afraid a tax won't be sufficient. Last year's poor harvest has left the city's coffers rather depleted, what with the need to buy grain from farther away. We will raise the tax of course. But we had in mind something more. An emergency measure." Frickhinger rubbed his palms on his thighs.

"Spit it out, man," I said.

"A loan," the councilman said at last. "We discussed a loan."

"No," said Salomon. "I'm not a moneylender."

"You're a Jew. In any case, it's... it's not a request."

Salomon was silent.

"You can't do that," I said. "You can't compel him to lend you money. That's robbery."

"We'll repay it within a year at a rate of five percent," Frickhinger said.

"And if I refuse?" Salomon said at last.

"Once again, it's not a request. This city has shown you and your family very generous hospitality. Surely you understand why this is necessary. If the armies aren't paid, they will take what they think they deserve. No one wants another Magdeburg."

I knew the look on Salomon's face well. I'd seen in it on my own father, pulling himself to his feet, just after he'd been knocked to the ground and spat on for the dozenth time.

"Very well," he said. "What amount?"

"Five hundred."

Salomon clenched and unclenched his fists in his lap. "I'll need two weeks."

The first of the armies arrived later that month. Ferdinand of Hungary set up camp a few miles away. He cut off the flow of water into the city, and soon the channel where the river ran was muddy and tepid. Insects buzzed around it, and the odor that rose from it was suffocating.

The wells and water pumps were too few, and people lined up for hours waiting to collect water for washing and bathing. To ensure there was enough to drink, the council tried to ration beer, but the order sent the city into uproar. Crowds gathered in front of the Burgermeisters' houses, threatening to drag them out of their beds and toss them in the swampy channel.

One morning, a fight broke out at the water pump outside of Salomon's surgery. We heard the shouting through the window and rushed out to see what was happening. A half-dozen women were piled on top of each other, reaching for each other's hair and throats and bellowing curses to make their husbands blush. Their pails and kettles had been discarded and overturned in the scuffle, and thirsty dogs lapped eagerly at the puddles they'd left.

The town watch stood by, unsure how to break them up. I looked to Salomon, who shook his head.

"Very well," I huffed. Picking up my skirts, I marched out to the women, shouting for their attention. But my voice was drowned out by their shouts.

The cabinetmaker's shop was on the same road, and he appeared at my side then, chisel in hand. He struck the water pump with the tool three times, and the combatants startled and separated.

I no longer remember what the matter was. Some woman accused another of cutting the line or some other such tiresome thing. I told them in plain terms what I thought of them, brawling over water.

What danger was there from the army, if we were determined to tear ourselves apart within a few days? They started to shout again, casting blame on each other. Konrad struck the water pump again, and the reverberations silenced them.

"If this siege goes on, you'll miss the days when all you had to fight over was water," I said. "Now line up. The cabinetmaker will fill your pails, one at a time."

But even as they lined up, the argument began afresh.

Konrad spoke: "You can line up as Miss Dorn says, or the watch can escort you to the gaol and bar you from drawing water here again."

At that, finally, they settled themselves.

Once the pails and kettles had been filled and the women sent away, Konrad turned to me. "You're friends with Eleonore Kästner, aren't you?"

"Nothing to do with Eleonore is any business of yours," I answered.

He nodded. "Of course. She's made me out to be a villain, I'm sure."

He still spoke with the same soft, unassuming demeanor as when I'd first met him.

"You didn't contest her story."

"No, I didn't. How could I? Her father is the deacon. Her stepmother's cloth business is a favorite of the council's. I lost my temper. I shouldn't have struck her. I'd just lost my father. I wasn't in my right mind. She took advantage of it to turn the whole town against me."

"You beat her bloody."

"I just think if you knew the whole circumstances, you'd have a little more pity for me."

"It's a mystery to me why you care what I think of you."

"Consider this: she was never interested in being my wife. I moved to this city, I left my father behind, so I could marry her. And where was she when he was dying? Who was she with? She was always looking for a way out. She found it. She provoked me into it. I'm not that man, but she poisoned my reputation. I can't get half the business I used to. The deacon won't even let me enter the church. I had to take my new bride to Augsburg to marry."

"Perhaps you should've stayed there," I said in parting.

He was asking me to pity him, and I might have. I knew well enough what the deacon's bad opinion could mean for a person in Nördlingen. But I couldn't forget how Eleonore's body trembled when she told me what happened to Georg; how like a ghost of herself she seemed. She had no proof, aye—no proof but a mother's instinct.

Not long after they cut off the water, the bombardment began. Ferdinand of Hungary set up his cannon on the hills outside town, and their shots hammered the walls day and night.

"Thunder?" Magda asked me. She was two and a half years old then and the very image of Eleonore.

Eleonore noticed the resemblance too, and the fact didn't sit well with her. From the off, she'd done her best to distance herself from Magda. After her return to Nördlingen, she preferred to find me alone or to wait until Magda was in bed. I told myself it was a practicality, the need to keep her ex-husband from learning the truth. I told myself she'd warm to her in time.

But the more Magda's features mimicked her own, the more uneasy Eleonore became. I observed a rigid tension in her body in Magda's presence, as if something in that small creature threatened her very being.

I tried to talk to her about it, but she dismissed my worries. "You're reading too much into it, Fi. I'm simply not the mothering type."

But I couldn't help but believe there was more to it than that.

Once the cannon fire started, I could hardly sleep. Not because of the noise—we were far across the city and the sounds of the bombardment were dull and distant. No, I couldn't sleep because I kept expecting to wake and learn that the walls had been breached.

How many times that month had it been said? "No one wants another Magdeburg."

Word came that the Protestant army was in Bopfingen, just a half day west of Pflaumloch. The garrison sent a message, pleading with them to attack Ferdinand before the city fell. But for days on end, they remained fixed in their position.

Meanwhile, we tried to carry on our day-to-day lives. I kept Magda close to me as I worked in Salomon's surgery—so close that the child protested, flinging herself on the ground and wailing because I wouldn't let her play in the street with the other children.

Every time someone invoked the name Magdeburg, images of a column of children, cut down on their way to taking refuge in the cathedral, appeared before my eyes. I couldn't let Magda out of my sight.

Day and night, the walls shuddered. We all grew tense. Rachel snapped at Salomon, and Salomon snapped at me, and one afternoon, I looked down at the scarificator in my hand and the patient's arm in front of me, and I couldn't remember what ailment I was treating or when I'd picked up the instrument. Had it been a few seconds or a minute that my mind had vacated my body?

I took Magda home, but she struggled to sleep with the sound of the "thunder" on the walls, and I lacked the will to force her. She was still awake when Eleonore came to visit.

"Aunt Nora," Magda said. "Magda scared thunder. Mama scared thunder."

"I'm sorry," I said. "She wouldn't go to sleep."

Eleonore exhaled and sat down on the bed beside us. "Well, Magda, I'm scared of many things. The thunder, too. I wonder if you could help me practice being brave."

"How be brave?"

"What we need to do is to be even louder than the thunder, so we can scare it off. Can you do that? Can you stomp your feet and shout as loud as you can?"

Magda slid down from the bed, hopped once, and gave a tiny shout. I covered my mouth to suppress a laugh. Eleonore looked at me with a knowing grin.

"That's right," she said. "Come on, Mama, it's your turn."

That night, we stomped and shouted until the family below us hammered on the ceiling. When we laid Magda in bed again, she was worn out from laughter and fell asleep in an instant.

"Thank you," I said to Eleonore, as we reclined side by side on the bed. "You say you're not the mothering type, but..."

"Fi, please."

"You're good with her."

"I had a younger cousin who was afraid of thunder, that's all."

Bursts of cannon fire popped off in the distance.

"It's not the 'thunder' I'm afraid of," I said.

"I know."

"There were babies in the Tross after Magdeburg. No one knew where they came from. They gave them to the women to care for. Orphans, I suppose. Their mothers and fathers killed during the sack."

Eleonore leaned against my shoulder.

"I don't know what will happen to me if I lose her," I confessed.

"You'll lose a part of yourself, too. A part you'll never get back. You'll wake up alive every day and wonder why."

Magda stirred, muttered a few words, and settled back to sleep.

"Do you understand?" Eleonore asked.

I nodded, but I couldn't say if she was talking about Georg or Magda, the one she'd lost or the one she'd given away. Perhaps it was both.

I said, "I used to ask myself, if I'd known ahead of time just how much it would hurt losing Isidoro, would I have chosen to love him less? I don't think I would have. If anything, I wish I'd loved him more. All I know is, it wasn't enough. It could never have been enough."

"It's terrifying, love," she observed.

"Aye." I held my hand out to her. "But it can't be helped."

"No, it can't," she said, fitting her palm into mine.

We stayed awake a while, sitting up in bed, listening to the bombardment.

By and by, my thoughts returned to Magdeburg. I turned to Eleonore. "If the soldiers storm the walls, you must surrender yourself to them. Let them take you out of the city. Offer to carry their plunder for them. Don't fight, even if they try to force themselves on you. Don't struggle."

"Fi—" she objected.

"No, listen to me. The women who were taken from Magdeburg survived. They were treated roughly, aye, but they lived."

"What about the church?"

"There have been massacres in churches before now. It's safer to let them take you."

"And what about you?"

"I have to stay with Salomon in the surgery. They're unlikely to kill us if they think they can press us into service. I'll keep Magda with me. If they take her, they must take me too."

Eleonore fell quiet.

"And if something happens to me," I continued, "if I'm killed, and there's no one to take care of Magda, you must…" My throat grew tight. "You must…"

"I'll take care of her," she said. "Of course I will."

That night as I prayed, I addressed my prayers to Isidoro directly. "I don't know how to stop this war from swallowing me up," I said. He was silent, but I have to think he was listening all the same.

Each day the siege dragged on, the council pressured the garrison commander to surrender the city. The commander sent another message to the waiting Protestant army and received the order to hold out for just "six days more."

Near the end of that six-day period, an excited shout came from the towers. Banners had been spotted on the horizon. Over the protests of both the commander and the council, the citizens flocked to the walls to see for themselves.

Relief gave way to despondency, then: the banners cleared the hilltops bearing the red-on-white cross of Spain. In the Swedish army's delay, the Spanish Ferdinand had arrived to meet his cousin.

On the twenty-sixth of August by the old calendar, the fifth of September by the new, the garrison reported movement on the southern hills. I took Magda and joined Salomon in his surgery. With some coaxing, I was able to persuade Salomon to send Rachel and the children to shelter in the church.

Finally, at the last hour, the Protestant army stirred to life. They marched, intercepting the combined Imperial-Spanish armies in the hills southeast of the city. The countryside erupted in sounds of battle. After the first day of fighting, they'd successfully driven the two Ferdinands back.

But from time to time, it happens that a patient on the brink of death shakes off the stupor of illness and, for a brief period, acts and feels as alive as if they'd never been ill at all. It's a terrible thing to witness, for it only serves to breed false hope in the minds of both the patient and the ones who are hoping and praying for their recovery. In truth, they are so near to death that they have become numb even to the pain of dying.

So it was with the Protestant army. After their initial success, disaster upon disaster befell them. While maneuvering in the night, their heavy cannon became stuck in mud, and the commotion of un-sticking them alerted the Imperial and Spanish forces to their presence. By morning, the enemy was prepared to counter their attack.

Those on the walls got a view of the next day's battle, though again the garrison and the council fought to keep the citizens away, for fear that a stray shot might strike one of them. The rest were left instead to hear the fighting—that indistinguishable cacophony of shouts and volleys and clashes of pike and sword.

In my time with the army, Catholic victory had always been accompanied by shouts of "Sancta Maria," but that day a different cry came over the walls. "*¡Viva España!*" the victors cried. *Long live Spain.*

At midday, the garrison commander ran up the flag of surrender and threw open the city gates.

26

The Quick and the Dead

1634

They say the dead are the fortunate ones, for they are beyond misfortune's reach. They have nothing left to fear, and not even the worms gnawing their bodies trouble them. Yet they also say that despair is a sin. To take one's own life is to refuse God's greatest gift. I've often wondered how both can be true at once.

After the battle of Nördlingen, some seventeen thousand lay strewn across the hills and forests where the fighting had been heaviest. Most of them remained where they'd fallen while wild dogs ran among them, picking at the meat. As usual, so too did more human scavengers, rifling through pockets for items of value—a button here, a belt buckle there, a handful of kreuzer or a razor. Then the crows did their work. As at Magdeburg, it was impossible to dig a grave wide enough for so many.

The surviving soldiers quartered in the city, and the conquering armies levied a hundred thousand gulden in *Brandgeld*, a sum far in excess of what the city could manage. After much pleading, Ferdinand of Hungary agreed to settle for half the price, which we all paid in heavy tax and plunder.

Still, we breathed relief for a spell. The water channel opened up again, and for the first time in weeks there was water enough for washing and bathing. The noxious odor that clung to the air dissipated. We started to think we living were the lucky ones after all.

Magda was of a spirited playful age, only dimly aware of the threat we all lived under. She perceived the war, if she perceived it, only through the worries of her elders—of Eleonore, Salomon, Rachel, and me.

I felt guilty for holding her so close during the siege, for dragging her to the surgery day after day, and in the days after I compensated with indulgence. I joined her on the floor of the apartment, playing games of her invention with her little ragdoll until late in the morning, and only then did I try to cajole her into dressing so I could go to work. She often refused, goading me into chasing her about the apartments while she squealed and hid, naked, beneath the table or the bed.

"*Mäuschen, Mäuschen*, say 'peep!'" I'd call.

"Peep!" she'd answer, her voice delicate as a snowflake, before giving herself over to peals of giggling laughter.

Then I'd catch myself thinking on the soldiers in the street, the high cost of bread, and the encroaching winter. I'd start to weep, wondering how I could protect her from such things, and the girl would crawl into my lap and nestle into me and shush me. "Don't cry, Mama. I good. I get dressed."

"Oh, *Mäuschen*, you are good. You are so good."

Love is terrifying, Eleonore had said. Aye. The only thing more terrifying is war.

A few days after the siege lifted, I found Salomon in the surgery talking to the councilman, Frickhinger. Their tone was low, their faces grim and ashen.

"What is it?" I asked.

"We were just arranging—" Frickhinger began.

Salomon interrupted him. "Go to Rachel," he said to me. "Tell her to take the children to my sister in Frankfurt. I suggest you go with them."

"What is it?" I repeated. I adjusted Magda in my arms, and my stomach roiled with a sick sort of dread.

"Do as I say!" Salomon snapped.

He did not need to say more. Disease had been spreading through the city for weeks, even before the armies' arrival, as the refugees from the neighboring villages arrived ahead of them. A rotten, stinking miasma had covered the city during the siege, rising up from the murky riverbed, so that it was hardly possible to walk the streets without gagging. Then the armies had come, bearing their own sick.

"It's the Pest, isn't it?" I whispered.

Salomon lowered his head.

Frickhinger spoke. "We're turning the building into a plague house. We have several afflicted already, and they need a place where they can be cared for. Konrad Lehmann and Widow Offenburg have offered to stay with the sick as plague master and mistress. The good doctor has just agreed to check on them twice daily and to give the plague master instructions on the correct treatment course."

"For a fee," Salomon added.

"Yes, of course," the councilman agreed. "For a fee."

I stared at Salomon while Magda wriggled in my arms. "Did they force you into this?"

"Absolutely not! I'm a physician, Josefine. This is what I swore an oath to do."

"And if you get sick? What will Rachel do? What will I do?"

Salomon shook his head. "Tell Rachel she's the best of women, and I hope she forgives me for all the times I was not a worthy husband."

I knew then that he was immovable.

I did as he asked. I went to Rachel and delivered his message, every word of it.

"He's finally given up all sense, has he?" She put her hands on her hips. "If he thinks for a moment I'm leaving him—"

"I don't know," I said. "But I think you should go."

"And if he goes and dies?"

"You have your children to think of."

She rubbed the back of her neck. "You're truly agreeing with him on this?"

"It doesn't matter whether I agree with him or not. You know what he's like. He swore an oath. What good is it for you to stay? You'll only put your life and the children's lives at risk. He'll do better work if he knows you're safe. He'll have a reason to stay alive."

"Curse him and his damnable oath," she said.

I left Rachel's and crossed the city to Eleonore's. Magda had sensed trouble and was resting her head quietly on my shoulder. I touched her back and felt the low rise and fall of her breathing as anxious thoughts whirled through my mind, rendering me light-headed.

Surgeons are arrogant by nature, believing that by cutting and probing and stitching we can mend the body, set the bone, and cleanse the suppurating wound. But plague is another matter. Even at my most prideful, I didn't have the first idea how to fight a plague.

My thoughts dwelt on Salomon, alone in the plague house. I joined Rachel in cursing him and his oath.

I can't say when I reached the decision, only that by the time I knocked on Eleonore's door, I was sure of it. Magda couldn't stay in the city, and I couldn't leave.

I said to her, "How would you like to stay with Aunt Nora for a while?"

She bounced in my arms, smiling with innocent excitement.

Eleonore was perplexed when I handed her the child and still more confused when I told her to take Magda and her family and leave Nördlingen. I knew I ought to explain myself, but I also knew if I told her the reason behind it, she'd be determined to talk me out of it. I'd no doubt she would succeed.

I kissed her on the mouth, heedless of who might be watching. "Take good care of her."

Magda reached for me, and I kissed her too. "Be good for Aunt Nora, *Mäuschen*. Mama loves you. I'll be back soon."

She was still reaching for me when I left. I kept my eyes fixed ahead of me, knowing that if I looked back, my heart—and my will—would dissolve.

Salomon of course tried to dissuade me. "No," he said. "I'll not hear of it. You have a child."

"You have four."

"I'm a doctor."

"And I'm a surgeon. You trained me, and I've learned plenty on my own since. I'm not going to let you do this alone, old man. So let's not waste any more time arguing."

"You're determined to break my heart, Josefine Dorn."

By and by, we converted the surgery into a plague house, with lodgings for the plague master and mistress on the uppermost floor, beds for the sick just below them, and space for operating and treating the worst cases on the ground.

We were joined that evening by Konrad Lehmann and Widow Offenburg, who'd volunteered to help tend the sick. The widow was past sixty, her children all grown, and she spent her days helping with the refugees in the Spital. Konrad, I supposed, was there to mend his damaged reputation.

When he first entered the plague house, his face was so pale and his hair so disheveled, I nearly mistook him for one of the ill.

"Is the cabinetry business so bad that you've come seeking death here?" I needled him.

"We have a common task. You might at very least pretend not to hate me," he said, rolling up his sleeves.

"I might. What are you doing here? Aren't you newly wed? Where's your wife?"

"Where's your little girl?"

"I'll ask you again, why are you here?"

"For the same reason you are. To help the sick."

"If you think that will ease your conscience," I said.

"Am I damned forever in your eyes because of a misstep? Can't a man be more than one mistake?"

"A mistake? Is that your name for murder?"

He leaned forward. "Hold now. What did Eleonore tell you?"

"She says you killed your infant son."

He clenched and unclenched his jaw. "What? I..."

"Is it a lie?"

Silence. He twisted a rag in his hands.

"Well? Is it?"

"I—I don't know," he said quietly.

"It doesn't seem like something that leaves much room for confusion."

"No," he said. His voice was distant. "No, it doesn't."

His shoulders slumped, and he retreated.

How he perplexed me. I think, in another life, he might have been easy to love. Once, as he held water to a dying man's lips, I caught myself calling him "Isidoro." My mouth filled with bile at the absent-minded comparison.

Was it the war that made him what he was, as it made all of us, in some way or other?

I'll never know. None of us will ever know who we might have been if there had never been a war. After peace, that was the first thing it stole from us.

The names of the dead stretch in every direction, from Hell to Heaven and back again. I sometimes wonder if God can name them all, or if he too struggles to hold them in memory across the years.

First, there were the soldiers, the ones the army left behind. On a good day, we lost two or three patients out of a dozen. Most days, the number was closer to six.

We instructed Konrad to stoke the fireplace hot to sweat the plague humors out of them and used rosewater and bundles of flowers to blunt the miasma's foulness. Sweat dripped into my eyes while I operated, and my mask prevented me from wiping it away. I lost a patient to blood loss because I couldn't see the vessel to make the ligature.

After the soldiers came the members of the Tross and the villagers from the surrounding countryside. Most of them were already weak and underfed. We lost six out of every ten. We burned herbs and bundles of sticks to fumigate the rooms.

The afflicted pleaded with us from their beds. Mostly they begged for prayers. The only prayers I knew were Isidoro's old Popish ones, but the sick were past minding. Salomon brought out an amulet with a small, dirty diamond set in the center and held it out for them to touch while I prayed over them. Some of them broke their fevers shortly after; others passed in agony, but quickly.

Next came the citizens of Nördlingen. The plague house filled up, and the council had to instruct people not to come anymore, but to remain at home and put a mark on their door if there was plague within. Every day the black sign appeared over more doors. Salomon and I visited as many as we could. We barely slept.

When I did sleep, my rest was fitful. I'd jolt awake thinking I heard Magda crying, only to blink into the dim silence of the empty bedroom and remember.

Baker Ruppel fell ill, as did most of his family. He and his daughters survived, but his sons and two of his grandchildren did not. The weaver, Daniel Wörner, died. So did several councilmen. For some, death was quick, but others were dragged slowly and painfully into oblivion.

One morning, eighty-five year-old Maria Holl was brought to the house. She was the keeper of the *zur Krone* tavern on the town square, and even in her old age, she had all the temperament of an unbroken bull. Her first day in the plague house, she asked to be sent home, declaring that she had every intention of living.

"That's well enough, but we can't send you home until you're recovered," I told her.

Still, she protested, complaining bitterly about the drink and the food and about being confined to her bed.

That evening, the plague mistress, Widow Offenburg, took me aside and said, "Best to let her go. If she says she means to live, she means to do it."

"Such willfulness won't hurt her chances," I said. "But it's better if she stays."

"Mistress Holl does not need chance. She has other means."

I looked over at Maria. For all her spirit, she was a small shriveled piece of fruit, her hair thin and gray. After much coaxing, she'd taken her medicine and was moaning in her sleep.

"What are you saying, Widow Offenburg?"

"I'm saying she knows the devil's art." The plague mistress jammed a poker into the stove. "She was nearly burned for it, too. Fifty-odd years ago. They put her to torture sixty times, but she wouldn't confess. They freed her after that. They had no choice. But they never did exonerate her."

"Perhaps she was innocent," I suggested.

"Bah. One needn't be guilty to confess. But to survive the torturer's methods, doesn't that require some form of witchcraft?"

When I returned the next morning, Maria Holl was propped up in her bed, defiant as ever.

"I told you," she said. "I mean to survive this."

"As you survived the torturer?" I asked.

She flashed a gap-toothed grin. "Aye, precisely so."

"Tell me, old woman. What's your trick?"

Her look turned sour. "It's no witchcraft, if that's what you're thinking."

"Then what is it?"

"I'm simply not ready to die."

"Is that all?"

I checked on her daily, and every day her condition was much the same. No better, no worse. We'd chat for as long as the unending line of patients in need of treatment allowed. She was full of stories, too many to write down—a woman who'd seen much in her long years and remembered it all.

But at the end of the week, she was white as lily petals and trembling. I looked into her eyes, but they were unfocused, drifting all around. She reached out for my gloved hand.

"It needed to end," she said.

I thought her delirious. "What needed to end?"

"The witch hunt. Every time they tortured someone, there was another confession. And every confession..." She pressed her lips together and swallowed. "Every confession meant more accusations. They asked me to name others. I couldn't have that on my conscience."

"So, you refused to confess."

She nodded. "I prayed to God. 'You know I'm innocent,' I said. Fifty-nine tortures. I can still feel them in my bones."

"My mother was accused of witchcraft," I confided. "But she wasn't so brave as you."

"She confessed, did she? You mustn't blame her for it."

"She killed herself."

Maria snorted. "I thought of doing that. But I was too afraid." She reached up and felt at the outside of my mask. "I wish I could see your face. I don't know if you are young or old. You sound young."

"I'm six-and-twenty."

"Young, then. I'm dying now, aren't I?"

"Yes, I believe so."

Her eyes glistened. "Stay with me?"

"I can't."

"No, of course not." She looked out at the other sickbeds. "There are too many of us. Well, remember me then."

When I returned the next morning, Maria's bed was already occupied by another woman.

After three weeks, Widow Offenburg fell ill. She passed a few days later. Konrad got sick as well. His sturdy frame lay prone in bed in a shuddering heap as the fever racked his body—a fallen giant.

"I suppose this is satisfying to you," he muttered to me. "I suppose you think this is what I deserve."

"I don't know what you deserve. I don't know why it matters to you what I think."

"Because you're her friend."

"Eleonore?"

"Tell me something. Did you see her when she was away in Nuremberg? She was gone for ten months. A very particular amount of time. Why not the whole year?"

My hackles rose. I didn't care for how he danced around the truth or the dark tone of accusation that hovered behind the words. "Forget Eleonore," I said. "You have a new wife. Think on her."

"Would you believe me if I said I don't remember what happened the night our son died? I was tired, so tired. He wouldn't stop crying."

"Enough," I said. "If you want absolution, seek a priest."

I left him and set to work treating the other patients and mixing up the remedies that the apothecary delivered.

For days Konrad lingered in that state, and Salomon and I began to count him among the dead. We sent a boy to inform his wife, and the young woman turned up at the house the next morning.

She was just as Eleonore had described her—slight and retreating. She seemed like she might startle at her own shadow. Did she know how her husband obsessed over his first wife? Had she seen his temper? Or was their relationship still in its sunny springtime?

We told her to go home, but she would not hear it. We advised her not to touch him, but she couldn't restrain herself. She took his hands—how they dwarfed hers. He smiled. I think it was only the second time I'd ever seen him smile.

In the end, we'd misjudged Konrad. He held on. The day after his wife arrived, he showed the first signs of improving. Within the week, he was well again and on his feet.

His wife, on the other hand, poor woman. She was stricken just as he started to improve, and she succumbed three days later.

By five weeks gone, I could no longer feel the deaths. The number had grown beyond meaning—fifty, one hundred, three hundred. It was no Magdeburg, but then the dead of Magdeburg hadn't reached out to me in their last moments pleading for relief; I'd not had to look into their fear-stricken eyes.

There was no time for funerals. The dead were not even wrapped in the sheets they died in, for we needed them for the next patient. They were tossed in a pit with sacks for shrouds.

Late one afternoon, there came a rapping at the plague house door. Salomon had just arrived a few minutes earlier for his night shift. I was in middle of giving him the report—who was newly arrived, who seemed likely to survive, who wouldn't last the night.

I answered the door, and there stood the deacon. A sharp, suffocating pain gripped my chest.

"Please," he said. "I need to speak to the doctor. It's urgent."

27

The Deacon

1634

The deacon stood with hands clasped in the plague house doorway, casting his gaze this way and that. His lips were pale and his eyes bloodshot.

"Well, man," I said. "Spit it out. What's the trouble? Is Eleonore well? What about Magda?"

"Eleonore took the child to Nuremberg more than a month ago."

I breathed again.

No, it was Margarethe, his wife, who'd fallen ill, struck down some two days before and growing worse daily.

Salomon promised to pay her a visit just as soon as he'd finished checking on the patients in the plague house, but when the deacon left, the physician turned to me: "I know you've been on your feet the livelong day, but I need you to accompany me. I cannot treat the deacon's wife alone. I dare not. Do you understand?"

"Of course." Where was I to go? My apartments were empty; no one was waiting for me there.

"Thank you."

All along the way, Salomon fidgeted, shaking his head and twisting up the curls of his beard.

"I don't recall you being half so anxious when Isidoro was lingering about your surgery in the Tross," I remarked as we passed in the shadow of the church.

"Your husband of blessed memory was one of God's righteous. The deacon makes me uneasy. I do not care for how he looms, nor for how his mouth does not move when he prays. A most unnatural manner."

"Isidoro was human enough for me," I said.

"Just help me keep the deacon's wife alive."

The deacon met us at the door with his Bible in hand and led us to his wife's bedroom. Margarethe lay on the bed, unmoving. If not for the intermittent flutter of her eyelids, I'd have taken her for dead already.

One of the purposes of the plague mask is to block out the noxious miasma that carries the disease, and one of its benefits is that it also blocks out many of the smells. Even so, I could tell the air in that room was foul when we entered.

Salomon ordered the deacon to open the windows.

"Margarethe, my dear," said the deacon. "The good doctor is here. And he's brought his assistant, Eleonore's friend."

The woman peered up at me through unfocused eyes. "Josefine Dorn," she said.

Her mouth formed the sounds only loosely, and they pressed up against each other and lost their shape. But the next sentence she spoke clearly enough: "I remember you from Nuremberg. You're the woman Eleonore loves."

I laughed uneasily. "Aye, she's a dear friend. I'm grateful to her for looking after Magda."

"They look very much alike, don't they? Her and the child."

"Yes," I admitted. "They do."

"Like mother and daughter," the woman went on, murmuring, more to herself than to me.

I looked over to the deacon, who stood with his hands clasped around his Bible and his gaze fixed on his wife. There was a faraway look in his eye that told me he'd heard little of the conversation that had just passed.

How many times have I seen that look in the eyes of those whose loved ones lie near death? They see the trial that is soon to come, and their spirit retreats from it. Their bodies are present, but their minds are drifting, elsewhere. There are times I'm grateful I didn't have time to see Isidoro's death coming.

"You must look after her," Margarethe continued, as Salomon began his examination. "Tell her to find a new husband. She's young yet, and she can still be happy." Then she turned toward the deacon. "We've been happy, haven't we, Peter?"

"Please, my dear. Don't speak as if you're dying. Not today." He looked to Salomon, his eyebrows arched, expectant.

Salomon moved around the woman, inspecting each of her hands and lifting the blanket to look at her feet, checking for signs of advanced illness. Then he turned toward me: "Josefine, a word with you, please. Outside."

I couldn't see his expression, but his tone filled me with dread. I followed him to the staircase landing, where he sat down heavily on the top step and removed his mask. He wiped the sweat from his face with his sleeve.

"There's nothing to be done," he said.

"Are you certain?" I asked, though I had no cause to doubt his judgment.

"The toes on both of her feet are completely black. Her neck is so swollen, it's a miracle she could even speak to us."

"We might still amputate," I offered.

"Both feet? Come now, Josefine. You saw her yourself. She'd not survive such an operation. And if she did..."

"She'd be lame, aye. But she'd be alive." I heard my foolish, hopeful priest's voice in the back of my mind as I spoke the words. *Life, Josefine.* But tell me now, dear priest, you've seen both sides of it—is it truly preferable to death?

"You're in earnest about this," Salomon said.

"You might at least talk to the deacon."

"If I kill her, Rachel and I will have to flee the city."

"If it comes to that, I'll be fleeing with you. You're family to me, both of you. Where you go, I go. You brought me here to help you save her life."

"I brought you so that the deacon couldn't turn around and say that a Jew killed his wife."

In all the time I'd known him, Salomon had preached prudence when operating, but he'd never once backed away from treating a patient out of fear. Yet just then his leg bobbed up and down on the step, and he twisted and tugged at his beard in anxious repetition.

I told him, "The man that taught me to be a surgeon wouldn't shy away from helping someone because he's afraid."

"Both feet," Salomon said with a shake of his head. Then he rose and donned his mask once more, returning to the room.

The deacon was sitting at his wife's bedside when we entered, his hands folded in prayer, eyes staring straight ahead. No sound came from his mouth; his lips did not move.

Salomon led him to the foot of the bed, where he lifted the blankets to reveal the woman's blackened toes. There was not a one of them that was not putrid with decay, from the tip to where they met the foot. The rot on the left foot was more advanced than the right, running near up to the heel. The deacon covered his nose and turned his head away.

In a low voice, Salomon laid out the two miserable choices that now presented themselves.

The deacon listened distractedly, his gaze flitting back and forth between his wife and Salomon. "Yes, do what you must," he said when Salomon had finished.

"Listen to me, man," Salomon said. "There is very little chance of this working out, do you understand? It will be very painful for her, and if it does succeed, she'll be lame. She'll not be able to walk for the rest of her life."

"I heard you the first time!" the deacon snapped. "I don't care. Do whatever you can. Save her!"

"No." The woman's voice was frail and quiet, so that I wasn't even certain I'd heard it at first. But she tugged on my cloak, and when I turned to her, she repeated it—a weak, but firm "No."

She looked up at me, straining to open her eyes. "Tell Peter I don't wish to be sawn up. Tell him I'm a Christian, and I'm ready to go now."

"No, Margarethe, please," the deacon pleaded. He fell to his knees at her bedside, grasping her hand with both of his. He addressed Salomon: "Don't listen to her. I'm her husband, and I say you must do what you can to save her."

Salomon shook his head.

I leaned close to her. "Mrs. Kästner, do you know what you're saying? If we do not remove the dead flesh, you will die. It's not a chance; it's a certainty. If we do, I won't claim the chance is high, but... but..."

"But God might yet use us to perform a miracle," Salomon filled in the words where I could not.

"No," she said. "I'm ready."

"Don't be foolish, woman!" the deacon shouted.

I raised a hand to quiet him, then turned once more to Margarethe. "Are you certain? What about Eleonore?" I pleaded. "Think on her. What will she do without you?"

She pressed her lips together into a thin smile. "What would Eleonore do with a lame stepmother?"

"You know she'd care for you. She loves you very much."

"*I* would care for you, Margarethe." It was the deacon, still kneeling at her bedside.

"No, the congregation needs you. In these times more than ever," Margarethe protested. She ran a hand along his cheek. "Please, Peter, I'm ready."

He broke down. It unsettled me to hear him sob. All my life I'd taken him for a distant and unfeeling man, one practiced at showing the appearance of kindness but without any of the sentiment. What other sort of man could have driven my father and I into the purgatory of the unsheltered road the way he had? Worse yet, it seemed he'd forgotten all about it. Yet there he was, and the keening, choking sounds of his broken heart sounded just like any other.

Salomon and I left them alone and waited downstairs. A short while after, the deacon came down and invited us to sit. He poured us beer, which our parched lips were all too glad to accept. We raised our masks just enough to put the cups to our mouths and drink.

"Thank you, and I am truly sorry," Salomon said.

"You're not to blame," said the deacon, his lips pressed together in a thin line. "The only one to blame is me. She wanted to go to Nuremberg with Eleonore and the child. But she wouldn't go without me, and I could not leave the congregation."

Salomon nodded. "You had your duty. I know something of that myself."

Eleonore's father went to the window and pulled back the curtain. The door of the church was visible across the square. "No," he said. "I swore an oath."

He sat down opposite us and folded his hands in his lap.

"I had a son," he explained. "His mother died birthing him. When he was just an infant, he caught the scarlet fever and died. The illness that took my son, I was afraid it would take my daughter too. I had just lost my wife, and the two griefs one after the other... I couldn't imagine a third. So, I swore an oath to God that I would serve the church for as long as I lived, just as long as Eleonore survived. She did, of course. She suffered just a little fever and then it passed. I don't think she even remembers it.

"Ever since then, I've given my time and my prayer to the congregation of this city. Other deacons have come and gone, but I've remained, ensuring that everything is in its place for the Eucharist, the baptisms, the funerals. For the Christmas celebration and the passion play. I married Margarethe, not out of love at first, but because her money meant that I could devote myself even more fully to the church. Love, affection, these things came after."

Eleonore's father took a sip from his cup.

"Surely the city has benefited from your service," Salomon ventured.

The deacon grunted. "This oath has cost me everything. I did everything I could to protect my daughter from wild influences, and still, she does what she wants. She hates me. I had her married to a good Christian man, hoping he'd have a pacifying influence on her, but he proved to be a brute, and now she has sworn never to marry again. One of my grandchildren is dead, and the other, whom my wife and daughter have conspired to keep secret from me, is being raised by a stranger." He glanced at me. I bowed my head, avoiding his gaze. Salomon said nothing.

Eleonore's father continued: "Each morning I wake up wondering what fresh sacrifice God will demand from me this day. No matter how much I give, it is never enough." He addressed Salomon. "Do the Jews believe that God is just?"

"I'd rather not speak for all Jews," Salomon said, uneasiness in his voice.

"Then I'll ask another way. Do *you* believe that God is just?"

"I believe that his wisdom surpasses our own. I believe that he wants us to live justly."

"Do you believe in Hell?"

"I've lived through war and famine and plague. So, I suppose I do. But not in what I understand to be the Christian sense, as a place of eternal torment."

"And what about Heaven?"

"Are you trying to catechize me, Mr. Kästner?"

"No. I'm sorry. I'm not. But do you pray?"

"Every morning and evening," Salomon answered him.

"Would you believe I haven't prayed in twenty-five years? Not for myself, at least. For the members of the congregation, of course. I pray for their requests—for good harvests, that the army will not take all the grain, that the city will be spared destruction for another year, that this or that ailment will pass, or that a marriage will produce children, and so forth. But I haven't been able to pray my own prayers since I made that damned oath. I suppose I'm afraid, although I can't say which frightens me more—the thought that God isn't listening, or the thought that he is."

"Yes, that is always a danger," Salomon said.

The deacon gave him a perplexed look.

Salomon cleared his throat. "When I was a boy, I spent several months dreadfully sick, and I prayed every day, asking God why it was that people get sick, and why God didn't make them better. Dangerous questions, those.

"My parents hired a doctor to tend to me, and in time I recovered. When I was better, I told the rabbi down the street about my prayers. I asked him, why is it that God did not make me well again? And the rabbi said, how do you know he didn't? And I said, the doctor made me well again. And the rabbi said, and who sent the doctor?

"That's when I realized that God meant for me to study medicine. Seven years of hard study, learning Latin and Greek and Arabic and memorizing plants and anatomies—not to mention all that my family had to do to afford to send me—all for praying! God has a wicked sense of humor."

"You are saying that if my prayers seem unanswered, it's because I have failed to do what God has called me to do."

"I am saying God's answers to our questions might be different than the ones we are expecting."

The deacon nodded. "Doctor, it seems that Margarethe is determined not to let you operate on her. Will you at least pray for her, since I cannot?"

"Of course," Salomon agreed.

The deacon stood then and escorted us to the door.

We returned to the surgery in low spirits. We'd spent the entirety of the afternoon with Eleonore's stepmother with little to show for it. Those were the deaths that pierced us most deeply; the ones we saw coming and could not prevent.

In the yard behind the surgery, we pulled off our masks and let the afternoon breeze cool our faces.

I took out Isidoro's pipe and filled it with tobacco.

Salomon puffed out his cheeks and exhaled. "He's a more bitter man than I knew."

"It was good of you to listen to him," I said. "I think he appreciated it."

He nodded, but I could see plainly that he was not consoled.

I leaned over and kissed him on the cheek, which drew a smile out of him.

And then I recalled the deacon's confession and how he'd looked at me when he'd spoken about his second grandchild. I wondered if Salomon had noticed.

I licked my lips. "What the deacon said, about his grandchildren..."

"So, it's true, then."

"Aye."

"You could have told me the truth."

"I know." What could I say? "I liked the lie better."

Salomon nodded. "That I understand."

Margarethe Kästner died the next day, with her husband the deacon at her side. Due to the plague, there couldn't be a funeral. But the deacon invited Salomon to join him at her burial, and he did.

Two months after the plague started, we noted with relief that we had fewer cases each day. Fewer black signs marked the city's doors. Fewer bodies lay moaning in our surgery. Fewer bells resounded through the streets, tolling death.

In part, we had the cooler weather to thank. The start of October had alternated between weeks of warmth and weeks of chill, but by the end of the month the first frost had settled on the fields and autumn had thrown the door open for winter. The cold air drove away the miasma that covered the city, bringing in sharp, fresh air and clarifying the water in the channels.

The other cause of the plague's retreat was, simply, that there were few people left to catch it.

Salomon and I were quick to hope and eager to be back in our loved ones' arms. By mid-November, we had, for the first time, no patients in the plague house. The building was quiet: no moaning or screaming bodies, just Salomon and I.

I tore off my cloak and mask and collapsed, exhausted, into a chair.

Salomon hobbled across the room to put his tools on the shelf. I assumed weariness was the cause of his limping; I'd spent so long on my feet each day, walking across the city, climbing staircases, and standing by the bedsides of the sick that my own feet were pocked with painful blisters and my shinbones ached.

He reached into one of the cabinets with his right hand and took down a copper pitcher. But when he passed the pitcher to his left hand, it slipped from his fingers and clattered to the floor. He lurched forward, then, leaning on the furniture for support.

I jumped up. He was breathing heavily, so I stripped off his mask and lowered his hood. Even through my gloves I could sense that his skin was burning. His face was pale and translucent as quartz. I removed the glove from his left hand. The fingers were black.

"How long?" I croaked. "How long have you been hiding this from me?"

"I didn't set out to hide it," he said.

"No, but you knew before now, didn't you?"

"I started feeling feverish two days ago. I didn't want to worry you."

I draped his arm over my shoulder and walked him to the chair. "Sit down," I ordered.

I donned my mask and cloak once more. My eyes were filmed over with a mix of sweat and tears, and I took a moment to blink them both away before returning to him and stripping off his boots and his other glove.

"Buboes?" I asked him.

"Yes," he said. "Left armpit and groin."

I stripped him of his jerkin and shirt. The buboes beneath his arm were small and filled with yellow bile. I pricked and drained them.

"I'll take your word for it about the groin," I said.

"I thank you for that," he replied with a faint smile.

Then we both looked at his hand. I took a knife and poked at the fingertips, but they had no feeling.

"You're going to have to take it," he said. "You're going to have to cut it off."

"No," I said. "You mustn't ask that of me."

"I can't very well do it myself, can I?"

I felt a strangling panic rise in me. "Damn it, old man, I'll kill you!"

"No, you won't," Salomon said. His eyes shone with a strange mix of fear and calm. "I trained you in how to do this. If you cannot do it, then God does not will it to be done. I told Rachel I'd return to her alive. Don't make a liar of me."

"No," I said again. "I can't." I said it, and in my heart I raged, for I knew there was no other course. I cursed Salomon—first, for getting sick and not telling me, and second, for ever giving me the skills to do what he now needed. I cursed God as well; I'd never asked to be his instrument.

"Please, Josefine," he pleaded. "Whatever love you have for me, forget it. If I've ever been a father to you, pretend it wasn't so."

"No," I protested. "Don't say that. Don't say that."

"You must. Forget you ever loved me. Treat me just as you would a stranger. Spare me no pain if it will save me."

I wished then that I could break apart, split into two halves, and leave my body. I wished I could float outside myself until the gruesome work was done. Back and forth across the surgery I went, preparing my tools, tying off Salomon's arm to cut off the flow of blood, fastening him to the chair, and placing a wooden bit in his mouth so he wouldn't bite off his tongue. I fetched a young man in from the street to hold my instruments and be my assistant. Then I muttered a prayer, halfway between a curse and a plea.

But when I opened my eyes again and saw Salomon, I froze. "I can't. I'm sorry. I can't."

"Nonsense. You're the only one who can. Now stop sniveling and do it. Do it, woman. Or else everything I taught you was a waste."

It was for my own sake he spoke to me so cruelly, but his words shocked me all the same. I blinked away tears and took knife in hand.

Oh, how he screamed when the knife sliced flesh. He tried to jerk free, but I'd tied him fast. I cut down to the bone and tied off the vessels, while his screams pierced my heart and rattled around inside it. I thought I was used to such screaming, but try as I might to make him a stranger, it was no stranger's voice I heard, no stranger's face that contorted in agony under the pressure of the saw as its teeth bit into bone.

I worked quickly. Two minutes is about all the human body can bear of such pain. I never knew two minutes could last so long.

Sometime in the night, I moved Salomon from the chair to a bed (I can't remember how) and then collapsed to the floor and blacked out with my back to the wall. I woke in this position, confused about where I was or how I'd arrived there. Then I heard him moaning in his fever and saw his bandaged arm resting on his stomach and remembered.

I don't know if the dead are the fortunate ones. What I do know is, they haven't the barest conception of how much a person might endure yet go on living.

28

A Loss of Vital Parts

1634-1635

Salomon recovered, but I did not. Only, I'd not been sick to begin with, so no one noticed.

The morning after the operation, I wrote to Rachel, but when I read the letter, I didn't recognize my own hand. She returned from Frankfurt a few days later, and we spoke through the plague house door. I told her I couldn't let her in until his fever lifted, and she cursed me for it.

During that time, I spoke to Salomon as his surgeon, and he answered me as my patient in curt, unadorned sentences. Our eyes did not meet even once.

The pustules on his neck diminished, but the fever clung to him. I checked his wound and found it suppurating, so I cleaned it and changed the bandage. Shortly after that, the fever broke. Rachel demanded to be let in.

"Leave us," Salomon said to me after she'd arrived. "You've done enough."

Rachel took over his care, and I went back to my apartments, alone. The place was musty, so I threw open the window over the pigsty. The breeze smelled strange, and it took me a moment to understand why. The air outside was sweet, fresh; the swine-yard below was empty. All the pigs had caught the plague and died.

Eleonore returned with Magda in December. I opened the door before she even had the chance to knock, having heard their voices in the stairwell. I scooped the child up and buried my nose in her curls, breathing her in. She giggled and squirmed in my arms. I went on squeezing her until she begged me to let her go.

Eleonore looked on me with a furrowed brow. I took her expression for grief.

"I'm sorry about your stepmother," I said to her.

"My father says you and Salomon did your best, and she died at peace. I couldn't ask for more." Then she asked, "Fi, are you well? I mean truly well?"

I couldn't answer her question. I wished desperately that I could. I wished I could find a way to take everything I'd seen and done and shrink it down until it was small enough to be contained in words, mere words. I still long for it; why else would I write this account, except to try, for the thousandth time, to do the impossible—to wring some meaning from all that I've seen and suffered?

"Of course," I lied. "You're back. Magda's back. Why shouldn't I be well?"

That night, after Magda was in bed, Eleonore and I joined ourselves together once again. As she ran her fingers along my back and parted my lips with hers, every nerve in my body shimmered and then burned.

And then it ended. Eleonore covered herself once more with linen and wool, and I was left to watch her, my skin cooling as the sweat on it dried.

"There is something I need to tell you," she said then, peering at me over her shoulder. "But I need you to promise me you won't be angry. Or if you are angry, promise you won't let your anger turn to resentment."

"You've built it up enough," I said. "Spit it out."

"I need your promise," she insisted.

"Very well. I promise."

She sat down at the edge of the bed, and I propped myself up on my side. "What is it?" I asked, impatient.

She bowed her head, kneading her hands in her lap. "When I was on the road to Nuremberg with Magda, we traveled for a while in the company of a Catholic priest. He was an older man, quiet, half-blind. Most of the other travelers paid him no mind, but Magda took a liking to him."

"She takes a liking to most everyone."

"She does," Eleonore agreed. And then she said, "I was afraid. You'd told me to leave so suddenly. You gave me Magda. I could not fathom what must be wrong that you would entrust her to me. And then, along the way, we started to see them. Survivors from the towns along the way. People who'd fallen ill on the side of the road, dying or dead."

I mumbled an apology, but she continued: "Nuremberg was days away at that point. I didn't know what might happen. People said that the armies had brought the plague with them, but what if it was in Nuremberg too? The priest was set to leave us. He was headed south, into Bavaria. I didn't have much time to think it over. I had to decide."

"What did you have to decide?"

"I asked him to baptize Magda."

My neck grew hot.

"I know you said you didn't want it. But I couldn't risk... what if she—or I—had caught the plague without the choice being made? What if brigands or murderers had attacked us on the road? What if she died, never having been baptized, and her soul went to Hell? Please," she said. "Say something."

"It wasn't your decision to make," I said.

"I know."

"You didn't even want her. You couldn't... you couldn't stand to look at her."

"That's not true."

"Why should you care where her soul ends up? What concern is it of yours?"

"What concern is it of mine? I lost a child, Fi. It's been nearly four years, and I still haven't woken up from that nightmare."

"You're not Magda's mother. I am."

"And if she'd died unbaptized, would you have forgiven yourself? Tell me honestly."

My anger was quicker than I was. "You weren't thinking of me. You were only thinking of yourself. Your conscience couldn't abide the fact that you'd given your daughter to a Godless heathen to raise."

"You're baptized. I'm baptized. Everyone we know is baptized, Fi."

"Salomon isn't."

"Are you planning to raise Magda Jewish, then? Or will you give her no God at all?"

"Look at the world. Look at this country. How am I supposed to teach her about God in such a place? The armies have trampled God in the dust. Who's left to pray to?"

"You've been through a terrible thing, Fi." Eleonore tried to embrace me, but I pushed her away.

Without pausing to dress, I crossed the room and opened the door. "You should go."

As she left, she turned to me. "I didn't do it to hurt you. Do you believe that at least?"

"You said it yourself," I replied. "Years ago. Perhaps we're condemned always to resent each other just a little more than we love each other."

Her lip trembled. "You don't mean that. I know you don't mean that."

After she was gone, I pulled on my nightclothes and climbed into Magda's bed. I draped my arm over her, and her small hand curled itself around three of my fingers. I couldn't sleep the whole of that night for the need to watch each rising and falling breath and inhale the sweet scent of her skin.

Was I Godless? No more or less than anyone in Germany could be considered Godless after near seventeen years of war. Our fathers and mothers were all dead, and what was left of their faith? They died with prayers on their tongues, and what did it profit them?

All those years of war, and what lesson did I have to teach my daughter? I'd cut off the hand of the man who'd given me everything. It had to be done. In order to survive, one must be willing to cut away anything that might sicken and turn to rot—love and faith and goodness among them. And once that's done, one wonders, what's the purpose of surviving?

Even so, I couldn't manage to give up on God, not entirely. I searched for him every night, running my fingers along my father's amber rosary beads. I prayed a litany of dead souls, starting with my mother, my father, and all the soldiers who had fought at his side and later perished—Bachmann and Stefano, Müller and Scheer, among others. I prayed as well for all the children that had been lost, for Dorothea and her infant, for Eleonore's murdered son, and for my own unnamed child. I prayed for Eleonore's stepmother, for Konrad's second wife, and even for miserable, drunken Gottschalk. I prayed for the twenty-five thousand murdered souls of Magdeburg. Most of all, I prayed for Isidoro.

Three years my priest had been gone. When he'd been alive, his faith had been more than sufficient to sustain the both of us. When he'd prayed, I'd begin to believe that God was not dead, only driven into hiding. The ambitions of wicked princes might have put goodness on the run, yet it had not been destroyed, not entirely, not so long as Isidoro was in the world to search it out and call it by name.

It was unthinkable that I was alive and praying for his soul each night; it was an outlandish cruel joke. When I'd finished praying for him, I asked him to pray for me. Perhaps he did. I like to think he was with me, in any case.

In Nördlingen, more than a thousand had died of the plague; hundreds more had fled, hoping to escape illness and the army alike in towns to the north, in Frankfurt-am-Main and in Strasburg. They took the plague with them to those cities, and the numbers of dead grew.

The following year brought rumors, sowing discontent throughout the city. The whispers held that the city's misfortunes, starting with the famine of 1633 and carrying on through the siege and the plague months, had only begun after the council had allowed the Jews to settle within the walls.

A second, still more vicious rumor followed the first—that Salomon had conjured the plague by sorcery, in order to enrich his doctoring trade, and that this was the explanation for why no one in his family had fallen ill.

Both rumors were as false as they were cruel, of course. Salomon had no more power to conjure a plague than I had to raise the ghosts of my mother, father, and husband from their scattered graves.

Nor could it be said that Nördlingen's fortunes were particularly cursed. The city had fared poorly, but what city in that part of Germany had fared well? The siege, though difficult, had been brief, cut short by the battle. The soldiers had left by year's end. And the plague that followed had spent itself quickly instead of lingering.

All through the war, the city council had bargained skillfully, trading the town's gold to spare its grain stores and the surrounding fields. Though the burghers resented the squeeze on their purses, they at least had food and wine on their tables. Their children were not slaughtered in their cellars; their wives were not boiled in their cauldrons.

That same year, the Imperial army laid siege to Augsburg for ten months, and by the time the city surrendered, it was said there was not a cat or a dog left alive within its walls, and the soldiers discovered pits of human bones within, stripped clean and sucked of their marrow.

No, by comparison, Nördlingen had been blessed.

But misfortune is misfortune. A man facing starvation isn't comforted to know that another's house has burned to the ground. The burgher whose unmarried daughter gives birth to a soldier's son nine months after the battle doesn't pause to give thanks to God that she was not killed instead.

The true causes of our misfortune were hundreds of miles away, in Austria, France, and Spain. They were in the palaces of the princes of Germany, who'd chosen at every turn to go on fighting without once contemplating the cost. It was pointless to lash out at them; so the people chose a closer target for their impotent rage.

Yet powerlessness, the war—these alone cannot account for the rumors, nor especially their viciousness. In Ellwangen, there'd been no need of a war to spur the hunting of witches in every hearth and home. My father and I had been driven out of Nördlingen long before the war escaped Bohemia.

No, for all that circumstances had rendered the people of Nördlingen desperate, desperation was not sufficient to explain the turning of the city's opinion against Salomon and his family. Such a turn required cruelty before all else.

On first hearing the rumors, I went to Salomon and Rachel's apartments. Salomon answered the door. He stammered out a greeting, and I did the same, unable to lift my eyes from the stump of flesh that peeked out beyond his sleeve. He caught me staring and hastily tucked it beneath his other arm.

Rachel found us there, and Salomon excused himself. He was tired, he said, and needed to lie down. His body had used up its strength in surviving, and he spent long hours in bed. He'd lost weight.

Rachel offered me a drink, and I told her what they were saying in the city. She paced, incensed.

"They invited him here to care for the sick," she said. "He did just that. He gave up his hand into the bargain. What more do those butchers want from him? A whole arm? A leg this time?"

I dropped my cup, splashing beer on the floorboards. "I'm sorry." I knelt to sop up the mess.

"No, Josefine, I'm sorry," she said. "Neither of us thinks… would you at least go to his room and see him?"

"I need to get back to the surgery," I said.

All through Salomon's recuperation, I kept the surgery running. Even when he was doing better, he couldn't be on his feet for long, so I took over the business, operating and mixing potions and prescribing cures. I hated every minute I spent holding a knife or a saw, and when I stitched a wound, I had to fight the rattling of my nerves.

But I couldn't well stop either; what would become of Salomon's livelihood, his family, if I stopped? I worked from dawn till twilight, wandering home at last light with Magda asleep in my arms, her head resting heavy on my shoulder. At night I was bone tired, but I couldn't sleep.

Since our argument about the baptism, Eleonore had left several letters for me. She repeated again what she'd said that night—that she was sorry for going against my wishes, but she'd not meant it to hurt me. She asked to talk.

"I am certain of two things," she wrote, "beyond any sliver of doubt: that I love you, and that if we were to sit down together and you were to confide all in me, I could be a balm and a salve to you. Will you let me?"

I wrote her a half-dozen answers, then tossed them into the stove.

To my dying breath, I'll swear, I never intended to sever myself from any of them. In my mind, it had already happened, the day I operated on Salomon. I couldn't see any way to reverse it.

One late evening in January, I heard the explosive crack of something heavy striking the surgery door and then bursting open. Next, I smelled smoke.

The fire grew more rapidly than I could act. As the smoke choked the room, I picked up Magda and ran out the back door and around to the front. I set her down in the street while I tried vainly to douse the fire with dirt and gravel.

The shopkeeper across the road emerged carrying a bucket, which he hurried to fill at the nearest water pump. He shouted out for help as he did, and if any of the onlookers hesitated, they jumped to his aid as soon as he reminded them that their houses would surely be next if the surgery was permitted to burn. Three more buckets were provided, and the others formed a line between the pump and the surgery, passing buckets up and down.

When the last of the flames had been extinguished, the door to the surgery had been burned away and the timber supports in front were damaged, causing the top of the building to sag. The inside reeked of smoke, and the heat had melted the glass jars nearest to the door.

Magda began to cry, and I picked her up, shushing her and trying to tease her into laughing.

Konrad stepped out of the crowd and inspected the doorframe. Then he approached me. "You'll need someone to prop up those beams. I can bring wood and board up the door, but you'll need a builder to repair the damage."

"Thank you," I said.

"You should be more careful, though."

"Careful? What the devil do you mean by that? It wasn't my doing. Someone threw something at the door. A lantern, I suspect."

Konrad shook his head. "People are talking. It used to be I was the most hated man in town. Now it's the Jew. You were fortunate the fire didn't bring the building down on your heads."

"Salomon's done nothing to deserve this, and you know it well. You saw how tirelessly he worked during the plague."

"Aye, I did. But they're saying he killed the deacon's wife, and what does the truth have on a story like that?"

"Take your insinuations elsewhere," I snapped.

"My apologies," he said. He was watching Magda, who gave a shy smile and hid her face.

"And what's your name, *kleine Dame*?"

"Magda," the child answered before I could discourage her from it.

"A sweet name. And you look so like your mother."

"Stay away from us, Konrad Lehmann," I warned him.

"Very well," he said with a thin smile. "I'll get to work on that door."

The next morning, I set out for St. George's church. I didn't know who'd set the fire, but I was sure I knew who'd spread the rumors. I'd seen it happen before.

I found the door to the church unlocked and the deacon inside. He was sitting near the altar, his hands clasped in his lap. The uninitiated observer would have thought him praying, but I knew different.

I set Magda in the back and instructed her to play with her ragdoll while I spoke to the man.

"It's time we talked," I said to him as I approached. The deacon gave a jump when he heard my voice.

I can only imagine what a wild sight I looked. I'd not washed since the fire and had barely slept. My face was smudged with soot, and my hair had not been combed since the previous morning.

"Mrs. Dorn, is all well?" he asked, rising from his seat.

"Not Mrs.," I corrected him.

"My apologies. Eleonore said you'd been married."

"It was an illicit marriage. My husband was a Jesuit, awaiting release from his vows. I never had the chance to use his name. Dorn was my father's name. Do you remember it?"

He rubbed his hands together and started to answer in the negative, but then he stopped and narrowed his eyes, studying my face.

"Do you remember me, Mr. Kästner?" I asked again. "I was ten years old when I first came to this city. My father cut my hair so that I could work as a baker's boy in Baker Ruppel's shop. I delivered you bread for the Eucharist every Saturday that year, from

November until the end of January. It was seventeen years ago now, but I thought you might remember."

He shook his head. "I'm sorry. I don't." There was regret in his voice. He was sincere in having no memory of me.

The wick of my anger sparked bright. I stepped closer to him. "Eleonore fell in the river that winter. I expect you remember that at least. She fell out of a tree."

His eyes grew wide; this, he remembered.

"You drove us from this city. You told folk my mother was a witch and ordered them to stop offering my father work. You told Baker Ruppel that I was no boy. My father joined the army after that. He was such a gentle man—you could hardly have imagined him a soldier. But what choice did he have? You saw to it that he had no choice. He was killed at Stadtlohn when I was fifteen. He left me an orphan."

"I didn't know," he stammered.

"Liar." I struck his chest with my palms. He was a tall man, much larger than I, but thin and frail. He stumbled a step back, toward the altar.

"I swear to you," he protested. "I never intended—"

"Damn your intentions! You're doing it again, now. You told folks that Salomon killed your wife!"

I took another step.

"I did no such thing," he said, standing his ground. "May God strike me down where I stand, I never said any such thing."

"Someone tried to burn his surgery to the ground last night."

"If they did, it was not on account of anything I said, on my oath—"

"Enough of your oaths!" A second time I shoved him, and he wheeled backward, his back against the altar.

"Please, Miss Dorn, calm yourself." He reached for me, gripping my shoulders.

"Don't touch me!" I tried to wrest myself free, but his hold tightened, and his fingers dug into my arms. "Let go of me!" I screeched. Magda heard my cries and ran toward me. I told her to stay put. The deacon let go.

"I am sorry about your father," the deacon said. "I remember him now. There was word from Ellwangen that his family had been involved in witchcraft. I only did what I thought was necessary to protect my congregation. To protect Eleonore. But I didn't start the rumors about the Jews."

"Then end them! You call yourself a man of God—act the part."

"I cannot control people's hearts."

"Horseshit. It's your calling to shepherd the people of this city. If you wanted, you could put a stop to the rumors with a single sermon, you miserable, faithless coward!"

Anger flashed across his face. "Miss Dorn!" he cried out, raising his voice for the first time since I'd started chewing him out. He took me by the shoulders once more. "Watch your tongue."

I wrenched myself from his grip. The force of my struggle sent him reeling backward. He fell, striking the back of his head against the wooden altar table. He stared up at me in wide-eyed astonishment from the ground. My heart hammered against my ribcage. I turned and ran.

Magda started to cry as I picked her up and fled the church.

In the fading intensity of my anger, the world shimmered. As I cut across the square, hundreds of pairs of eyes seemed to bore into me. I know now that this was as likely as the dead rising from their graves, but at the time, my conscience was a-torment imagining their judgment on me.

I heard a woman's voice behind me, shouting my name. I thought it must be Eleonore, but I didn't turn to see.

How my hand falters now, as I try to write out these events. How the nerves flare and then grow numb. I've taken to my desk for three evenings straight, until the candle has burned to a nub and the voice of my lover has called me to bed, and each evening I've left the page as empty as when I started.

There's a telling of this tale in which I turn back. I enter the church and I apologize to the deacon and tend to his injured head. Then I kiss Magda's cheeks and wipe away her distressed tears and we both go to Salomon and Rachel's. I tell Salomon I'm sorry, too. I'm sorry I couldn't save his hand or his surgery. I'm sorry that the world is such an unkind place, full of faithless priests and ungrateful burghers. I'm sorry I wasn't a better daughter—to him or my father.

Then I go to Eleonore and I rest my head in her lap and confess everything. I lay out the whole of my life to that point, marking out the moments where the cuts were made, the ones that severed nerve and muscle and bone, leaving me scattered across Germany in pieces. I confide it all to her, and I let her be a balm and a salve.

Instead, I walked Magda back to the apartments as she sobbed frightened tears. There I poured her a cup of warm goat's milk and sat her on my lap, telling her favorite story, *Rotkäppchen*. Her tears turned to giggling as I lowered my voice in imitation of the evil wolf. Then she leapt from my lap and ran to hide, daring me to search for her.

"*Mäuschen, Mäuschen,* say 'Peep.'"

When she'd tired herself out, I laid her in bed for a nap.

I was convinced that we couldn't stay in Nördlingen. Not after what I'd done to the deacon. I didn't know where we would go, but I was strangely untroubled by the thought. I'd find a way; I'd always found a way.

While Magda slept, I prepared a bag, filled with everything I thought we might need for the road—blankets and clothes and matches and what little food we had in the larder. I fastened a small kettle to the bag with rope. Then I lay down in bed next to the sleeping child.

I'd only intended to rest by her side until she woke, but as the morning's fever pitch of anger and fear receded, weariness settled over me like a heavy blanket. I dozed and then I slumbered, not waking even when Magda rose from bed and settled on the floor playing.

It was a pounding at the door that first jarred me awake. By then it was sundown. The rooms were dark. I lit a candle and approached the door carefully. In the stupor of sleep, I'd nearly forgotten my argument with Eleonore's father, but when I saw the bag I'd packed, every shameful detail returned to me. I was so certain that the person at the door was the magistrate, come to arrest me for attacking the deacon, that I didn't think to check who it was.

It was not the magistrate. It was the cabinetmaker, Konrad Lehmann. I blinked at him, trying to make sense of his presence. Understanding came sluggishly, a moment too late.

He charged into the apartment, covering my mouth with one hand and yanking at my hair with the other, until tears filled my eyes.

"Be quiet," he said. "Keep quiet and I won't hurt you."

He pinned me against the wall. In panic, I shouted and bit and kicked, but he was too strong for me. He clasped his hands around my neck and started choking the breath out of me. I kneed him in the stomach with all my strength. He cried out in pain and released me, and I toppled forward, gasping for air.

Then something solid struck the back of my head, and my skull erupted with pain. My last waking thought was of Magda.

29

The Black Nail

1635

When the world returned, just a few blinks of an eye later, it was fractured, and the air was filled with a terrible singing. I had the notion to rise and throttle Konrad, but I could barely lift myself upright without feeling the need to empty my guts. It was better that I couldn't; he would have killed me for sure.

"The devil take you," I muttered. "And hang you from a tree. Let buzzards pluck out your eyes and wild dogs devour your liver. May you—"

He kicked me in the ribs, and I heaved my insides out on the floor. Magda was wailing in his arms, crying out *Mama, Mama*. The sound scraped my soul from my body.

"Hush now, little one," he said to her, his voice honey sweet. "This woman is not your mama, but a thief, a child-snatcher. She took you away because she has no husband, no children of her own, and it made her warped and mad. But it's over now. There's no need to cry. I'm your father, come to take you home."

Magda quieted.

"*Mäuschen*," I said, gritting my teeth and trying to stand.

His boot met my ribs a second time, causing me to taste blood. He left me with the warning, "Do not follow and do not send anyone else to follow, or you will be mother to no one."

Then he was gone, and Magda with him.

My memory of what came next is unreliable. I lay on the floor clutching my stomach. For years now, I've insisted that a rat scurried in front of me while I laid there. I remember it pausing to sniff at my boot before disappearing into the straw. Only now, as I write it out, I realize that it couldn't have been. The floor of those rooms was not lined with straw. There were no rats. I am forced to conclude that the rat must have come later.

There *was* an animal at the apartments that night. Not a rat, to be sure, but a crow. It tapped on the window, startling me out of my wounded daze.

Whenever my mother used to dream of crows, she read it as an ill omen. If you'd ever seen the way they descend in great flocks on the battlefields after the fighting's done, you'd understand why. The tumultuous screeching, the beating of wings—you cannot hear it without thinking on your own death. But is it death that follows the crows, or do the crows follow death?

But I'm racing ahead of myself. At the sound of the crow's tapping, I climbed to my feet. The bundle I'd packed for me and Magda lay where I'd left it. Her clothes were inside. Konrad had dragged her into the winter night only in what she was wearing.

This was the thought that shook me out of my stupor—the thought of her shivering in the cold, without even her coat. I stumbled into the street, shouting Magda's name and beating my fists against every door I saw.

I was well out of my senses by then. I went from neighbor to neighbor, rousing them from their first sleep of the night. They hollered at me to shut my mouth and go to bed. They told me to lay off the wine.

One couple, a cobbler and his wife, did try to show me kindness. They opened their door to me, the raving woman on their step, and invited me to come in, sit down, and have a drink until I'd calmed myself. I turned away their hospitality; it was not what I wanted. I wanted them to shake off their sleepy movements and rise to action, to lift even a single a finger to help my daughter.

"Please, you must calm yourself," the wife pleaded. "We cannot help you if you don't calm yourself."

When I'd exhausted the meager kindness of my neighbors, I made my way to Konrad's house. I hammered on the door, but of course he didn't answer.

So, I hurled rocks at the window until it broke, and then I climbed through, slicing open my arm on the jagged glass. I wrapped the wound hastily with a linen cloth I found in his living room. Then I scoured the house for any sign of him or Magda.

When it became clear he wasn't there, I took to tearing the place apart. I turned the furniture over. I rifled through the cabinets and the drawers. I took down the dishes from the shelves in great handfuls and smashed them on the kitchen floor. I think it was then that I started screaming—screaming as I clawed at the curtains, screaming as I overturned chairs, screaming as I pulled books from their shelves and ripped out the pages.

The ruckus drew the attention of the city watch. They came knocking. The glow of their lanterns danced outside the broken window. There were three of them. I ran out into the street, and one of them seized my injured arm. The wound throbbed in time with my beating heart, but I gritted my teeth and demanded he release me.

"Are you mad, woman?" said one. "What were you doing in this house?"

"Looking for my daughter. This devil's son took my daughter!"

"Aye, she's mad," said another.

He held the lantern close to my face, and the flame writhed in front of me, seductive, mesmerizing.

"Probably drunk as well," said the third.

"No, not drunk," I protested. But neither was I the master of my senses.

I struck out at the man that held me, battering him with my free fist until he cried out, cursing, and let me go.

"Steady yourself," said the first one. "Tell us where you live, so we may see you home safe."

"No!" I can recall shouting. "I can't go home. I must find Magda!"

I ran, but in just a few strides one of the watchmen caught me and lifted me clean off the ground. I threw my head back and struck him square in the nose.

He let go as he shouted in pain, and I resumed running. Next I remember, I'd arrived, breathless, at the nearest city gate. I demanded to be let out, convinced that Konrad had fled the city. The watchmen caught up yet again and proceeded to debate with the gatekeeper.

"If she wants to go so badly, I say let her," said the one with the injured nose. He held his hand to it still, blood dripping between his fingers.

The gatekeeper refused. "And leave her to be torn apart by wolves or raped by brigands?" he said. "Not on my conscience."

"Why not, if that's what she wants?" spat the other.

The first watchman, the one who'd tried to steady me, spoke to me in a measured tone. "You say this man took your daughter, yes? If he's out there, you'll not find him tonight. It's too dark, and the roads are unsafe. Come with us. We'll see you're taken care of, and then in the morning you can tell us all about it."

He extended his hand to me. His voice sounded like mercy, and even in that state, I wasn't too far gone to take it. But as soon as my hand clasped his, he pulled me in, grappling me against his much larger frame.

"Watch that skull of hers," warned one of the others. I thrashed and kicked, but he squeezed all the tighter. The place where Konrad had kicked me screamed with pain.

"Let me go," I gasped. "I must find Magda. I must find my daughter."

"Aye. In the morning. We'll all go looking for her in the morning."

They had me overpowered. "Please," I said, my voice growing weaker. "Let me go."

"So you can tear through the city disturbing the peace? Not likely. A night in the gaol will return you to your senses."

My strength flagged, and by the time we reached the gaol, I was too weak to plead any longer. I was sure then that the crow had been an omen, and that the death it foretold was my own.

They shoved me inside one of the cells, built to hold three or four. But this night, I was alone in it.

"Who is it?" the gaoler asked.

"A madwoman," said the watch. "Found her raving in the street."

The gaoler grunted and slammed the door.

"Salomon ben Judah," I said quietly, as the key clanked in the lock.

"Did you say something?" the gaoler asked.

"Salomon ben Judah, the doctor. I need to see him."

"Are you sick?"

"Just tell him that Josefine Dorn needs to see him."

He looked to the watchmen, muttering an exchange I couldn't hear. The watchmen shook their heads, shrugged their shoulders, and left.

I collapsed into the corner of the straw-lined cell. That must have been when the rat scurried across the floor, sniffing my boot. My foot twitched, and the rat startled, burrowing into a pile of wet straw.

My head, arm, and side ached. I unwound the cloth from my forearm and traced the wound with my fingers. I remembered my mother's face, framed in the doorway of our house in Ellwangen, putting on a false expression of happiness. How many times, since the plague, had I done the same for Magda, hiding my cracks behind a feigned smile? She'd sensed them anyway; children always can.

I thought about the day my mother died, how she'd looped a rope over the rafters of my father's workshop rather than be confined to a cell, rather than seeing her family burn. Had she had a vision of crows beforehand, I wondered.

What can I say for my frame of mind then? Magda was gone. I was convinced of that. I'd seen her through siege and plague, and still it wasn't enough to keep her. Madness, love, call it what you will—some take one look at it and retreat; some lash out at what they know they cannot control; and some are swallowed up by it. Sitting in that cell, I felt myself being swallowed up.

I didn't have a rope, but I patted the straw and found a bent nail sticking out from the floorboards. I gave it a tug, but it wouldn't budge. In desperation, I clawed at the board, splintering the rotted wood with my fingernails. Finally, the nail broke free.

A man's voice spoke to me from a neighboring cell, so faint, it might have been the wind.

"So, they think you're mad, too?"

"Aye," I answered him. "But I'm not. At least I don't think so."

"No, neither am I," said the voice. "What did you do?"

"I broke into a man's house."

"Why?"

"He took my daughter."

"That's enough to drive anyone mad."

"And you? What did you do?" I asked the stranger.

"They said I blasphemed. They said I was stirring revolt."

"Were you?"

"Not much of a revolt. Just myself and three of my comrades. We stormed the town hall during a council meeting. My friends all ran off, though. So, it was just me then. It wasn't my idea. God, he spoke to me in a dream. He gave me a message. I was just following his orders."

"And what was the message?"

"That he's not real. That we are fighting over nothing and no one. That the war should end. The princes should till the fields, and farmers should feast on roasted lamb. That no man is greater than any other."

"God told you that God is not real?"

"The God we call God is not real."

"How do you know that it was God that spoke to you and not the devil?"

"Because he was weeping. He was in pain. He just wanted the war to end."

"The war's never going to end."

"They'll hang me. Then there'll be no more war for me."

I looked at the nail in my hand, warped and rusted. It would make a miserable death. But then, it would be over. All the sorrows of this life, all the miseries of war, they would reach their end. What horrors could Hell hold that weren't already here on earth?

"Do you think I'm mad?" the stranger asked from his cell.

"No, I think you've had enough. I have too. I've had enough of war, and I've had enough of being kicked when I'm down, and I've had enough of people turning cold on each other."

"Aye. That's just it, isn't it?" came the voice. And then he asked, "Will you pray for me?"

Of all the questions he could have asked!

"Aye, I will."

I closed my palm around the nail and slipped it into my pocket.

I don't know if there's a God or if he answers prayers or any such thing. I don't know if he's Protestant or Catholic, Jewish or Muslim. Isidoro imagined him seeing only the goodness, blinded by the beauty of how it all ends. I like to think that if there's a God at all, he's one of us mad ones, weeping in a straw-lined gaol cell somewhere, tossing and turning in the sickhouse, or splayed on a battlefield, eyes glassy, face streaked with blood, watching the crows overhead while he waits for his comrades to bring him home.

I still have that nail. I keep it in a little locked box with Isidoro's prayer book, his lock of hair, his clay pipe, and my father's rosary.

Some time that night, I heard the gaoler's key turning in the lock. The bars sang out like chimes as something solid, something metal struck them. I looked up. In the doorway stood Salomon, sconced in shadow, rapping against the bars with an iron hand. "Little warrior," he said. "Get out of that cell, will you? It's time you came home."

On the way out of the gaol, I looked for the stranger in the neighboring cell. In the far corner lay a featureless heap. Whether it was a man or a pile of straw, I could not say.

30

Out of the Wilderness

1635

The walk back to Salomon's was a long one, marked by a weighty and uneasy silence. It seemed we'd forgotten how to talk to each other ever since the day I took his hand.

"Magda..." I began, but my voice faltered.

"I know," he said. "How do you suppose I found you in that hole? You're fortunate. Your neighbors were very upset by your behavior—enough so, that they went looking for anyone who might know you."

I said nothing.

"They stirred up the whole quarter. There must be a dozen people out searching for you and for any sign of that scoundrel, what's his name?"

"Konrad Lehmann."

"The plague master?"

I nodded.

"He's the girl's father, is he? Be honest with me. Enough secrets."

"Aye, he's Magda's father." The admission felt like betrayal.

Salomon shook his head. "I just don't understand why you didn't come to me and Rachel *before* you got yourself arrested."

"I wasn't in my right mind," I confessed.

"No, I imagine you weren't. But you had us beside ourselves. Sick with worry. I haven't seen Rachel so green since her morning sickness with Judith. I would've thought you were trying to kill us both."

"I'm sorry."

Inside their apartments, Rachel embraced me. Then she wiped the grime from my face and sat me down at the kitchen table. "Damn you, Josefine Dorn," she muttered over and again.

Salomon unraveled the cloth from around my wounded arm and clucked his tongue at what he saw. Dirt and dried blood clung to the cut in dark brown clumps. He daubed the wound with a wet cloth, and the cut bled afresh. "You know better than this."

He went to get needle and thread while Rachel poured me a cup of wine. I had no stomach for it, but I drank it anyway, knowing that I would be grateful for its numbing qualities when Salomon began to work. Then I nodded to him that I was ready.

He weighted my arm in place with his iron hand and stitched with the other. I jerked as the needle pierced my skin, but Rachel held my shoulders, steadying me.

All the while I stared at the axled joints of his metal limb. It was a clumsy mechanism, especially compared to the dexterous way in which his right hand moved the needle.

I gritted my teeth and emptied another cup of wine. The drink loosened my tongue. "You shouldn't have asked me to do it," I said, still staring at his metal hand.

"What are you carrying on about?" he muttered, his attention focused on his work.

"You shouldn't have asked me to take your hand and replace it with that... that counterfeit contraption."

Salomon gave the last stitch a tug. Pain coursed up and down my arm.

I grunted. "You saved my hand, remember? After I smashed it on that whoreson's face. What was his name? Gerhard. You saved my God-damned life, and for what? Why did I survive when my father died? When Isidoro died? So I could butcher you like the fatted calf? You should have left me in the Tross. You should have left me to die of disease or birthing some soldier's bastard."

Salomon stared at me, mouth hanging open. "Nonsense," he said. "This is the wine talking. A melancholy humor. You're in pain and you're afraid for Magda. Both are understandable. But you cannot mean these vulgar things. You know it had to be done. You know you were the only one I'd have trusted to do it. It was a gift that you were there that day."

His words were well-intended, I knew. He sought only to console me. Yet they had the opposite effect. They incensed me.

"Do not call it a gift!" I shouted. "It was no gift!"

All color left his cheeks. He looked back at me, pale and shaken. "Where is this coming from, Josefine? Why are you shouting?"

"Salomon, my love." It was Rachel. "You talk too much sometimes. Listen to her a while, why don't you?"

"Very well," he said, coughing once, sheepishly. "Go on, then. I'll listen."

I swallowed, wetting my tongue. "You ought to have told me the moment you felt ill. You should never have let the sickness reach that stage. You should never have laid it on me. Don't you understand what kind of choice it was you gave me? Whatever I did, I would lose you. If I didn't cut, you would die. But to cut, I had to make you a stranger. I couldn't look on you as a father anymore. What child maims their parent? How was I supposed to come to you tonight? Perhaps it was a gift to you, but it was poison to me."

"Is this the reason you've been withdrawing from us of late?" Salomon turned to Rachel. "Rachel—did you know she felt this way?"

"I had my suspicions—but no, I hardly imagined the depths of it."

"You should have come to us," he said to me.

"How could I?" I asked. "You'd just lost your hand. You'd just recovered from plague. You wouldn't even look at me. How could I come to you with my petty complaints?"

Salomon unfastened the metal hand and massaged the stump of his arm. "Here I thought you were ashamed of me for this." He paused and shook his head. "But it turns out you've been wandering in the desert this whole time, lost."

I was shivering. Rachel rose from the table, disappearing into her and Salomon's bedroom.

"Josefine," Salomon said. "Will you forgive this old man?"

"How can you ask me for forgiveness?"

"It's only a hand. I have a spare. If I'd known you felt this way, I would never have left you to yourself. I admit, it was difficult for me at first; I was ashamed for getting sick and for not telling you sooner. I thought you of all people would understand. The plague took my hand, not you."

"I wish I knew how to live with it."

"I wish I had some answer for you."

"In time, my love." Rachel returned with a blanket and wrapped it around me, folding me in her arms. "The answers will come in time, I'm sure. What matters is you're here now and you're safe. The rest will come in time."

Salomon fastened the false limb back onto his forearm. "Do you know what my one regret is?"

I shook my head, exhaling a ragged breath.

"That I never did learn to play the harpsichord." He flashed his teeth beneath his whiskers, and I smiled in spite of myself.

"There," he said, beaming with mischievous pride. "That's a start."

The neighbors I'd roused had gone to Salomon. Then they'd gathered the folks who knew me to search the city for both me and Magda. It was a motley lot, comprised mainly of neighbors, people I'd treated at one time or another, and folks who remembered seeing me with Magda in the street. One person had witnessed my argument with the watch, which is how Salomon had come to find me in the gaol. While he was fetching me, the rest had split into search parties, looking for any sign of Magda or Konrad.

We waited up into the night as the search parties brought back their reports. I paced back and forth in Salomon and Rachel's living room until at last, Salomon barked at me to sit down, as my agitated movements were compounding his own anxiety.

Rachel sat beside me, holding my hand and offering reassurances, but we both jumped to our feet at each knock at the door.

As the night wore on, even Rachel's nerves started to fray. "It's not so large a city. How long could it take?" she exclaimed. The sound woke their youngest, Esther, and Salomon took her back to bed.

In the small hours, we'd as much as given up hope on hearing anything before morning. Salomon talked of going back out, but Rachel wouldn't hear of it. Finally, there came a knock at the door. Salomon answered, and a woman's voice spoke: "Did you find Josefine? We think we know where Konrad's taken Magda."

It was Eleonore. Rachel and I rushed to the entryway.

Eleonore's cheeks were pink with cold, and her cloak and hair were flecked with large, wet snowflakes. The deacon, her father, was with her, his hands clasped in front of him, lips pressed together in a grim, stoic expression. Only his eyes betrayed any emotion—worry, I thought.

"Where is she? Where's Magda?" I demanded.

"Fi," Eleonore said. "You're here. Thank Heaven." She stepped forward to embrace me, but caught herself. Then her gaze fell on my bandaged arm.

"It's a scratch. It'll heal," I said. "But what's this about Konrad? About Magda?"

"A witness saw him heading in the direction of the Reimlinger Gate, so we questioned the gatekeeper. He confessed to accepting a bribe to let Konrad through," she explained. "He did not see Magda, but he said Konrad was pulling a handcart on foot. Most likely she was in the cart."

"So he's left the city?" I asked. "We're sure of it?"

She nodded. "On the road south. My guess is he plans to go to Augsburg."

"We need to go." I made for the door, but the deacon interposed himself, blocking my way.

"Please, deacon, step aside," I said. "I must find my daughter."

"Miss Dorn," he said evenly. "We are all very concerned for young Magdalena. But it would be sheer recklessness to go out into the open road at this hour. I'm sure the good doctor would agree."

"Indeed," said Salomon. "It's out of the question. We know which way he's headed. That's enough. We'll ready ourselves before dawn, ride out first thing in the morning, and overtake him."

"She's out there! How am I supposed to wait? If it were your children, would you wait? Eleonore—"

She shook her head. "They're right, Fi. It's blackest night out there, barely a sliver of moon through the clouds, and the snow is falling more heavily by the minute. Even with our lanterns, we're only able to see a few feet in front of us, and that's in the city, with buildings everywhere to catch the light. If we went out there now, we'd be no use to Magda or anyone."

"Lehmann can't have gone very far either," the deacon hastened to add. "Our best chances of bringing Magda back safe are to do as the good doctor says. Leave at daybreak and overtake him."

The sound that came out of me was unholy. My knees buckled and I started to fall. It was the deacon, standing nearest me, who propped me up.

Eleonore came up beside me and took me from him. "Fi, listen to me. We will find them both. God help me, we will find them."

"She doesn't have a coat," I stammered.

"He won't let her freeze. He may be reckless and mad, but he didn't take her only to let her freeze." Eleonore looked to Rachel and Salomon. "She's exhausted. She needs rest."

"Take her to our bed." Rachel gestured toward the stairs.

Eleonore led me to the room. By then I was too weary to protest. All night long, my nerves had burned bright, and now they were depleted, smoldering wicks.

"How did you know Magda was missing?" I asked her when we were alone in Rachel and Salomon's bedroom.

"Salomon sent word."

"Of course," I murmured. "He knows you're Magda's true mother. Your father told him as much."

"Enough of that. You are Magda's true mother."

"I'm not either. Even if we catch up to Konrad, he has more claim to her than I do."

"Hush." She led me to the mattress and pulled back the blanket, motioning for me to lie down. I lowered myself belly-first onto it, too tired to even undress myself.

Eleonore climbed into the bed beside me and ran her fingers through my hair, turning me onto my back as she did, and kissing me on the lips.

Wordlessly, she undid the laces of my bodice. Piece by piece, she stripped me bare. A great black bruise had formed below my right breast where Konrad had kicked me in the ribs. Amid all the other pain and turmoil of that night, I'd forgotten it, but when Eleonore slid my blouse off, I winced. She leaned forward and blew tenderly on the spot.

Then she planted kisses up and down my naked skin, soft and warm and tender.

"Someone will hear," I said in half-hearted protest.

"Not if you're quiet," came the reply.

She wrapped us both in the blanket afterwards while I listened to the sound of the winter wind rattling the windowpane and tried not to think of Magda. We heard voices and movement in the rooms below us, but no one on the stairs. They were none the wiser.

"I want you and Magda to come live with us," Eleonore said then.

I didn't answer at first, convinced I'd heard her wrong.

"I hate your silences," she said. "You might at least say something—even if the answer's 'no.' I'm a grown woman. I can bear it."

"You want Magda and me to live with you and your father?"

"That's what I said."

"Eleonore, please. I can't stomach another of your fantasies right now."

"I ran out of fantasies long ago. I'm in earnest."

"Your father would never stand for it. Even if we do manage to hide the truth from him. I knocked him to the ground this morning. I told him I was the girl who pulled you out of the river, and then I shoved him into the altar."

She stifled a laugh. "I know. I saw the whole scene. I called out to you, but you didn't hear me. He came to me afterward and apologized for not being a better father, can you believe it? If you ask me, someone ought to have shoved him sooner."

"We'll burn if they catch us."

"If they catch us. What's to suspect about a widow and a divorced woman living together? And why should that stop us, anyhow? The soldiers take what they want. Why shouldn't we? I'm deadly serious, Fi. I've had enough of waiting for permission to be happy. There's so little happiness left these days."

"And if we don't find Magda? Or if Konrad's hurt her?"

"We'll find Magda."

"You can't know that."

She sighed. "No, of course I can't. That's the very matter. I can't know a thing. I can't know if there will be another siege, another battle, another plague. I can't even know if we'll be good for each other, but I hope we will. I'm willing to try it if you are. Come live with me."

"You always dreamed of leaving this city."

"Yes, but you always dreamed of staying."

I stared at the shadows on the ceiling, as if trying to read the future in them.

"Stay here," she urged once more, "with me. Make my home your home. And if the worst happens—if we don't find Magda, then at least we won't have to bear it alone."

What is loving? I know what it's not. It's not a battle to be won, or a debt to pay, or even a forest at peace. No, it's something meaner and more common, caked with dirt and smelling of sweat and vinegar. It's a thing you choose out of sheer stubbornness, not knowing where it will take you or how it will end up.

Eleonore watched me thinking, her lips slightly parted, hopeful. I'd run out of reasons to say no, so I said, "Yes."

31

God Help Us Night and Day

1635

We gathered at the Reimlinger Gate just before dawn. Salomon, the deacon, Eleonore, and four others: an old African mercenary by the name of Anton, a pair of brothers, Franz and Johann, who served on the city watch, and Unsinkable Chayim, who'd moved to Nördlingen just a few months before the siege. He brought a pair of asses to carry our packs.

Rachel left the children in her eldest daughter Hannah's care and walked with us as far as the gate.

"I do miss it sometimes," she confessed, looking up at the fading starlight. "Sleeping under the open sky. Strange, isn't it? You forget the hard parts. The long marches, the damp sinking into your skin, fucking some stinking soldier for a handful of gulden."

"You never liked me using that word."

"It was far too crass for an eleven-year-old's tongue."

"I was good as grown. I was taking care of myself already."

"Aye, you were. I remember when I first saw you. What a skinny little blade of grass you were. The other camp women said you wouldn't make it through the winter. Oh, but you were made of stouter stuff. Every morning, right about this time, as I was going to sleep, you crawled out of that tent of yours, schlepping a kettle near half your size down to the river. Every night, I saw you huddling by your fire, trying to keep warm."

"I had no blanket."

"Every day it was the same thing, you and that kettle, sloshing water as you went, with that giant of a dog trailing behind you. Cooking porridge and boiling scraps of meat. Foraging for fennel and mushrooms and radishes to make up the shortfall in your father's ration. Sitting by the firelight, sewing patches in his clothes and repairing his boots, while your own toes dangled over the soles of your shoes. Alone, almost the whole time."

"My father had to drill. And I wasn't alone. I had the runt."

"I'm not passing judgment on your father. We didn't see eye-to-eye, but I'll not speak ill of the dead. I know something of having a choice between bad and worse. But that first winter, I kept asking myself—is this child never going to ask for help?"

"You helped me. You brought me blankets."

Her expression darkened. "Aye, and what would you have done otherwise? I simply couldn't stand it anymore. I couldn't stand watching you shiver yourself to sleep each night. I couldn't stand listening to those ill-tempered gossips placing bets over how many more months you'd survive." She shook her head. "Why didn't you ask for help?"

I shrugged. "We'd not encountered many people in our travels willing to help us. And those that did, well, their help didn't go far or last long."

"And what's your excuse now, I wonder."

"Is that why you came with me this morning—to chide me?"

"Someone must. Salomon won't do it because he feels guilty for asking you to operate on him. Your friend Eleonore won't because, well, she's afraid she'll drive you off, I suppose. I expect if your priest was here, he'd have some words to say about it. Perhaps you'd even listen to him. But he's not here, so it falls to me. We've always been honest with each other, haven't we?"

"Aye, we have."

"I've lived by my own wits, and I know what it's like to believe you can only ever rely on yourself. I know what it does to a person. How it starts to feel as if you're responsible for carrying the whole world on your back. You have some addled idea that it's shameful to ask for help—that you must carry everything alone, including me and Salomon.

"The deacon told us about your argument. We don't need you knocking over clergymen on our account. You're no longer that child in the Tross, hauling a kettle half her size down to the stream to make her father's porridge, do you understand? Look around you. God knows, we don't have much to offer against the darkness of this world. But I have to believe it's worth something. It's only hopeless if we let it tear us apart."

We'd arrived at the gate.

"Well, then, here we are," she said. "Think on what I've told you?"

"Aye, I will."

She planted a kiss on my forehead. "Good luck and God be with you, *Häschen*." It was a nickname I'd not heard since before my father's death. "Come back safe."

The sky was kissed with the blush of dawn as the gatekeeper ordered the doors to the city opened wide.

That morning the road was quiet, the sort of stillness that seemed to portend something, though none of us could say what.

Anton and Salomon were the talkers of the group. They'd both spent time in Italy, and soon they were lost to swapping stories and chattering about this or that place none of the rest of us had ever seen.

Unsinkable asked me if I wanted to ride one of the asses. He was no longer so boyish as when I'd known him. He'd put on weight, and his beard was longer, but he was still handsome in his way. I teased him about it, how he'd aged, how we'd both aged.

"I have the blessing of a wonderful, Godly wife who keeps me well-fed," he laughed.

They'd been married seven years, he said. They had no children. But he spoke of her with warmth.

"I'm sorry for dragging you away from her," I said.

"Think nothing of it. When Salomon told us about your little girl, Rivka said I had to go."

Less than a mile outside the city, a black-and-brown wire-haired bitch trotted up behind us, following our group. She appeared to have some wolf in her, but she was tame enough.

One of the young men, Johann, chased her off, and she loped away into the woods, only to appear again behind us a half a mile later. His brother Franz picked up a stone and readied to throw it at her.

"Leave her be," I said. "She isn't harming anybody."

"She's likely diseased," he protested, but he tossed the stone aside.

The bitch walked behind us from then on. Once or twice, I tried to approach, holding out a crust of bread in offering, but she was a skittish creature, and she jumped away whenever any of us drew close. I noticed, however, that her teats were swollen. I supposed her pups must have been long gone, for her to follow us as far as she did.

In the town of Reimlingen, we found confirmation that a man pulling a cart with a young girl in it had passed through just after sundown, though the man had been unwilling to say where he was going. I grew irritable at the lack of information, but Eleonore urged me to take comfort that we were going in the right direction.

Shortly outside that town, we saw wheel tracks turning away from the main road and cutting across a fallow field. We paused there to debate our course. I was eager to follow the tracks, but Anton, the veteran, hesitated. Any delay might prevent us catching up to Konrad before nightfall. It seemed to me that it was entirely too early in the day to think about nightfall.

"If he means to reach Augsburg, he'll stay on the road," Eleonore agreed.

"It's only a guess that he's gone to Augsburg," I argued.

In the end we decided to split the party. Though he'd been against leaving the road, Anton accompanied Salomon and me into the field, while the others continued further along with Eleonore and the deacon. We left both donkeys with them.

As we walked, we heard swishing in the low grass behind us. We stopped, and the bitch stopped a few feet away, panting. When we resumed walking, she followed us.

The day was bright, and the air was clear. We'd not gone far before we scented wood burning and sighted smoke rising beyond the tree line at the meadow's edge. An anxious hope rose in me as we approached. Anton stalked ahead, disappearing into the trees. A short while later, he gestured for us to follow.

It was a narrow strip of woods, separating one field from the other. The cart tracks ended there, near the remnants of a firepit. There wasn't an ember left of the fire. Anton poked at the ashes with his dagger.

"If they were here, they moved on hours ago," he said. "The smoke we smelled must have come from further on."

Voices drifted over the next field—laughter. "We should go on," I said. "If there are farmers nearby, someone may have seen them."

Anton grumbled, but he led us onward. Unlike the first field, this one had been ploughed and planted as recently as autumn. Sprouts of winter wheat peeked up from the furrows. Midway across the field, the veteran stopped.

The source of the smoke was a cookfire in front of an old farmhouse. The fire was surrounded by a dozen men and women, but not one of them wore the look of any farmer I'd known. They were armed, man and woman alike, with swords, daggers, and pistols strapped to their waists. Several of the men were missing eyes or limbs. Swine and goats milled about the yard, but the animals scattered when the bitch came into view.

"Brigands," said the mercenary.

Salomon nodded. "Let's go back to the road before they take notice of us." He turned to go back the other way, but two of the men from the group were already walking in our direction. They called out a greeting, and seeing no other choice, Anton called back.

"Are you lost?" the men asked as they drew close.

One of them walked with a limp. The other had a scar that split his lip in two.

"We're looking for a man and a girl," I answered them. "We think they may have camped the night in yonder woods."

"What of them?"

"The girl is the young woman's daughter," Salomon answered. "The man is a villain; he's taken her, though he has no claim to her."

"A sorry story," said the one with the limp. The other whispered something in his ear. "The girl. Would you say she was about three years old? Brown hair? Always clutching a little blue ragdoll?" the first one asked.

"Aye, that's her," I confirmed. "Have you seen her?"

The one with the scar nodded. "Man came knocking at the door during the snowstorm. Child was crying of cold. My missus gave them a place to sleep in the barn, along with blankets and goat's milk for the little one."

Salomon eyed the weapons strapped to their sides. "What sort of folk did you say you are?"

The first one smiled. "Farmers, of course. This is our field, and those over there are our livestock."

"Did the man tell you which way he was headed?"

"No," said the scar. "They set out again at sunrise. Did not linger long enough for breaking the fast or for conversation. Begging your pardon. We saw no harm in offering hospitality to a man and his daughter, especially in this day and age, when the road is crawling with wicked sorts."

"You did no wrong. I'm glad she was warm," I said.

The first man nodded. "Aye. I pray you find your daughter soon. Might we give you a bit of meat for the road?"

They walked away, and the one with the limp shouted to the others around the fire. One of the women went behind the house and a short while later, she ran out to us, carrying a little bundle. She was a hardy woman, looking doubtless much older than her age. "Goose, freshly slaughtered this morning, and a bit of cheese," she said, and then she handed me a small gray coat. "And something for the little one should you find her. I sewed it for my youngest, but wouldn't you know, he grew an inch in the autumn and it doesn't fit him anymore."

Anton thanked them for their aid, and we returned to the road, puzzling over the encounter. As for whether the men were brigands, as the mercenary first suspected, or farmers, as they claimed, I could not say. In recent years, I've heard tell of soldiers throwing down their pikes and their muskets to take up farming on the very lands they'd once plundered. I suppose it's possible to imagine anything in Germany these days.

By mid-morning, the three of us had caught up to the others once again. I shared the meat and cheese and we made a breakfast of it. As we walked, I broke apart a piece of bread and left the crumbs on the trail for the dog, and she scooped them up into her mouth eagerly. The young brothers gave her wary sideways glances and kept their distance.

At Hohenaltheim, we spoke to the Count of Öttingen's huntsman, who said Konrad had asked him to point the way to Donauwörth. The huntsman told him that the most direct way was to take the shepherd's road through the foothills, east and slightly south until he reached the River Wörnitz, then follow that river to Donauwörth. But the easier path would be to head northeast to Harburg castle-town and follow the river south from there.

Once more, our party descended into argument, with each person having a compelling reason to go one way or the other. In the end, we drew straws. Salomon took the short straw, so he chose: we would take the more direct route.

At this point, the flat farmlands gave way to foothills, and the road became riddled with treacherous rocks. The deacon struggled, and we were forced to slow our pace.

"Should we pause to rest?" Salomon asked him.

The deacon's face was beaded with sweat and his chest puffed in and out, but he shook his head "no" and pressed onward in defiance.

To pass the time, the mercenary Anton struck up a marching song, one he'd learned while serving in the Saxon army under the Swedish banner. The two watchmen joined in, and before long, Salomon, Unsinkable, and I had learned the refrain:

Threadbare soldier
In our proud array

March on, soldier
God help us, night and day!

Eleonore looked at me like I was half-mad, but there's nothing like a song to urge weary legs onward on a long march, and soon enough, she was singing too. Only the deacon kept his silence.

Along the shepherd's road we saw the usual signs. Little settlements lay abandoned and what livestock had been left roamed wild.

In one of the last fields before the valley rose up into mountain, we found an abandoned dovecote giving off a terrible stench. The brothers Franz and Johann looked inside and came out retching.

Salomon and I went in after them, covering our noses, and found two rotting corpses—young women from their dress—already food for worms. I cannot say how they died; I suppose it's likely they had taken shelter there to hide from the soldiers and caught their deaths.

"A dead animal?" Unsinkable Chayim asked when we returned.

"Something like." I told him what we'd found.

The deacon bowed his head: "Dear God, if the soul is still in the state that it can be helped, then I pray that you would be gracious to it."

"Amen," I said, crossing myself.

As we went further into the wooded foothills, however, the signs changed. Here and there, we followed a strip of beaten path that brought us to a cluster of houses deep in the woods that had been left more or less untouched. In one of these settlements, a woman asked if we were soldiers.

Unsinkable laughed. "Do we look like soldiers?"

I asked her what she knew of the war. She said they'd heard tell of it, but they didn't know where it was. Was it in these parts, she asked. They'd not seen Konrad in that village or in any of the others that we passed through, and we started to fear we'd chosen the wrong way.

We found the main road again about halfway between Harburg and Donauwörth. It was late in the day. The hills had made our progress slow, so we stopped in a nameless village to rest and regroup. Our legs and feet ached, and the bitch had left us miles back, wandering off into the wood for a nap or to chase some creature.

The deacon sat down on a stump to pull off his boots, and there was blood on his stocking. Salomon and the other men made their rounds in the village to ask after Konrad and to see if any of the villagers would aid us in the search. I knelt in front of the deacon to tend to his foot.

"You ought to have said something," I chided him as I peeled off his sock and inspected the blisters. "You could have ridden one of the donkeys awhile."

"I don't know how to ride," he confessed.

"What's there to know? It's an ass, not a charger. You balance on top, take a scruff of its mane in your hands, and Unsinkable holds the reins. He's been working with animals his whole life. He won't let you fall." I'd packed herbs and ointment in my bag along with a set of surgical tools, just in case, and I started preparing a treatment.

Eleonore paced a little distance away from us with her arms crossed around her middle. The deacon watched her while I worked.

"It's my fault," he said to me. "All of this. Margarethe's death. Lehmann. God's punishing me for my sins. For my lack of faith."

I wrapped a bandage dipped in Egyptiac around his foot.

He winced and grunted with the pain. "You might have warned me it would sting."

"It doesn't hurt any less if you're expecting it," I said.

He pulled his sock back on and replaced his foot gingerly in his boot.

"Why didn't she tell me about Magda?" he asked.

I exhaled. It wasn't a question I knew how to answer. "You know, my father and I were never any good at talking to each other," I said. "It wasn't easy for us after my mother's death drove us from our home. We were all each other had left. I think we were each afraid of saying the wrong thing. I think we were afraid of how much we could hurt each other if we told the truth."

"I am dearly sorry about your father," he said.

"You can tell him that in the life hereafter," I said.

He nodded. "You've still not answered my question. You know my daughter's heart as well as anyone. She trusted you with her child, but she didn't tell me. Why?"

"The closest I came to telling my father the truth was on the day he died. He'd been nursing an injury for months, and I tried to convince him not to fight. I tried to tell him that I didn't need him to be brave or honorable; I didn't need him to die for me. I needed him to live, to be there with me. But I had no practice telling the truth, so it came out mean and ungrateful. I called him a coward."

"'The truth shall set you free,'" he said.

"No, deacon." I shook my head. "Salomon is much better at this than I am. That's not what I'm saying. The truth, it won't free you. The truth is a wound. Leave it untended and it festers and rots until it kills you. What frees you is the healing. But you can't begin to heal if the wound stays hidden, and if you leave the wound untreated too long—well, sometimes it's too late."

"I see," he said.

I packed away my ointments and stood. "I'll tell you one thing, deacon—I don't believe that God is punishing Magda for your sins or mine or anyone else's. The only person who's to blame is Konrad Lehmann. It's his sin we're answering for."

I joined Eleonore waiting for the others. If she'd overheard any of our exchange, she said nothing about it.

In that village again we found no sign of Konrad. I grew convinced that we'd taken the wrong path. Salomon reproached himself for the choice, but he wasn't to blame; there was no way he could have known any better. We didn't have much daylight left, and we were stuck once more on a dilemma—whether to go on, or double back in case we'd passed him. It was true he was just one person to our eight, but he was pulling a cart and a small child.

In the end, we decided to split up. The greater part of our group decided to use the remaining light to trek back along the road toward Harburg, in hopes that we had accidentally overtaken them. Meanwhile, the young brothers, Johann and Franz, would go ahead toward Donauwörth.

Eleonore urged her father to stay in the village, but he refused. He insisted that his foot was feeling better and that he was fit to walk. Unsinkable Chayim took one of the donkeys with us.

We'd walked less than half an hour when we came across an overturned cart along the side of the road, its contents scattered and ransacked. Anton drew his weapon and crept into the woods, searching for signs of a waiting ambush. Moments later, he cried out: "Over here! Come quickly."

I ran in the direction of his voice, outpacing all of them. The mercenary stood over Konrad, who lay with his back propped up against the trunk of an old, gray-barked tree. His face was pale and covered with sweat, and his chest rose and fell with each difficult breath. His left leg was broken, the lower half bent at a perpendicular angle to the upper.

"Where is she?" I demanded. "Where's Magda?"

"Don't know," he muttered. "Run off."

I stooped in front of him, opening my pack. I laid out my surgical tools, my ointments, my bandages, and I proceeded to cut away the leg of his trousers. The bone poked through the skin.

"Pretty, isn't it?" he said.

"As pretty as you deserve," I said. "What happened to you? How long ago?"

"An hour, maybe two. Hard to see the sun through these trees. It was thieves. I tried to run, but the cart tipped. They had horses. They ran me down, trampled my leg. I crawled here, looking for Magda."

Unsinkable arrived next, and Eleonore and Salomon followed shortly after. Salomon had to pause to catch his breath, but Eleonore launched herself at Konrad as soon as she saw him.

"Where is she, you bastard?" she shouted, shaking him by the collar. "What did you do with her? It wasn't enough for you to murder one child?"

She beat his chest with her fists, but Anton pulled her away.

"Murder?" Konrad shouted. "What the devil are you talking about?"

"You. You killed him. You were so sure he wasn't yours. You throttled him in his sleep."

"No! You're wrong. It's all wrong!"

"Then tell me what happened. Why didn't our son wake up that morning?"

"It was a mistake!" Konrad's expression was contorted, from pain or regret or a mix of each, I couldn't tell. "I didn't... I didn't mean it. He wouldn't go to sleep. I just wanted him to go to sleep, but he kept on screaming. I couldn't get him to stop." He was weeping by the time he finished. The rest of us looked, one to the other, unsure what to make of the confession—all except Eleonore, whose jaw flickered with fury.

"You bastard," Eleonore hissed.

"It was a mistake," he repeated. "You had no business keeping the girl hidden from me."

"I did it for her protection."

"You did it so you could divorce me. You had it out for me from the start. Then you as good as stole my daughter from me."

"You were mad. Listen to yourself. You're still mad. I never had it out for you. I was never against you, Konrad."

"You didn't love me."

"I needed time."

"You provoked me, again and again and again."

The air between the trees rang as their argument grew ever more pitched.

"Yes, it's always my fault," Eleonore shouted. "Georg was my fault, too, is that right? If I'd loved you more, then you wouldn't have shaken him till his face turned blue!"

The deacon limped up behind us, through the dead leaves. He wore a wide-eyed, haunted expression. "What did you do to my grandson?" he spoke through gritted teeth.

Konrad was too fixed on Eleonore to answer him. "Aye," he said to her. "It is your fault. My soul may be the one that's damned for it, but you're not blameless. You never did care to have a child. Least of all mine. A husband has the right to affection from his wife. To understanding. Companionship. But you had none to spare for me or for my son. You were a lazy mother and a faithless wife."

"No. I may not have loved you, but I was not faithless."

"It doesn't matter now. You win. The victory is yours. I hope it's worth it to you. You've destroyed me. Good luck finding the girl. She ran off hours ago."

Salomon joined me by Konrad's leg. I counted three, and together we reduced the broken bone back in place. Konrad's cries echoed across the treetops.

"Don't bother saving him," Eleonore muttered. "He's not worth your troubles."

"I swore an oath," Salomon answered.

"She's right, though." It was Konrad. "It's a waste of your time. You're just going to drag me back to Nördlingen to hang."

"Enough from you," I spat. "Unless you plan to tell us where Magda is."

He cried out again as Salomon adjusted his leg.

"You look for her," Salomon said to me. "Go on. I can tend to him from here."

Four of us spread out into the woods—Eleonore, Anton, Unsinkable Chayim, and myself. The deacon remained behind with Salomon. He'd not stopped staring at Konrad.

The forest floor was dappled with shadow and golden light; it might have been beautiful, but for the urgency brought on by the sinking sun. We considered the leaves and branches, looking for signs of a trail. But Magda was a small child, and her passing left little discernible trace.

An hour later the tree trunks were turning black in the fading light, and we still hadn't found her. Anton and Unsinkable called us back, but I was unwilling to give up the search. I pushed onward, till I heard a choked sound a few feet away from me. It was Eleonore, sitting amid the roots of a beech tree, sobbing.

"He always wins," she said as I drew near. "That bastard always wins. It wasn't a marriage we had; it was a war. He takes everything good and destroys it."

"No," I heard myself saying. "To Hell with him. You mustn't believe it. Whether we find her or not, he hasn't won. There are things he can't ever touch. Things I won't let him have. Our memories of her. The day she was born, you remember, when I held her that first time and knew I wanted to be her mother? Her first steps, her first words, her first sickness, the first time she called you Aunt Nora. I'll be damned, I'll spit in God's eye before I let Konrad have any of them. You said it yourself—whatever happens, we'll bear it together. Christ knows, I haven't the faintest idea how, but it's the only thing I have left to hope on."

I slid into the roots beside her and held her.

An urgent, anxious whine came through the trees, a few paces ahead of us. It broke the silence then stopped. I waited, listening.

The whine came a second time, and I rose to follow it. It led me to a place where the ground sloped downward, coated in half-melted snow and dead pine needles.

At the bottom of the slope was the wire-haired bitch from earlier, pacing and whimpering. She stopped only to lower her head and peer beneath a thicket canopied by a fallen tree branch. She let out another high-pitched whine and then barked at me.

"Where have you been?" I asked her. "Are your pups in there?"

I wended my way down the slope, but the wet earth gave out beneath me, and I slid most of the way, till my skirt was covered in mud. The fall startled me, and I paused to catch my breath before approaching the dog.

The bitch's tail wagged.

"What do we have here?" I asked her.

I knelt, and I found myself looking into a pair of wide brown eyes. Human eyes. Eyes I did not need any light at all to recognize.

I reached out with a trembling hand. "*Mäuschen, Mäuschen,* say 'Peep,'" I whispered.

A moment later came the small reply: "Peep!"

Magda crawled into my arms. "Yes, that's right," I said. "I'm here. I'm here now. Your mama's here." She embraced me, holding fast to the back of my cloak.

"Mama," she said. "I was being quiet. I hided."

I pressed my face into her hair and wept into her small body. "Oh, Magda. Yes, you hided. You did a very good job of it. You were very quiet. I'm sorry it took so long for me to find you."

"Don't cry," she said. "I'm very good at hiding."

I tried to stand, but my limbs had gone weak. I shouted Eleonore's name as loud as I could. She gave a joyous shriek when she saw us and came tumbling down the slope. At the bottom she hugged us both. Magda burst into a fit of giggles.

By and by, we made our way back to the others. Salomon shouted a prayer of thanksgiving when he saw us, and Unsinkable Chayim joined him. Even the stern-faced mercenary, Anton, grinned.

We were all so caught up in the joy of the moment that we did not notice the deacon.

We did not see him limp over to where Konrad lay slumbering after the ordeal of having his leg wrenched back into place, stitched up, and splinted.

We did not see him reach into my bag and remove the surgical knife.

We did not see him nudge Konrad awake.

We did not notice the deacon at all, until we heard him say, "You killed your son."

"Aye," said Konrad, slow and blinking away sleep. "That's right. I killed him. I'm a damned and wretched man. Pray for my soul, deacon?"

"You'll find no friends waiting for you in Nördlingen. Only the hangman's noose."

We saw the knife then. We saw the deacon press the handle into Konrad's palm and close his fingers around it.

"What about redemption, deacon? Is there any way I can be forgiven?"

"Think on your daughter. Do what's best for her. Don't subject her to a trial. Spare her the pain of having a criminal for a father."

Konrad looked from Magda to the deacon and finally to the knife. "I'll give my regards to the devil for you."

The mercenary lunged for the knife, but he was a step too slow. I turned Magda's head aside, shielding her eyes and ears, just in time.

The blade was made for cutting flesh. It cut deep as the cabinetmaker drew it across his throat. He gave one last, strangled breath and slumped over.

32

Now All the Woods Are at Peace

1650

More than three years it's taken me to write this. If I'd known what a tortuous labor it would turn out to be, I never would have started. Now, I mean to end it. Eleonore is particularly glad of it. She says this writing business has possessed me like a wicked spirit. She's not wrong. I have been at times moody and intractable while writing this. I'll be glad to be free of it.

On the way back to Nördlingen, I carried Magda until my arms grew stiff. By and by, Eleonore insisted I give her up a while and rest. The girl clung to me, unwilling to be parted. But when she saw it was Aunt Nora waiting for her, she relaxed her grip and laid her tired head on Eleonore's shoulder. She was asleep by the time we arrived in the little nameless village, where Johann and Franz were waiting.

The half-wolf bitch continued to follow us. We brought her back to Nördlingen and Eleonore named her "Lady," as she did not wish for me to call her "bitch" indefinitely.

Not long after our return, Magda and I moved into Eleonore's house. I took the risk of confessing the nature of our relationship to Rachel as the two of us packed my things for the move.

She interrupted me before I could finish. "You and Eleonore have a special friendship, that much is plain. There's no law against friendship. As for the rest—as for what happens in secret, *discreetly*, behind closed doors—it's not for me to know, is it?"

"No, I suppose not," I said. "But do you understand?"

"Understand what? Love? No one understands love. But you didn't betray me and Salomon when we asked you to keep the secret of my conversion, so if you're asking if you can trust me, you can. Just please be careful about the deacon. He is not like to be so understanding when it comes to his daughter."

She snapped the dust out of the tablecloth she was folding and packed it away. I took that to mean she was done with the conversation.

In the house, Magda and I each had a room to ourselves, but Eleonore slipped into my bedroom nightly. As for the deacon, he relished having his granddaughter close, and if he suspected anything about me and Eleonore, he said nothing.

Rachel's advice proved wise as ever. Discretion goes a long way these days. Now and again, someone makes a stray comment, insinuating something, but such words are not paid much mind. It seems folk are no longer so afraid of sin as they once were, nor of blasphemy—so long as you take pains to keep it out of view.

As for the years after, they continued in the usual way. Regardless of confession, we all prayed for the war to end. After the Swedish king's death, people cared less and less who had the victory. And after the battle of Nördlingen, there was little talk of Protestant or Catholic armies. The armies belonged to the Empire, France, Sweden, and Spain, and who could say which was the worse?

Despite our prayers, the war went on. We went on, too—those of us who could. The rest we carried with us, in memory.

In 1635, Rachel gave birth for the fifth time. It was to be her last child, she declared. They named him Benjamin.

Around that same time, a man in Bopfingen was overheard confessing to setting the fire at Salomon's surgery. For starting a blaze that might have burned a quarter of the city to the ground, he was brought before the judge and given the usual sentence of hanging.

From the scaffold, the man claimed to be repentant and asked Salomon for his forgiveness. "May your God forgive you," was Salomon's answer, just before the platform opened and the man's body fell with a jerk and a twist.

After the hanging, the city moved on. The anger toward the Jews faded, as did the rumors.

In 1641, the deacon died unexpectedly. He'd been complaining of a weakness in his body for a few days, but neither Salomon nor I could identify anything at all wrong with him. We gave him herbs and sent him on his way. He collapsed in the church on a Saturday afternoon while preparing the altar cloths. He did not awake again.

Magda screamed when I told her. She was nine years old by that time, and the deacon had been a doting grandfather to her. Her response to his death was to tell me that I was wrong, the deacon had not died, and it was my job to go operate on him and save him. Her anger eventually subsided, but not before she'd spent the days leading up to his funeral with her hands balled into fists in her lap, refusing to speak.

Eleonore played the role of the dutiful bereaved daughter in front of the burghers, but in private she approached the burial arrangements with stoical practicality. "Just this last thing," she said to me, "and I'll be free of him."

The two of them had tried on a few occasions over the years to speak to each other and form an understanding, but each time old grievances intervened, and their conversations turned to arguments or else fizzled into icy silence.

After the funeral, Salomon invited Eleonore to come and sit in mourning at his and Rachel's house. He and the deacon had become close friends. Every week, they met at the tavern to play a game of Trictrac after Sunday services were over. To my surprise, Eleonore accepted Salomon's invitation.

All that day, she sat in silence, speaking nary three words until just before it was time for us to leave. She broke down sobbing then, like a pot boiling over. She heaved out years of festering emotion in wet, choked gasps.

For my part, the deacon is on the list of souls I pray for each night, and I was surprised to find an emptiness left by his passing.

The war went on. There were good years and bad; years of want and years when we found good profit in selling to the soldiers as they passed through. In 1645, the French army clashed with the Emperor's at Alerheim, southeast of the city. For a month afterward, we quartered a French soldier and his family. The soldier's wife was a German woman from the Rhineland, an officer's daughter, born and raised at war.

That same year, the city gave some of the Jewish families permission to resettle in Ellwangen, and Unsinkable Chayim and his wife made the move. Salomon and I rode out to visit them after they'd settled in.

It was an uneasy feeling, being in that town again. It was no less desolate than I remembered it. The armies had plundered it down to the last grain. I found the spot where we'd buried my mother, but there was no sign that a grave had ever been there. My father's tannery, too, had long since been destroyed.

Shortly before I began the writing of this account, the Bavarian army bombarded the city from the nearby hilltops, igniting the roofs in the weavers' quarter. More than a dozen houses burned to the ground before the fire was put out. They've still not been rebuilt.

Finally, in 1648, about a year after I started writing, France, Sweden, Denmark, Spain, and the Empire all put pen to a treaty. Peace, they declared. But two years on, the armies are still among us. They won't go until they're paid. Mutinies break out on the regular and need to be put down with gunfire and skirmishing. Now the generals sit in Nuremberg and argue over who pays what, and we wait to see if the war will continue. It is a storm that can't be stopped.

So, here we are. Have I found what I was looking for? Was my foolish priest right? Was God hiding in those ways and years, working in my life all along? Who can say? Perhaps when I die, I'll finally know the answer. Perhaps Isidoro will be there to tell me himself.

I think of him still, looking for goodness. I think of Rachel and her talk of holding back the darkness. The war is persistent, eternal; it moves according to its own dreadful logic. If this one ever ends, there will surely be another. How often it has tried to kill us; how often it has succeeded. And those of us who've survived this far—we'll never know who we might've been if we'd been allowed to live in peace.

So, what, then? If peace comes, if the armies finally go home, what can I tell Magda? If this war ends, we must imagine a different world. We can't build peace out of the stones of war.

So, I carve out new stones, and I pile them up: Look for goodness. Do not let the darkness turn you, one against the other. Give without expectation of repayment. Don't let your resentment grow greater than your love. And if you find a moment of peace, of respite, wherever you might find it, hold onto it. Hold onto it, and don't let anyone convince you to trade it away for anything. Though soldiers come to plunder it, though princes claim to fight for it, hold onto it, keep it safe in the one place all the soldiers and all the princes in the world can't reach, in the depths of your soul.

I suppose that's all then. I suppose that's where I end. The only thing left to do is to sign it.

I thought I'd finished this account, but yesterday a thing happened which has prompted me to sit at my writing table for I hope the final time.

We were gathered in Baldern by Bopfingen for the marriage of Salomon and Rachel's youngest daughter, Esther, to the grandson of the rabbi there. It was a very fine celebration, with the bride looking especially happy.

Salomon was only a little sour—he wasn't ready to give Esther up, and though he respects the rabbi, he considers the groom Jakob a dimwit.

Rachel, for her part, seemed more relieved than anything: "These wedding contracts are always such a bother. So many details to negotiate. I can't rest easy until the wedding's done."

Eleonore and I joined the celebration, as did Magda. She is eighteen now—a spirited, clever young woman—and she spent much of the night flirting with the young men.

"She takes after you," Eleonore remarked.

Magda was dancing with the groom's younger brother.

"I should hope not, or we'll have to check the barns before the evening's done," I replied.

Eleonore reached out and brushed a lock of hair from my face. "Look at you," she said.

"I've gone completely white. I look like an old crone."

"You look wise."

I laughed. "Certainly not."

"Oh, the things I've done just to see that smile," she said. Her hair is streaked with gray now; her skin is creased around her jowls and eyes. But there is still that mischief in her from when we were children. She can still make me damn myself with a touch.

"I never imagined reaching forty," I said.

"I plan to live to a hundred," Eleonore declared. "What do you say? Shall we go *check the barn*?" It took me longer to grasp her meaning than I care to admit.

We returned to the party some time later, after we'd done picking the straw from each other's hair. By then, Salomon was deep in conversation with one of the Count's representatives. By and by, he drummed his metal hand against the wedding canopy to draw the attention of the gathering.

"Today," Salomon said, "we celebrate not just one, but two joyous occasions. The wedding of my daughter and this news, fresh arrived from Nuremberg." He cleared his throat. "The generals..." his voice wavered. "The generals have reached an agreement. The armies will disband effective immediately. It is therefore... it is therefore my great privilege to announce that the war is, finally, truly, at an end."

Well, we were all in very good cheer from that point on. There wasn't enough wine to slake our thirst nor enough dancing to tire us out.

But now, here I am, in the low morning light, my head more than a little sore from the jubilations, and it still feels like a dream: peace. More than thirty years I've waited for it. What will we do now? How will we live when there is no *Brandgeld* to be raised, no threat of cannon fire bombarding the city, when we can walk Germany's roads again in peace?

Hold onto it.

Last night, as the party was dying down, I wandered to the edge of town, and looked out on the woods, where the spruce trees stood like black sentinels. I stared into it and strained my ears to hear, not knowing at first what I was searching or listening for.

What I heard was unexpected, a sound I couldn't remember hearing since I was young.

Magda found me. "There you are, Mama. Aunt Nora has been looking for you."

"I'm sorry," I said. "I needed some quiet. It was a fine party, wasn't it?"

"Well, it should be." Magda leaned against me. "Esther told me what her father-in-law spent on it. Salomon was contracted to pay half, plus the dowry." Magda's two years older than Esther, and an inch taller than me. Her face is round and her hair is dark like Eleonore's, but Eleonore is not wrong—her temperament is very like my own. She takes the measure of everything. She does what needs to be done. She survives.

"You don't think her new husband is a little... simple?" I asked.

"Oh, but that's just how she wanted it. This way, she may let him believe he has the run of things while she has her way."

"Poor man," I laughed. "He has no idea what he's in for. What of you? Is there someone from tonight that you favor? A stupid young man you can twist around your finger?"

"Oh, heavens, no. I want someone with means and the wits to keep them."

"That's not all there is, you know."

"Oh, Mother," she sighed. "You can be so sentimental sometimes. I'll not have a man who dies and leaves me with nothing, like Father left you. Aunt Nora has already said that the cloth business will pass to me when her time comes. I won't have a fool squandering away my inheritance, either."

"Your father didn't leave me with nothing," I said quietly.

"Yes, I know, your little treasures."

"More precious things than that," I said.

"I'm sorry. I didn't mean to touch a sore spot. I didn't know him. I wish I had."

"I wish you had too. He was not like us. Not at all pragmatic like you or me or Aunt Nora. But not sentimental either. He would've known what to do with this peace we now find ourselves with. He would've known how to celebrate it and to keep it."

We walked back to the wedding together. As we arrived, Salomon and Rachel were the only ones still dancing, and the musicians had long packed up their instruments. Esther and her new husband had already departed for their home in the city.

Eleonore readied the wagon for our return, and Salomon and Rachel's sons, Daniel and Benjamin, climbed aboard. Their older daughters, Hannah and Judith, already had husbands and families of their own, and they'd left hours earlier.

Salomon and Rachel broke off their dance to join us. As we rode back into the city, I listened to the wheels turning in the dirt and once more looked to the woods, to watch the treetops rustle against the sky. The moon shone bright. I turned to Magda.

"Peace," I said. "When you are ready to take a husband, find a man who brings you peace."

She rolled her eyes. "Very well. And what's peace?"

I watched the trees crawl by, and it took me back to those long marches through hilly wooded lands, to the sound of thundering boots, the lurching of carts bearing heavy guns, the marching songs echoing among the branches. The birds fell silent at the army's approach, the small creatures ran and hid.

"Well, Mama?" Magda asked again, breaking into my thoughts.

"It's patience," Eleonore said. "Every day, a little more patience."

Rachel laughed. "I'll second that."

"It's a quiet study, so I can catch up on my reading," Salomon said.

"It's when Daniel goes to Italy and I finally have a room all to myself," Benjamin declared.

Daniel, who is readying to follow in his father's footsteps by taking up study in Padua, spoke up: "It's a cartful of Protestants, Jews, and Catholics riding home from a wedding, laughing." He smiled at Magda, and in the low light, I thought I saw her blush.

"Come, Fi," Eleonore urged. "Give us your answer."

"Listen," I said, then. Everyone fell quiet. Into the silence came the chirping of frogs, the owl's cry, and the rustle of the squirrel and the hedgehog in the bushes. "There," I said. "Do you hear it?"

"You've gone mad, Mama," Magda laughed. "I don't hear a thing."

"Hush," I said. "Don't talk. *Listen.*"

Hold onto it.

Josefine Dorn
Nördlingen, July 1650

Author's Note

In the time it took me to finish this book and prepare it for publication, two wars started, one in Ukraine and another in Israel/Gaza. As in Josefine's war, civilians, many of them children, have borne the brunt of the suffering. Each year these wars last, those children get older. One day, they will be the adults responsible for running their countries. Will they try to build something new, or will they look back with bitterness and fear, hoping to use violence to reclaim a vision of an idealized past?

The Peace of Westphalia that concluded the Thirty Years War was one of Europe's many "never again" moments. Never again will we make religion the cause of such bloody, protracted, senseless conflict! But as C.V. Wedgwood so insightfully observed, "They wanted peace and they fought for thirty years to be sure of it. They did not learn then, and have not since, that war only breeds war."

If you enjoyed this book, please tell others about it. Ask your local library to stock a copy. Leave a review on your website of choice. Every bit helps this book reach more people.

Acknowledgements

A novel may have one author, but it is rarely the work of a single person. Josefine's story would not have been possible without the support of countless people who championed the book and helped make it better, as well as the numerous sources and inspirations that a writer of historical fiction relies on to give their imagined characters a foundation in truth.

I'm indebted to my beta readers, Matthew Cropley, Emma Holliday, Elisa Mader, Elizabeth Vail, and Sarah Vanacore for their direct, helpful feedback, and to Cecily Blench for her critique and edits.

The historians and archivists whose work informed Josefine's story are too numerous to name here. Still, I want to highlight a few:

The portrayal of Nördlingen in this book would not be nearly so complete without the generations of curators, archivists, and preservationists responsible for keeping so much of the historical character of the city in tact to this day. I'm especially indebted to the Stadtmuseum Nördlingen and the Stadtarchiv Nördlingen. Christopher R. Friedrichs' comprehensive study *Urban Society in an Age of War: Nördlingen 1580-1720* proved essential to contextualizing that information.

Rachel's conversion was one of the trickiest parts of the book to write. While there is a wealth of sources on Jewish conversion to Christianity, conversion in the opposite direction is under-documented and under-discussed. Paula Tartakoff's *Conversion, Circumcision, and Ritual Murder in Medieval Europe* is one of the only English-language books that addresses the subject, and her chapter formed the basis of those scenes in the book. I hope more scholars will take up the topic in the future!

For insight into the daily lives of people during and after the war, I relied on a number of documentary histories, in both German and English, including *Peter Hagendorf: Tagebuch eines Söldners aus dem Dreissigjahrigen Krieg* edited and transcribed into modern German orthography by Jan Peters, *The Memoirs of Glückel of Hameln*, translated by Marvin Lowenthal, and *Plague in the Early Modern World: A Documentary History* edited by Dean Phillip Bell.

There are so many more resources I could name, but I'll limit myself to one more: C.V. Wedgwood's *The Thirty Years War* remains as timelessly perceptive and compassionate a history of the war as it was when it was first written.

I firmly believe that anyone who sets out to write a book about war should not do so without first reading Kurt Vonnegut's seminal anti-war work, *Slaughterhouse-Five* and internalizing its lessons. Sadly, few writers seem to have heeded Vonnegut's warning against glamorizing war. I hope Josefine's story has gone some way to correct that balance.

Finally, my wife Nina has been with this book from draft one, when the story took a very different form, providing her honest critique and quickly becoming this book's first champion. Writing a novel is often lonely and emotionally trying work; Nina made it much less so.

Milton Keynes UK
Ingram Content Group UK Ltd.
UKHW012155300124
436918UK00002B/23/J

9 783910 998025